Nicolaes Berchem, Ambrosius Bosschaert the Elder, Isaack Koedijck, Adriaen Coorte, Jacob Backer, Willem Heda, Paulus Potter, Jan Baptist Weenix, Aelbert Cuyp, Jan van Goyen, Jan Davidsz de Heem, Jacob van Ruisdael, Balthasar van der Ast, Emanuel de Witte, Jan Steen, Jacob van Ruisdael, Simon de Vlieger, Jan van der Heyden, Frans van Mieris the Elder, Adam Pijnacker, Willem van Aelst, Philips Wouwerman, Gerard  Porcellis, Jacob van Ruisdael, Willem van de Velde the Younger, Hendrick Avercamp, Jan van de Cappelle, Gerrit Dou, Rembrandt, Frans Hals, Karel du Jardin, Adriaen van Ostade, Salomon van Ruysdael, Jan Both, Jan Lievens, Rachel Ruysch, Willem van de Velde the Elder, Aert van der Neer, Esaias van de Velde, Salomon de Bray, Pieter Claesz, Gabriël Metsu, Nicolaes Berchem, Ambrosius Bosschaert the Elder, Isaack Koedijck, Willem Heda, Paulus Potter, Jan Baptist Weenix, Aelbert Cuyp, Jan van Goyen, Jan Davidsz de Heem, Jacob van Ruisdael, Balthasar van der Ast, Emanuel de Witte, Jan Steen, Jacob van Ruisdael, Simon de Vlieger, Jan van der Heyden, Frans van Mieris the Elder, Adam Pijnacker, Willem van Aelst, Philips Wouwerman, Gerard Houckgeest, Nicolaes Maes, Jan Porcellis, Jacob van Ruisdael, Willem van de Velde the Younger, Hendrick Avercamp, Jan van de Cappelle, Gerrit Dou, Rembrandt, Frans Hals, Karel du Jardin, Adriaen van Ostade, Salomon van Ruysdael, Jan Both, Jan Lievens, Rachel Ruysch, Willem van de Velde the Elder, Aert van der Neer, Esaias van de Velde, Salomon de Bray, Pieter Claesz, Gabriël Metsu, Nicolaes Berchem, Ambrosius Bosschaert the Elder, Isaack Koedijck, Adriaen Coorte, Jacob Backer, Willem Heda, Paulus Potter, Jan Baptist Weenix, Aelbert Cuyp, Jan van Goyen, Jan Davidsz de Heem, Jacob van Ruisdael, Balthasar van der Ast, Emanuel de Witte, Jan Steen, Jacob van Ruisdael, Simon de Vlieger, Jan van der Heyden, Frans van Mieris the Elder, Adam Pijnacker, Willem van Aelst, Philips Wouwerman, Gerard Houckgeest, Nicolaes Maes, Jan Porcellis, Jacob van Ruisdael, Willem van de Velde the Younger, Hendrick Avercamp, Jan van de Cappelle, Gerrit Dou, Rembrandt, Frans Hals, Karel du Jardin, Adriaen van Ostade, Salomon van Ruysdael, Jan Both, Jan Lievens, Rachel Ruysch, Willem van de Velde the Elder, Aert van der Neer, Jan Both, Esaias van de Velde, Salomon de Bray, Pieter Claesz, Gabriël Metsu, Nicolaes Berchem, Ambrosius Bosschaert the Elder, Isaack Koedijck, Adriaen Coorte, Jacob Backer, Willem Heda, Paulus Potter, Jan Baptist Weenix, Aelbert Cuyp, Jan van Goyen, Jan Davidsz de Heem, Jacob van Ruisdael, Balthasar van der Ast, Emanuel de Witte, Jan Steen, Jacob van Ruisdael, Simon de Vlieger, Jan van der Heyden, Frans van Mieris the Elder, Adam Pijnacker, Willem van Aelst, Philips Wouwerman, Gerard Houckgeest, Nicolaes Maes, Jan Porcellis, Jacob van Ruisdael, Willem van de Velde the Younger, Hendrick Avercamp, Jan van de Cappelle, Gerrit Dou, Rembrandt, Frans Hals, Karel du Jardin, Adriaen van Ostade, Salomon van Ruysdael, Jan Both, Jan Lievens, Rachel Ruysch, Willem van de Velde the Elder, Aert van der Neer, Esaias van de Velde, Salomon de Bray, Pieter Claesz, Gabriël Metsu, Nicolaes Berchem, Ambrosius Bosschaert de Oude, Isaack Koedijck, Adriaen Coorte, Jacob Backer, Willem Heda, Paulus Potter, Jan Baptist Weenix, Aelbert Cuyp, Jan van Goyen, Jan Davidsz de Heem, Jacob van Ruisdael, Balthasar van der Ast, Emanuel de Witte, Jan Steen, Jacob van Ruisdael, Simon de Vlieger, Jan van der Heyden, Frans van Mieris the Elder, Adam Pijnacker, Willem van Aelst, Philips Wouwerman, Gerard Houckgeest, Nicolaes Maes, Jan Porcellis, Jacob van Ruisdael, Willem van de Velde the Younger, Hendrick Avercamp, Jan van de Cappelle, Gerrit Dou, Rembrandt, Frans Hals, Karel du Jardin, Adriaen van Ostade, Salomon van Ruysdael, Jan Both, Jan Lievens, Rachel Ruysch, Willem van de Velde the Elder, Aert van der Neer, Esaias van de Velde, Salomon de Bray, Pieter Claesz, Gabriël Metsu, Nicolaes Berchem, Ambrosius Bosschaert the Elder, Isaack Koedijck, Adriaen Coorte, Jacob Backer, Willem Heda, Paulus Potter, Jan Baptist Weenix, Aelbert Cuyp, Jan van Goyen, Jan Davidsz de Heem, Jacob van Ruisdael, Balthasar van der Ast, Emanuel de Witte, Jan Steen, Jacob van Ruisdael, Simon de Vlieger, Jan van der Heyden, Frans van Mieris the Elder, Adam Pijnacker, Willem van Aelst, Philips Wouwerman, Gerard Houckgeest, Nicolaes Maes, Jan Porcellis, Jacob van Ruisdael, Willem van de Velde the Younger, Hendrick Avercamp, Jan van de Cappelle, Gerrit Dou, Rembrandt, Frans Hals, Karel du Jardin, Adriaen van Ostade, Salomon van Ruysdael, Jan Both, Jan Lievens, Rachel Ruysch, Willem van de Velde the Elder, Aert van der Neer, Esaias van de Velde, Salomon de Bray, Pieter Claesz, Gabriël Metsu, Nicolaes Berchem, Ambrosius Bosschaert the Elder, Isaack Koedijck, Adriaen Coorte, Jacob Backer, Willem Heda, Paulus Potter, Jan Baptist Weenix, Aelbert Cuyp, Jan van Goyen, Jan Davidsz de Heem, Jacob van Ruisdael, Balthasar van der Ast, Emanuel de Witte, Jan Steen, Jacob van Ruisdael, Simon de Vlieger, Jan van der Heyden, Frans van Mieris the Elder, Adam Pijnacker, Willem van Aelst, Philips Wouwerman, Gerard Houckgeest, Nicolaes Maes, Jan Porcellis, Jacob van Ruisdael, Willem van de Velde the Younger, Hendrick Avercamp, Jan van de Cappelle, Gerrit Dou, Rembrandt, Frans Hals, Karel du Jardin, Adriaen van Ostade, Salomon van Ruysdael, Jan Both, Jan Lievens, Rachel Ruysch, Willem van de Velde the Elder, Aert van der Neer, Esaias van de Velde, Salomon de Bray, Pieter Claesz, Gabriël Metsu, Nicolaes Berchem, Ambrosius Bosschaert the Elder, Isaack Koedijck, Adriaen Coorte, Jacob Backer, Willem Heda, Paulus Potter, Jan Baptist Weenix, Aelbert Cuyp, Jan van Goyen, Jan Davidsz de Heem, Jacob van Ruisdael, Balthasar van der Ast, Emanuel de Witte, Jan Steen, Jacob van Ruisdael, Simon de Vlieger, Jan van der Heyden, Frans van Mieris the Elder, Adam Pijnacker, Willem van Aelst, Philips Wouwerman, Gerard Houckgeest, Nicolaes Maes, Jan Porcellis, Jacob van Ruisdael, Willem van de Velde the Younger, Hendrick Avercamp, Jan van de Cappelle, Gerrit Dou, Rembrandt, Frans Hals, Karel du Jardin, Adriaen van Ostade, Salomon van Ruysdael, Jan Both, Jan Lievens, Rachel Ruysch, Willem van de Velde the Elder, Aert van der Neer, Esaias van de Velde, Salomon de Bray, Pieter Claesz, Gabriël Metsu, Nicolaes Berchem, Ambrosius Bosschaert the Elder, Isaack Koedijck, Adriaen Coorte, Jacob Backer, Willem Heda, Paulus Potter, Jan Baptist Weenix, Aelbert Cuyp, Jan van Goyen, Jan Davidsz de Heem, Jacob van Ruisdael, Balthasar van der Ast, Emanuel de Witte, Jan Steen, Jacob van Ruisdael, Simon de Vlieger, Jan van der Heyden, Frans van Mieris the Elder, Adam Pijnacker, Willem van Aelst, Philips Wouwerman, Gerard Houckgeest, Nicolaes Maes, Jan Porcellis, Jacob van Ruisdael, Willem van de Velde the Younger, Hendrick Avercamp, Jan van de Cappelle, Gerrit Dou, Rembrandt, Frans Hals, Karel du Jardin, Adriaen van Ostade, Salomon van Ruysdael, Jan Both, Jan Lievens, Rachel Ruysch, Willem van de Velde the Elder, Aert van der Neer, Esaias van de Velde, Salomon de Bray, Pieter Claesz, Gabriël Metsu, Nicolaes Berchem, Ambrosius Bosschaert the Elder, Isaack Koedijck, Adriaen Coorte, Jacob Backer, Willem Heda, Paulus Potter, Jan Baptist Weenix, Aelbert Cuyp, Jan van Goyen, Jan Davidsz de Heem, Jacob van Ruisdael, Balthasar van der Ast, Emanuel de Witte, Jan Steen, Jacob van Ruisdael, Simon de Vlieger, Jan van der Heyden, Frans van Mieris the Elder, Adam Pijnacker, Willem van Aelst, Philips Wouwerman, Gerard Houckgeest, Nicolaes Maes, Jan Porcellis, Jacob van Ruisdael, Willem van de Velde the Younger, Hendrick Avercamp, Jan van de Cappelle, Gerrit Dou, Rembrandt, Frans Hals, Karel du Jardin, Adriaen van Ostade, Salomon van Ruysdael, Jan Both, Jan Lievens, Rachel Ruysch, Willem van de Velde the Elder, Aert van der Neer, Esaias van de Velde, Salomon de Bray, Pieter Claesz, Gabriël Metsu, Nicolaes Berchem, Ambrosius Bosschaert the Elder, Isaack Koedijck, Adriaen Coorte, Jacob Backer, Willem Heda, Paulus Potter, Jan Baptist Weenix, Aelbert Cuyp, Jan van Goyen, Jan Davidsz de Heem, Jacob van Ruisdael, Balthasar van der Ast, Emanuel de Witte, Jan Steen, Jacob van Ruisdael, Simon de Vlieger, Jan van der Heyden, Frans van Mieris the Elder, Adam Pijnacker, Willem van Aelst, Philips Wouwerman, Gerard Houckgeest, Nicolaes Maes, Jan Porcellis, Jacob van Ruisdael, Willem van de Velde the Younger, Hendrick Avercamp, Jan van de Cappelle, Gerrit Dou, Rembrandt, Frans Hals, Karel du Jardin, Adriaen van Ostade, Salomon van Ruysdael, Jan Lievens, Rachel Ruysch, Willem van de Velde the Elder

This publication was produced to accompany the exhibition
Made in Holland: Old Masters from an American Private Collection

Royal Picture Gallery Mauritshuis, The Hague
4 November 2010 through 30 January 2011

This exhibition was possible thanks to the support of
the Turing Foundation, the Friends of the Mauritshuis
Foundation and NIBC

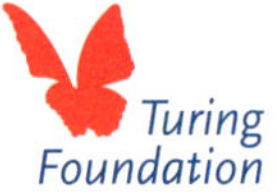 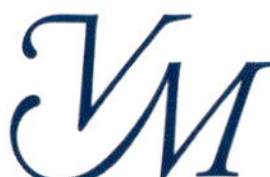 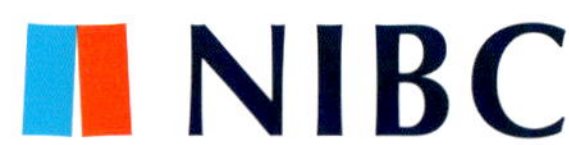

Made in Holland

Highlights from the Collection of Eijk and Rose-Marie de Mol van Otterloo

Quentin Buvelot

Royal Picture Gallery Mauritshuis, The Hague
Waanders Publishers, Zwolle

Content

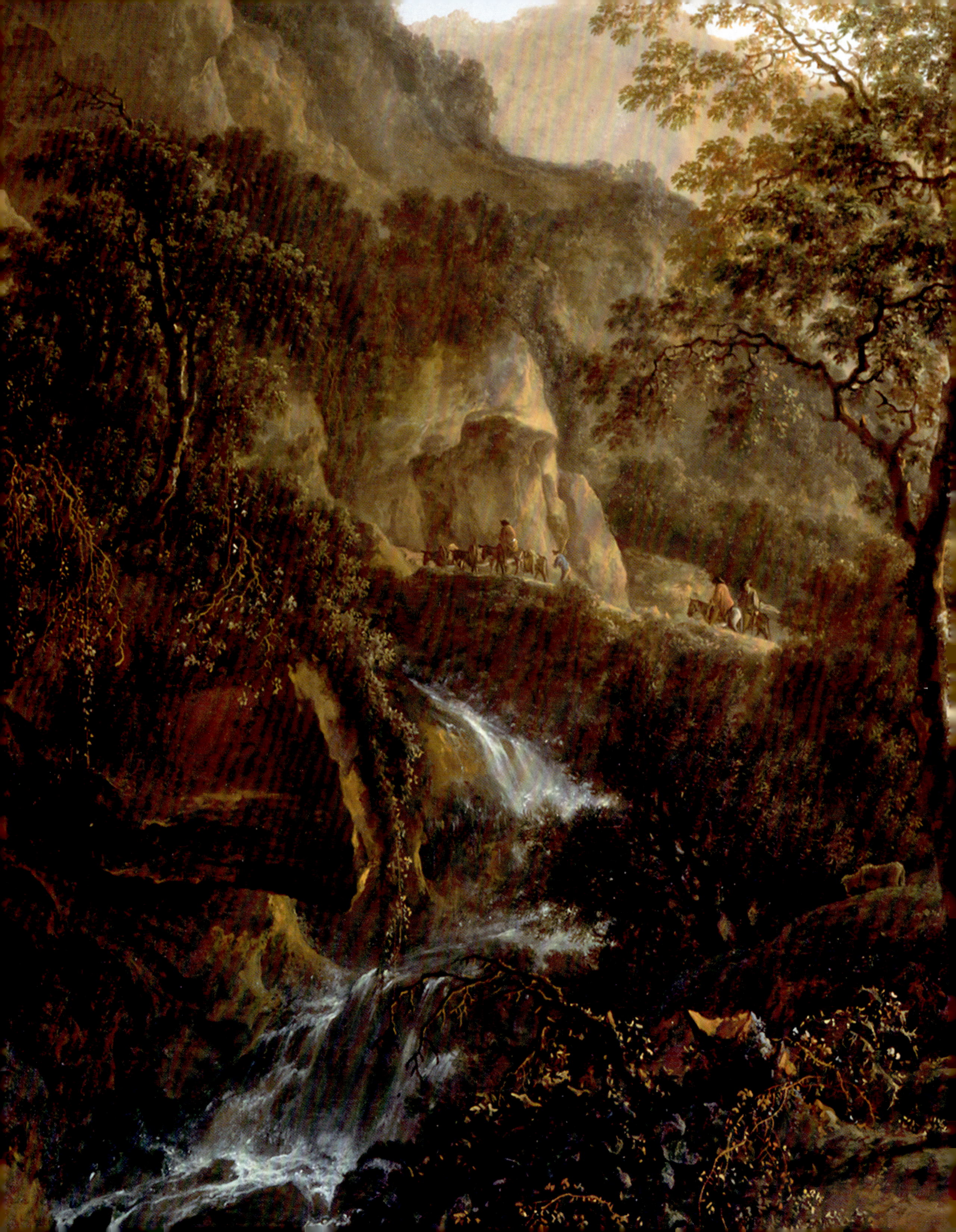

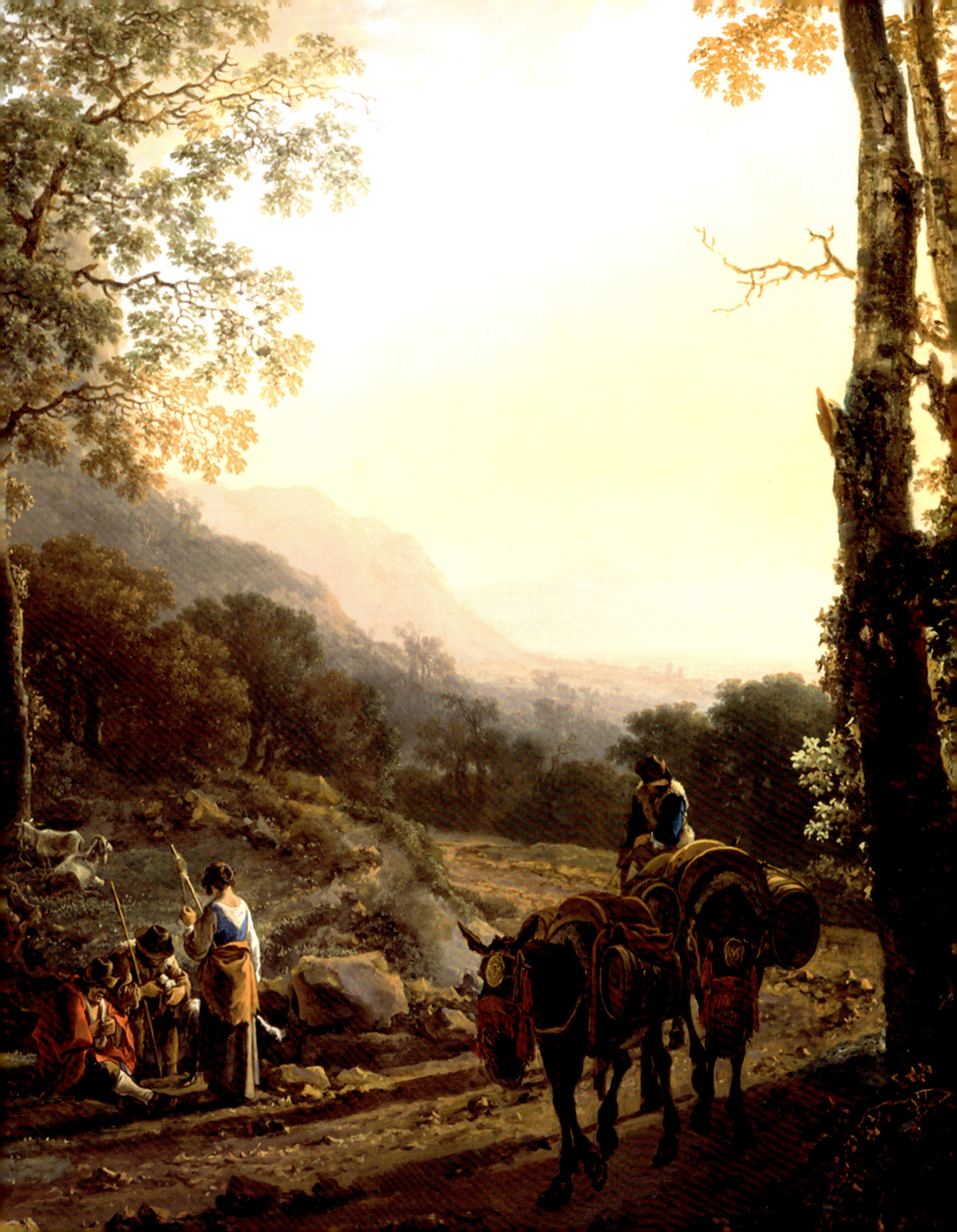

Preface

At the Mauritshuis, we think we have good reason to be proud that we are the first museum to display a selection of highlights from Eijk and Rose-Marie de Mol van Otterloo's collection of Dutch Golden Age paintings. The couple, originally from the Netherlands and Belgium, has put together a magnificent collection of paintings: all are of outstanding quality and on a par with those in leading museums in New York, Washington, London and Amsterdam, as well as The Hague. Since the paintings were originally destined to hang in private homes, the exhibition is in its element in the intimate rooms of the Mauritshuis, which was built in the seventeenth century – when the selected paintings were made – as the residence of Johan Maurits (1604–1679), count of Nassau-Siegen.

Our visitors are not always aware of the important role that private collectors have traditionally played in the activities of the Mauritshuis. Since 1822, much of the collection has been acquired through donations and bequests. In addition, loans from private collectors have long enhanced the permanent presentation, some temporarily and others on a permanent basis. Loans provided by private collectors are an indispensable part of many exhibitions in the Mauritshuis.

The Van Otterloos have been amongst the most generous lenders to the Mauritshuis in the recent past. We are now more grateful than ever for their willingness to part with their much-loved paintings for the duration of this exhibition, and we are quite sure that visitors to the exhibition will feel the same way. The exhibition could never have taken place without sponsors. The Turing Foundation provided crucial support at an early stage. NIBC also provided generous financial assistance for the exhibition and for a special educational project. The Friends of the Mauritshuis Foundation, who have long been an indispensable mainstay of our museum's activities, also provided indispensable funding.

The 44 paintings featuring in the exhibition in The Hague were selected by the Senior Curator Quentin Buvelot, in close collaboration with the collectors and their advisor, Frederik J. Duparc, the former director of the Mauritshuis. After the exhibition closes here in 2011, the entire collection of paintings will be shown, together with a smaller selection of antique furniture and decorative art, in the Peabody Essex Museum, Salem. This larger version of the show will travel on to the Fine Arts Museums of San Francisco and subsequently at the Museum of Fine Arts in Houston. We are grateful to the staff of the Museum of Fine Arts in Boston, where a number of paintings from the collection are usually on display. They undertook several minor restorations and improved the frames of a number of works. Jean Woodward coordinated these tasks, and made new digital reproductions of the paintings available to us.

Many members of staff at the Mauritshuis have worked tirelessly to make the exhibition a success. Deputy Director Victor Moussault and project leader Pia Westgren were closely involved, as were all the members of the project group. Indemnity for the insurance was obtained from the Ministry of Education, Culture and Science through the Netherlands Institute for Cultural Heritage. The insurance for the exhibits was arranged by Aon Artscope Nederland.

This publication was compiled by the exhibition's curator, Quentin Buvelot. He pulled off the difficult feat of crafting texts that are both scholarly and entertaining. In doing so, he drew on the recently published catalogue of the Van Otterloos' paintings, with contributions by Frederik J. Duparc and others. As ever, we were grateful to have the library and photograph collections of the superb Netherlands Institute for Art History (RKD) in The Hague at our disposal for catalogue research.

Made in Holland is about the subject of collecting in general, and more specifically, about collecting Old Masters in our own time. For three months, one entire storey of the Mauritshuis will be transformed as if it were the house of Eijk and Rose-Marie de Mol van Otterloo. And in that house, we will have a unique opportunity to discover many treasures that are rarely displayed in public. We hope that we will be able to welcome our visitors with the same warmth and generosity as the collectors have shown to all of us at the Mauritshuis.

Emilie Gordenker
Director

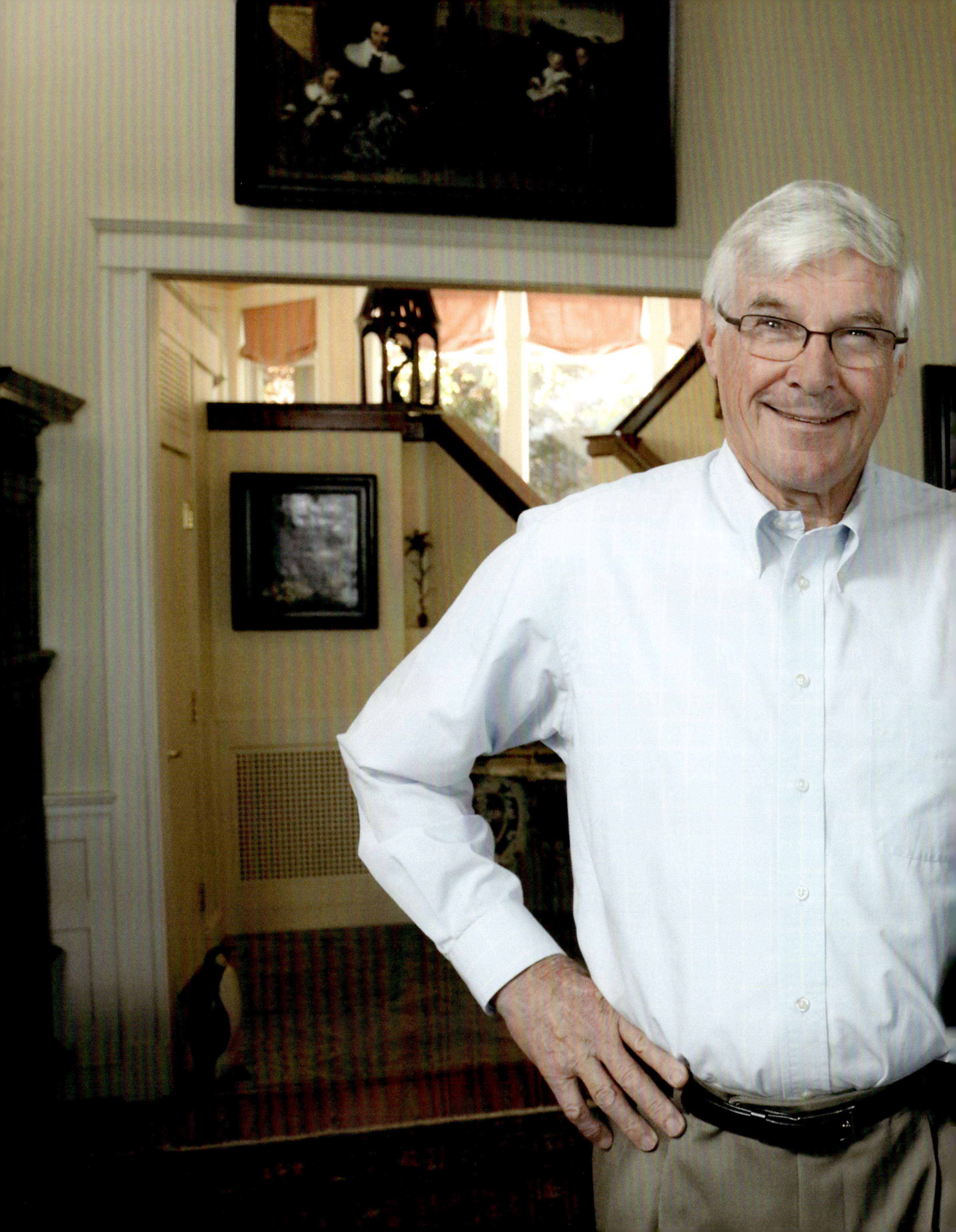

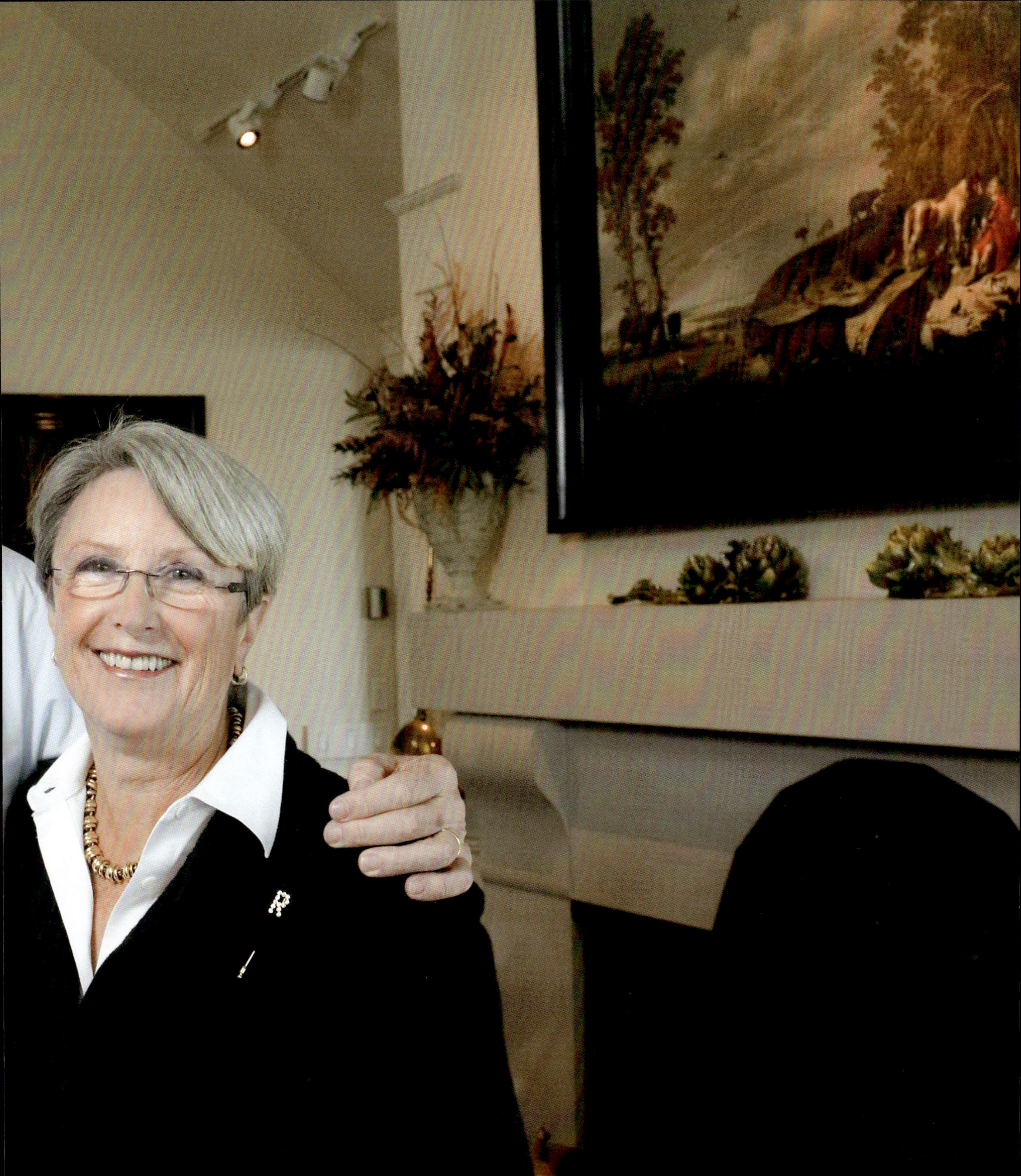

A Passion for the Golden Age

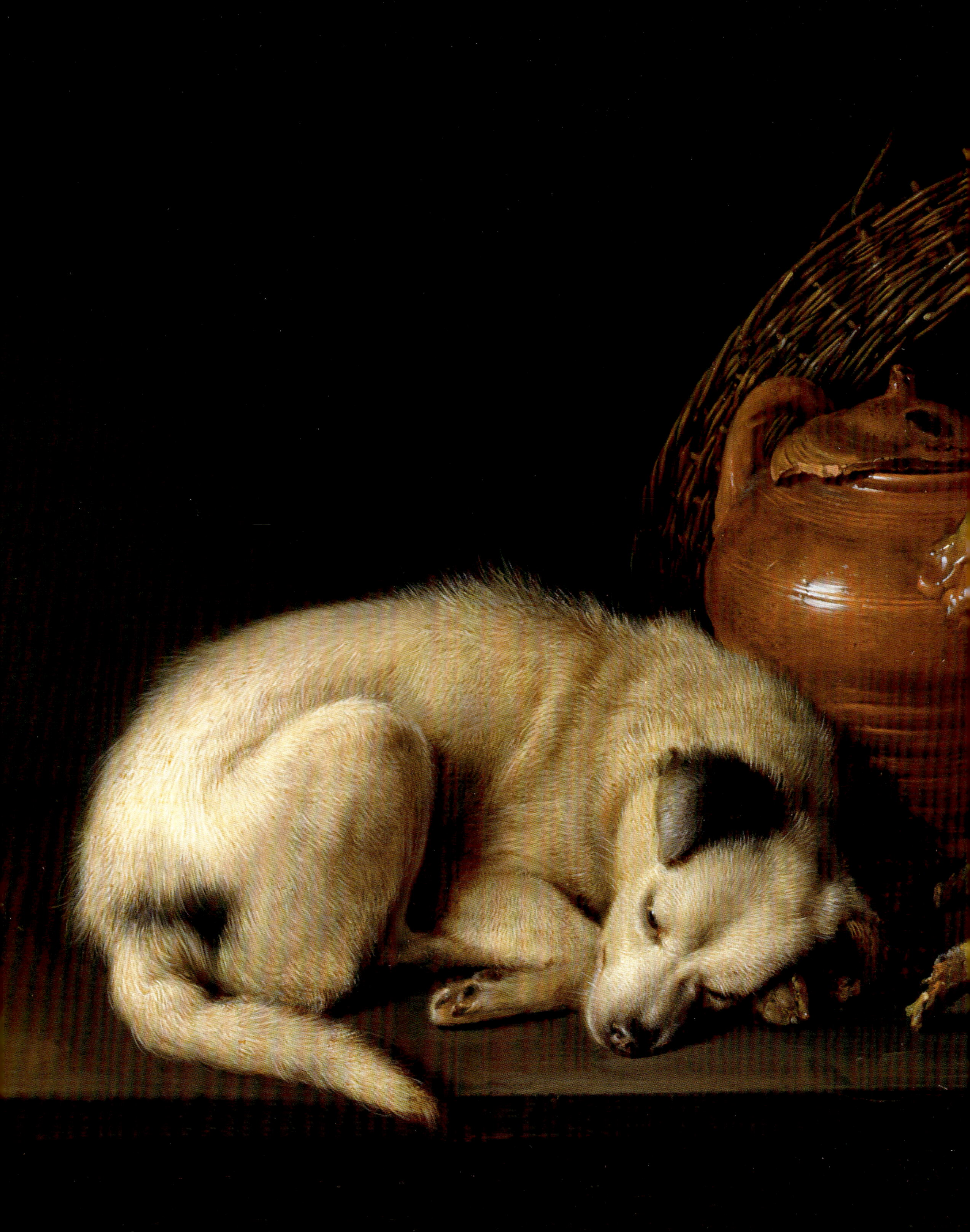

Many masterpieces by painters of the Dutch Golden Age are still in private hands. They can be found all around the world in collections that are generally not open to the public. Now the Mauritshuis has a unique opportunity to display a representative selection from one of these private collections, and a particularly remarkable one: that of Eijk and Rose-Marie de Mol van Otterloo. It is the first time that they have presented their collection in public. The occasion may prompt many questions: How old is their collection? How was it built up over the years? What are the collectors' backgrounds and who are their main examples? Do they do everything themselves, or do they seek advice from others? And is their collection now 'complete'? This introduction sets out to answer these and many other questions.[1]

The collection's 'home base' is on the east coast of the United States, a region where several other collectors live who have focused on Dutch art produced in the Golden Age.[2] Visitors to the couple's climate-controlled modern house will find themselves facing famous Dutch masters like Paulus Potter, Jan Steen, Gerrit Dou and many others (fig. pp. 12–13). It is striking that the works not only present attractive scenes, but that each one, without exception, is in outstanding condition, a criterion that the couple have emphasised more and more over the years. The paintings are displayed in an interior that is in part furnished with fine items of furniture, utensils and objects of decorative art from the same period. Still, notwithstanding all the care lavished on the interior, the house is no museum: it is truly lived in. The couple's children and grandchildren enjoy coming to visit, and have long since come to take these beautiful surroundings for granted. Rose-Marie de Mol van Otterloo explains: 'We live with our collection. This is our home'. This makes the house an ideal place to lose oneself in reveries about the past. After all, these paintings were originally made to be hung in private homes, and in a modern home such as this one, too, they can clearly be seen to fine advantage.

The collection has never been together in one place before: the couple lend generously, both to exhibitions and to permanent presentations at museums. Museum directors and curators always find the owners obliging when applying for loans for an exhibition. Anyone who studies the exhibition history of these paintings will see that they are frequently selected for major shows in all parts of the world.

The 'visible world'

A sweet, fluffy mouse or an appealing little dog, winter landscapes or summer scenes
with shepherds, a woman eating porridge or a fiddler, a portrait of an old lady or a
tronie of a young girl: all the main genres of seventeenth-century Dutch painting are
represented in the collection. The couple clearly feel a connection with the 'visible
world': besides landscapes, which account for the largest part of the collection, we also
see portraits, still lifes and genre paintings.[3] There are also a number of history paintings,
but scenes from classical antiquity or Greek mythology are almost completely absent.[4]
The Dutch landscape is well represented, including three works by the greatest landscape painter of the Golden Age, Jacob van Ruisdael, that demonstrate this artist's
versatility: the Van Otterloos purchased a winter landscape, a woodland scene, and a
panorama. The work of Salomon van Ruysdael, Van Ruisdael's uncle and one of his
teachers, is also well represented, with two paintings (see p. 21, fig. 3). In the summer
of 2008, the collector couple acquired a splendid winter landscape by Aert van der Neer.
It presents a delightful picture of a snow shower, a motif very seldom depicted. This
magnificent painting is shown in The Hague with the winter scenes of Van Ruisdael
and Jan van Goyen, and the 'winter painter' Hendrick Avercamp. An unexpected high-
light is *Orpheus Charming the Animals*, a large landscape by Aelbert Cuyp, showing a scene
based on a passage in Ovid's *Metamorphoses*. One of the rare history paintings made by
the Dordrecht landscape painter, this is among his earliest works.

Besides the low-lying Dutch countryside, we also see the Italian landscape depicted
in work by Italianate artists such as Nicolaes Berchem, Jan Both, Karel du Jardin and
Adam Pijnacker. Seascapes by father and son Willem van de Velde the Elder and the
Younger show the Dutch Republic as a seafaring nation. Lovers of seascapes are also
well catered for: there are paintings by Jan van de Cappelle, Jan Porcellis and Simon
de Vlieger. In the still life section, it is striking that three of the painters, Balthasar van
der Ast, Ambrosius Bosschaert and Adriaen Coorte, were active in Middelburg; all their
works are executed on a small scale. The collection also includes work by famous still-
life painters such as Jan Davidsz de Heem, Pieter Claesz and Willem Heda. In the portrait
section, our attention is immediately drawn to a group of masterpieces by Rembrandt
and Frans Hals. A family portrait by Jan Baptist Weenix, who is famous largely as a
landscape painter, is very rare. Besides portraits, we also find *tronies* painted by Jacob
Backer, Jan Lievens and Salomon de Bray. A *tronie* is a type or character study; these studies
of young women were never intended as portraits, but constitute excellent material for
comparison with work by the portrait painters mentioned. Everyday life is at the heart
of the work produced by painters such as Jan Steen, Nicolaes Maes, Adriaen van Ostade
and Frans van Mieris the Elder. Church interiors by Gerrit Houckgeest and Emanuel
de Witte show the surroundings in which Dutch society practised its religious life.

The History of a Collection

After their marriage in 1974, Eijk and Rose-Marie de Mol van Otterloo started by collecting not paintings but antique carriages and English sporting prints for their attractively furnished farmhouse in New Hampshire. 'We collected everything related to horses and farms: utensils, and art and decorative arts made of wood and silver', says Rose-Marie. After they moved to a seaside house, this collection was no longer in an appropriate setting, and the couple were ready for something new. It was Peter Sutton – then curator of European painting at the Museum of Fine Arts in Boston, and now director of the Bruce Museum in Greenwich, Conn. – who encouraged them to start collecting Dutch and Flemish masters from the seventeenth century. In the late 1980s, Sutton not only introduced them to collectors, dealers and art fairs in Europe and the United States, but also helped to familiarise them with the works that were offered for sale. In these early years, they collected eagerly and enthusiastically, buying at auctions as well as in the art trade. They started with landscapes by Nicolaes Berchem and Jan van Goyen.[5] Some paintings are still in the collection today, including the still lifes by Bosschaert and Coorte, but many others have been sold (see also below). One exception is a painting purchased in 1993, which was soon exposed as a copy after Jan Steen's famous painting *The Poultry Yard*, in the Mauritshuis. These days the collectors can smile when they recall this purchase, which they keep as a souvenir, but it was a sobering experience at the time. Over the years, as they studied and compared works of art, they developed an increasingly discerning eye. Their activities eventually resulted in one of the most important private collections of seventeenth-century Dutch paintings in the world. Some Flemish paintings, such as an early landscape from 1609 by Jan Brueghel the Elder (1568–1625), supplement the Dutch works in art-historical terms (fig. 1).[6] A major source of inspiration was the superb collection of Dutch paintings from the Golden Age built up by the late Edward and Hannah Carter, whose collection is now preserved at the Los Angeles County Museum of Art. The Van Otterloos saw this collection of 35 paintings, predominantly small cabinet pictures in perfect condition, as posing a challenge, and set out to build up a similar or even better collection of their own.[7]

To build up a collection of this quality, one needs not only the necessary budget, but also a certain expertise in the field of art and an understanding of its market. From October 1995 onwards, Simon Levie (born in 1925), former director of the Rijksmuseum in Amsterdam, was closely involved with the collection's growth in an advisory capacity. On this informal advisorship, Eijk de Mol van Otterloo says: 'Those days, we were being offered so much that we couldn't see the wood for the trees. What's more, everything looked equally beautiful to our eyes. We didn't want to do anything stupid, and so we knew we needed help'. From then on, they deliberated carefully over every purchase, as is clear from the detailed correspondence between Levie and the collectors.[8]

1

Jan Brueghel the Elder, *A Village Scene with Figures*, 1609. Copper, 22 × 32 cm. Acquired in 1995.

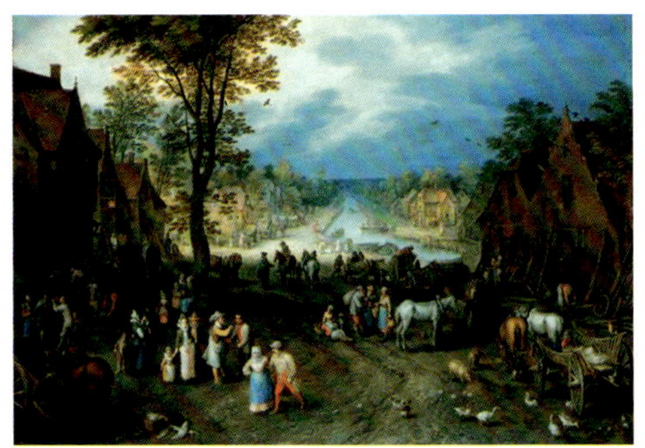

That diverse factors played a role in their purchases is clear from a short list that Eijk de Mol van Otterloo sent to Levie: the collectors wanted to know everything about the subject of the painting, the importance of the artist, the work's place in the artist's oeuvre, its rarity and provenance, its condition, and – last but not least – the asking price. Whenever they were considering buying a painting, they looked closely at the condition of the canvas or panel. Some of the paintings were in excellent condition when they purchased them; in other cases, they have had them restored. In the latter case, the appearance of new purchases has been radically improved by removing yellowed layers of varnish and replacing old retouches. There are many examples, such as a history painting by Claes Moeyaert (1591/92–1655) that is completely unknown in the art-historical literature, which turned out, after restoration, to have been preserved in superb condition (fig. 2).[9] The appearance of another painting, Jan van de Cappelle's *Boats in a Calm* from 1651, was also greatly improved by treatment in a restoration studio.

The collection gradually became more cohesive, since purchases were assessed partly for their relationship to the paintings that were already present. The couple also looked to the future. In 1996 Levie started on a plan devoting systematic attention to the collection as a whole. Since the collection was intended to give a representative picture of the Golden Age of Dutch painting, this plan also identified gaps, in exactly the same way as a museum would analyse its holdings (see also p. 22). The main exponents were identified for each genre on the basis of thematic classification, and of these masters, only the finest works would be considered for purchase. This precisely formulated collection plan enabled the Van Otterloos to weigh their decisions on new purchases more carefully. It is obviously impossible to draw up a 'shopping list', since they are always dependent on what is offered for sale, but a 'wish list' is always useful. In September 1997 the collectors made an important purchase: they acquired Aelbert Cuyp's *Orpheus Charming the Animals* for a large sum of money. To make this purchase possible, they sold several works that were of relatively inferior quality or less well preserved, a decision that they made with painstaking scrupulousness. That was not the only time that paintings were replaced by other, better works to raise the average quality of the collection. In a different case, one still life by Willem van Aelst was exchanged for another, which the collectors saw as a more attractive picture. The quality of the collection was steadily improved: the couple purchased less, and what they bought was of the highest quality, even though prices continue to rise.

In 2005 the collection was elevated to a higher level with the purchase of Rembrandt's portrait of Aeltje Uylenburgh (1632), since then the collection's undisputed *pièce de resistance*.[10] Rose-Marie de Mol van Otterloo calls this painting, which came from the celebrated Rothschild collection, 'the jewel in the crown of our collection' (on the painting's provenance, see pp. 90–91). To purchase the Rembrandt, a process that took some three years, the Van Otterloos again sold a group of paintings – 18 works in total.

2

Claes Moeyaert, *Esau Selling his Birthright to Jacob*, c. 1630–1635. Panel, 68 × 83 cm. Acquired in 1994.

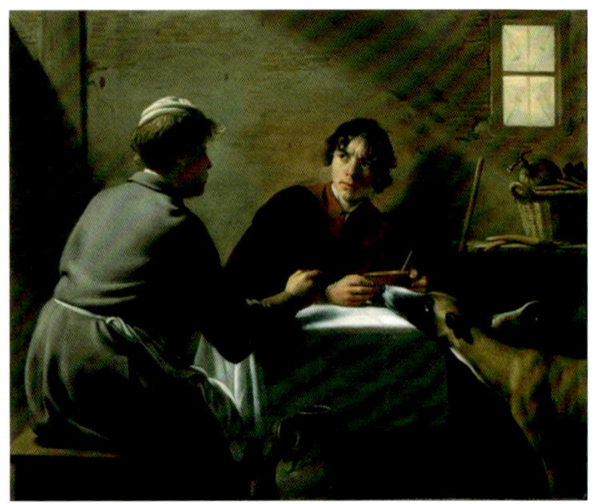

Two advisors were involved in this radical decision: Levie himself and Frederik J. Duparc (born in 1948), who was the director of the Mauritshuis at the time and who succeeded Levie as the couple's advisor in 2009. When it came to deciding which works should be sold, the lists of suggestions that Levie and Duparc drew up separately from one another (in addition to the Van Otterloos' own list) each contained 18 paintings, and proved to be almost identical, with just one exception. Pictures by artists including Jan van der Heyden, Jan Miense Molenaer, Salomon van Ruysdael and Philips Wouwerman were sold. Eijk found parting with these works more difficult than Rose-Marie, whose verdict was crystal-clear: 'once they [the paintings that were sold] were gone, I thought that our collection was more beautiful and more cohesive'.

'Aeltje' has never in fact been hung at home, but has always been displayed in public: in 2005 it was shown for some time in the Mauritshuis, opposite Rembrandt's famous *Anatomy Lesson of Dr Nicolaes Tulp*, also dating from 1632, after which it moved to the Museum of Fine Arts in Boston in the spring of 2008.[11] Eijk and Rose-Marie enjoy the attention that 'Aeltje' commands among enthusiastic museum-goers. This was not the only painting to be sent straight to an art gallery after its acquisition. In 2006, Salomon van Ruysdael's *River Landscape with Ferry*, dated 1649 (fig. 3) was transferred on long-term loan to the Rijksmuseum in Amsterdam, which had been obliged to return a similar painting dating from the same year to its rightful owner.[12] When the Van Otterloos bought Jan Both's large landscape, the artist's greatest masterpiece, in 2007, they imme-diately transferred it to Los Angeles, to the J. Paul Getty Museum, which had tried to buy the work for its own collection. Another leading American museum, the National Gallery of Art in Washington, also usually displays a number of paintings from the collection, including *An Elegant Company in a Garden* by Esaias van de Velde.

The Van Otterloos' ongoing activities prove that collecting seventeenth-century Dutch paintings has in no sense come to a standstill.[13] Everyone who takes an active interest in the Golden Age knows that a vast number of paintings of superior quality were produced in that period. That explains why major works continue to appear on the market, even some by great names such as Rembrandt, Hals and Steen, although the supply is definitely declining. Timing is of the essence when seeking to acquire attrac-tive, superior paintings of this kind, since there will always be competition, from private collectors as well as from art galleries with ample means. That opportunities still abound is clear from the recent acquisition, in 2008 and 2009, of successive masterpieces by Aert van der Neer, Esaias van de Velde, Gabriel Metsu, Salomon de Bray and Pieter Claesz. Virtually unknown works by great masters are occasionally discovered, such as the appealing *Resting Dog* by Gerrit Dou, which lived a concealed existence for a long period of time. When sold at public auction in 2005 it fetched a very high price, the highest ever paid at auction for a Dou. Both Eijk and Rose-Marie felt 'love at first sight' for this painting.

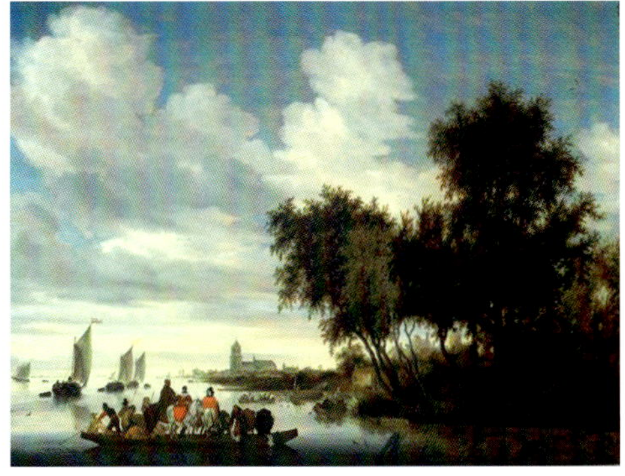

3

Salomon van Ruysdael, *River Landscape with Ferry*, 1649. Panel, 91 × 126 cm. Acquired in 2006 (on long-term loan to the Rijksmuseum, Amsterdam).

The Future

The project launched some time ago to publish Eijk and Rose-Marie de Mol van Otterloo's collection in an official catalogue has since been completed. This voluminous book includes all the 67 paintings belonging to the collection in 2010,[14] even the most recent acquisitions, such as the delightful tronie by the classicist painter Salomon de Bray and the still life by Claesz. The publication of this catalogue should by no means be taken as an indication that the collection is now 'complete'. When asked about their plans, the collectors say that they still have a 'wish list' of future acquisitions. While not divulging too much detail, they mention a few names that are still missing from the collection: Hendrick ter Brugghen, Pieter de Hooch, and Judith Leyster – three artists whose work is extremely rare and is therefore seldom offered for sale. Still, one never knows what the future may bring.

The Van Otterloos are also deliberating about the best future location for their collection. For they are determined that this collection, their life's work, will be preserved intact. The children know that they will not inherit the paintings. How and where the couple wish to make the collection permanently accessible to the public in the future has not yet been settled, although they hope that it can be preserved in its entirety in a foundation in the United States, the country that made all this possible. The current exhibition provides a fine opportunity to contemplate this destination in more concrete terms. In Eijk's words, 'It will help us to decide what we're going to do with the collection in the future'.

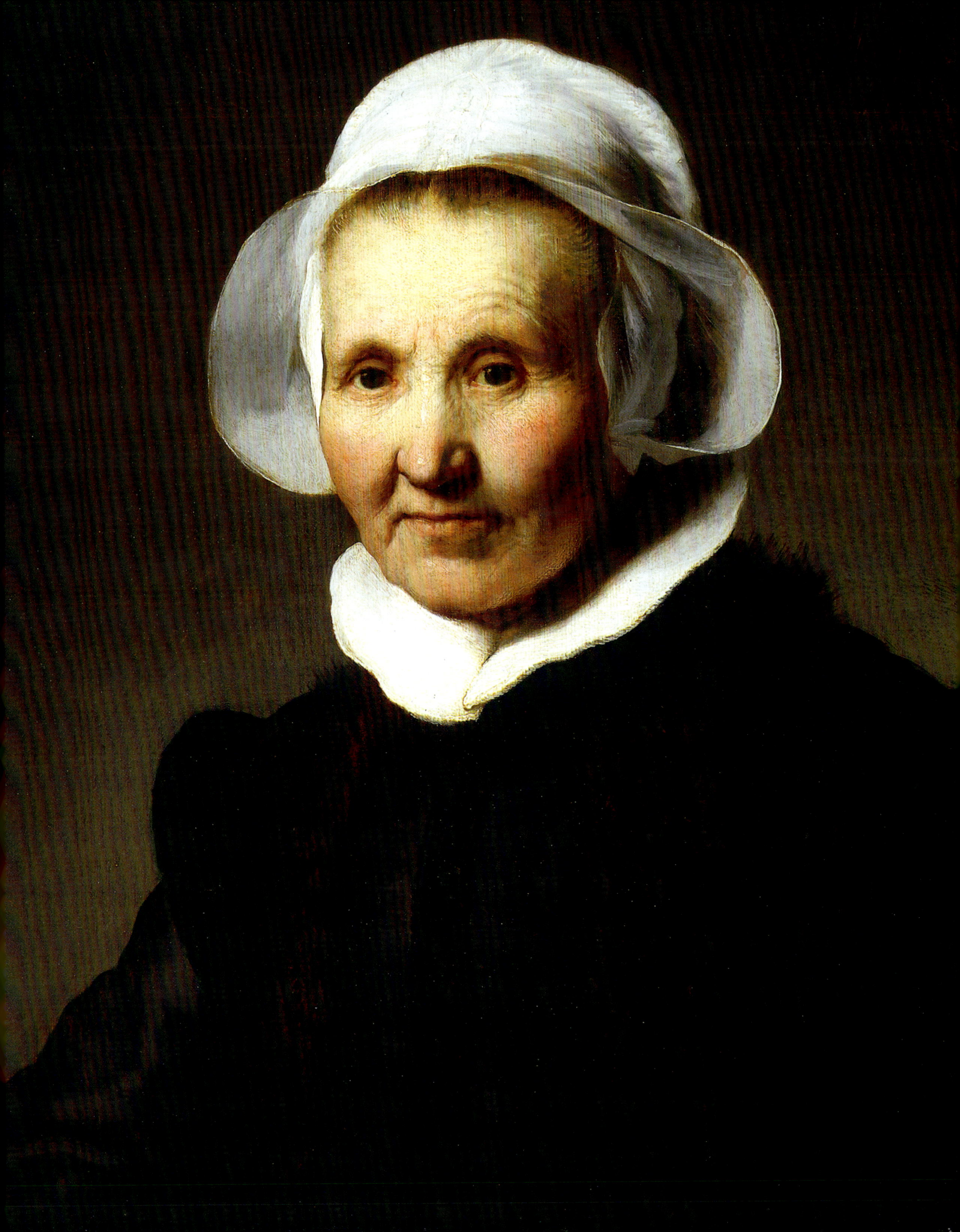

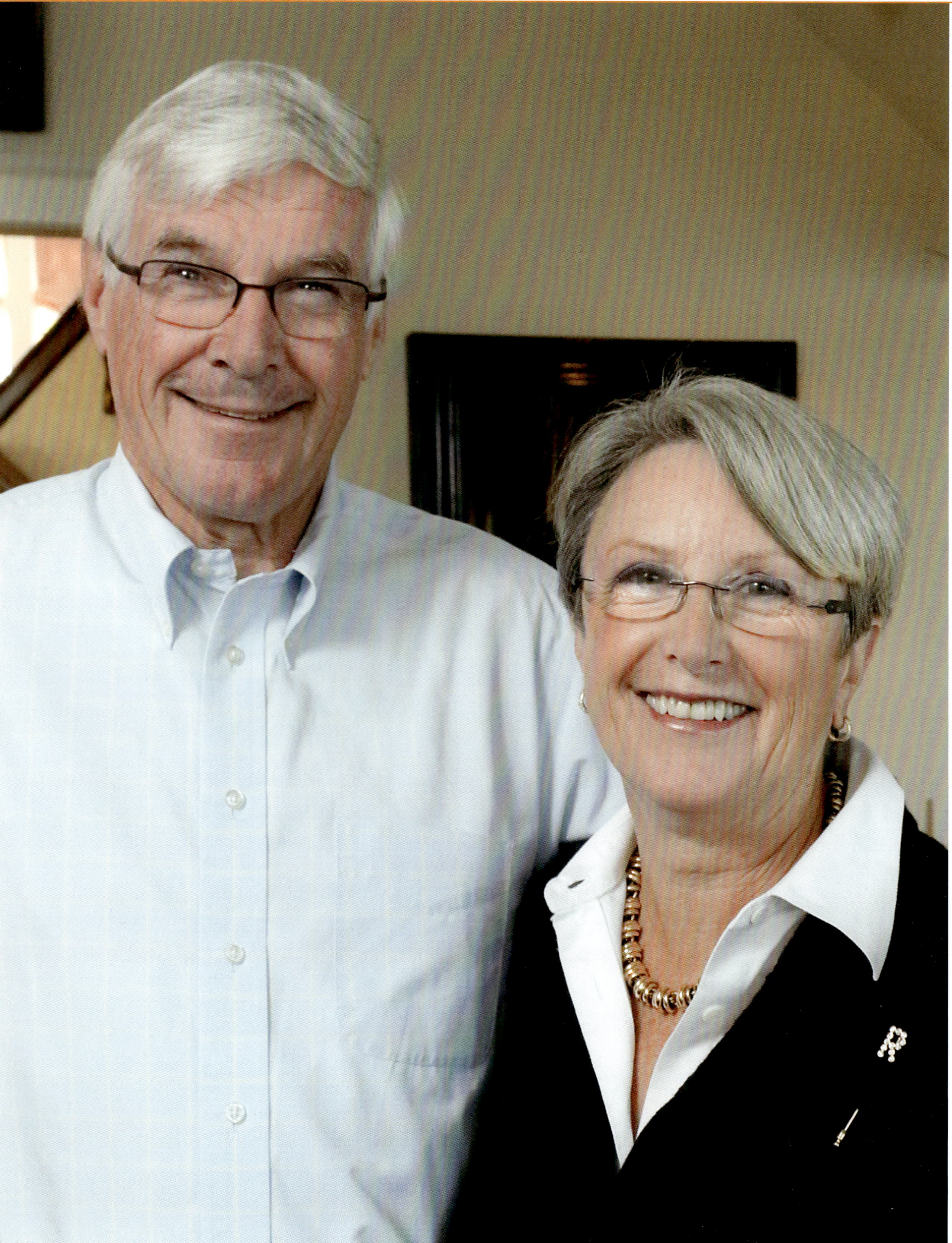

On Eijk and Rose-Marie de Mol van Otterloo

Eijk de Mol van Otterloo (born in Amsterdam in 1937) is an American investment expert. But he was raised in Amsterdam, where his school often organised visits to the Rijksmuseum, in the course of which he and his fellow pupils at the Montessori Lyceum would be told a story about one of the paintings in the collection. 'The visits to the museum always made a big impression on us, even though we did not always understand those explanations about diagonal lines or light and shade'. He studied economics at the University of Amsterdam, and then moved to the United States, where he took an MBA at Harvard Business School. He subsequently worked at Keystone Custodian Funds, Inc. and Phoenix Mutual Life Insurance Company. In 1977 Eijk de Mol van Otterloo established an investment company in Boston together with Jeremy Grantham and Dick Mayo. This company, which started life as Grantham, Mayo, Van Otterloo & Co LLC, is now known simply as GMO. In 2010, the company has offices in Boston, San Francisco, London, Zürich, Sydney and Singapore.

Like her husband Eijk, Rose-Marie de Mol van Otterloo-Jacobs (born in Kinrooi in the province of Limburg in Belgium in 1945) is a great art lover. She can reminisce enthusiastically about her childhood school trips to the main museums of Antwerp and Brussels, under the wing of an inspiring teacher. In October 1974 she married Eijk de Mol van Otterloo in Hartford, Connecticut. They have children, and now, to their great delight, grandchildren. Eijk and Rose-Marie are loyal members of the Museum of Fine Arts (MFA) in Boston, where some of their paintings have been displayed on loan since the spring of 2008, including Rembrandt's *Portrait of Aeltje Uylenburgh*. In 2003 the couple donated five etchings by this master to the museum, besides which they also sponsor a paintings conservator there. Eijk sat on the Board of Trustees of the MFA for many years, and Rose-Marie is now a board member herself. She is also vice-president of the board of the Peabody Essex Museum in Salem. Among her many public responsibilities is the management of the Van Otterloo Family Foundation, set up in 1997 to support special education programmes. The couple also contribute to various other charities worldwide.

For a comprehensive overview of the collection, readers are referred to
F.J. Duparc et al., *The Collection of Eijk and Rose-Marie de Mol van Otterloo*,
New Haven-London 2010. This catalogue also contains the full provenance
details, exhibition history and literature of the paintings described here.

Highlights

from the Collection of Eijk and Rose-Marie
de Mol van Otterloo

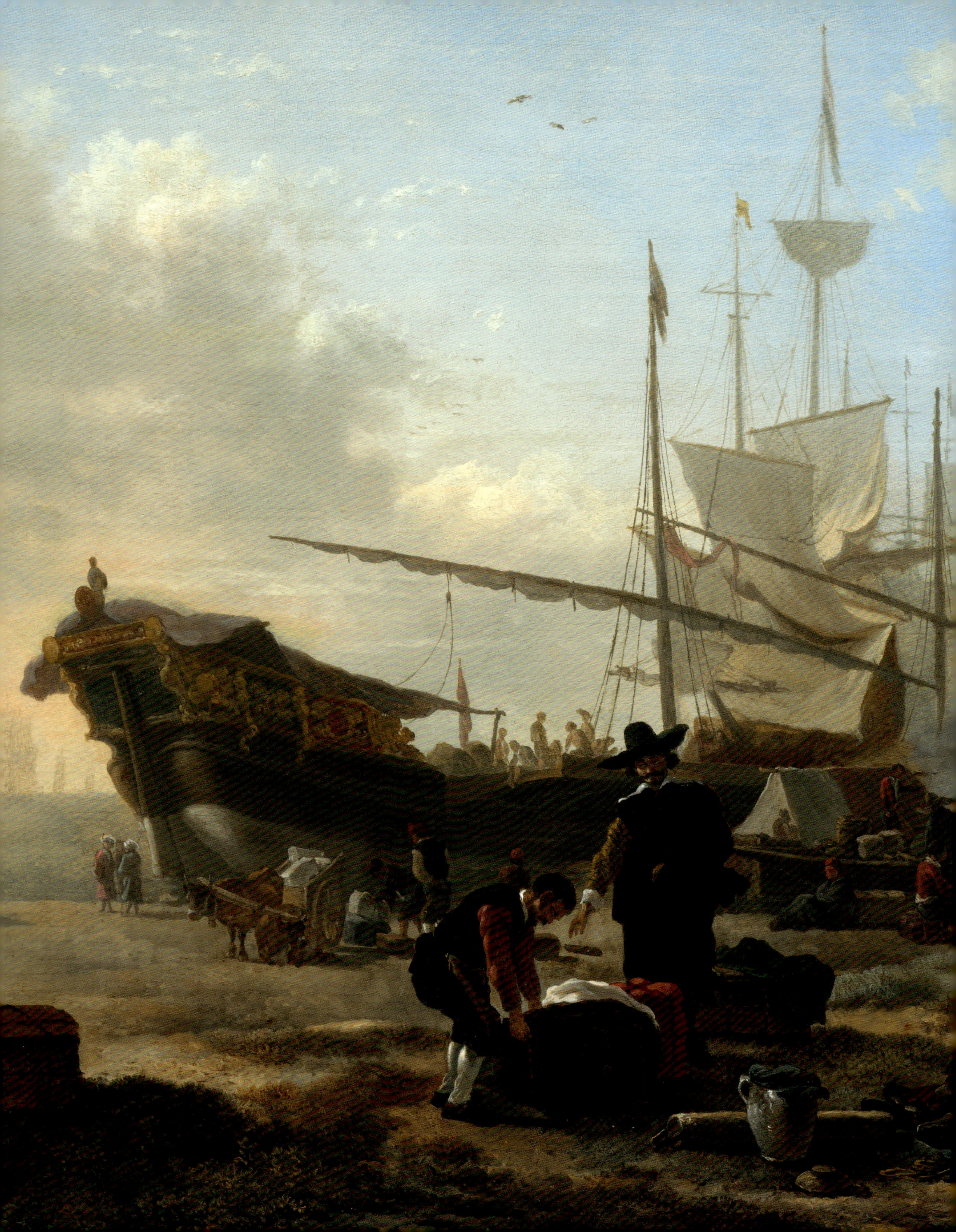

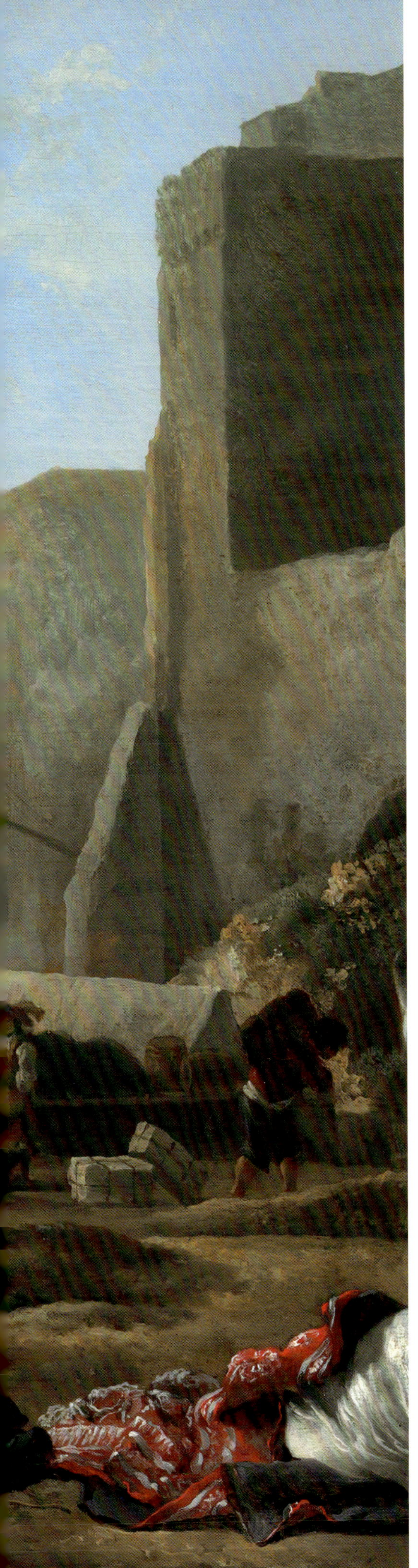

Landscapes & Seascapes

Landscape painters abounded in the Golden Age. Like the still life painters of the day, they developed highly specialised areas of expertise: some confined themselves to such motifs as ice scenes, cityscapes, seascapes or moonlit landscapes. The characteristic landscape of the Dutch Republic with its numerous rivers was recorded in countless paintings, drawings and prints. This Dutch landscape originated in the work of artists who had been active in the Southern Netherlands in the sixteenth century, and who had fled to the North after the fall of Antwerp. Such is the realism of these scenes that we are sometimes inclined to forget that painted landscapes were always created in the painter's studio. Not until the nineteenth century – with the production of oil paint in tubes – did artists start painting in the open air.

Besides countless motifs from rural Holland, Dutch landscapes of the Golden Age also featured motifs derived from landscapes further afield. Allart van Everdingen (1621–1675) went to Norway and Sweden in 1644, for instance. But no seventeenth-century landscape painter travelled as widely as the Haarlem artist Frans Post (1612–1680). At the end of 1636, Post set sail for Brazil, in the service of his patron, Count Johan Maurits of Nassau-Siegen (1604–1679), today known chiefly as the man who commissioned what is now the Mauritshuis, in The Hague. After he returned to the Netherlands in 1644, Post again settled in Haarlem, where he enjoyed a monopoly on Brazilian landscapes to the end of his days. Most artists sought inspiration rather closer to home, however. Italy had for centuries been the land of dreams for artists from the north. Many seventeenth-century Dutch artists crossed the Alps, whether seeking the remains of ancient civilisation or driven by curiosity about the art of the Renaissance and Baroque. *En passant* they discovered the golden light that played over the often arcadian landscape. Many also visited France, sometimes lingering there on their way to Italy.

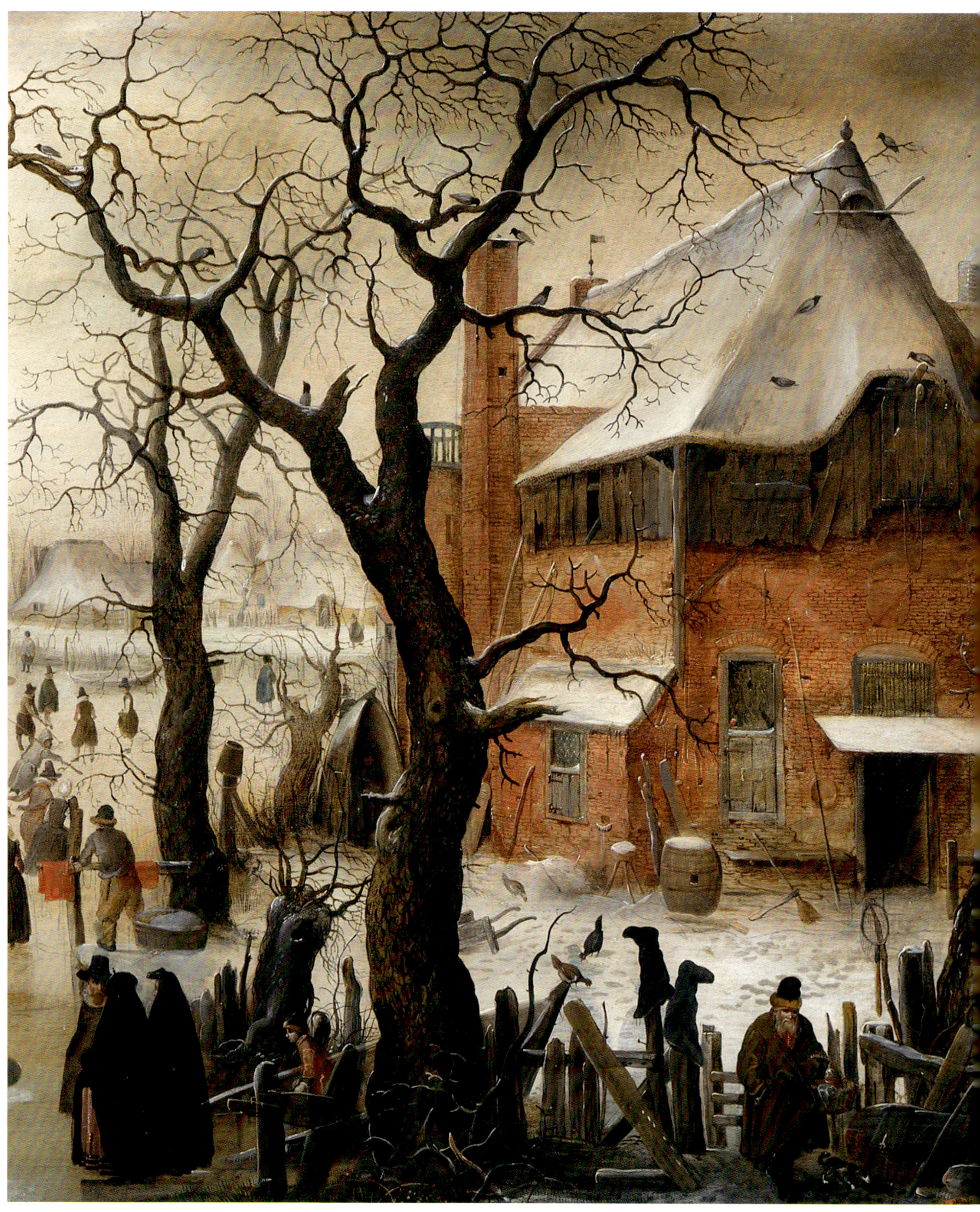

Landscapes

Hendrick Avercamp
Winter Landscape with Skaters
c.1610–1615

Hendrick Avercamp (1585–1634) was the
first Dutch artist to specialise in drawing
and painting a genre that became typical
of the painting of the Golden Age: skating
scenes. Under a grey sky, a frozen canal
in a village provides the setting for this
wintry scene. With great attention to
anecdotal details, Avercamp painted
numerous little figures, whose meticulously rendered clothing shows them to
be from all walks of life. In the foreground,
our attention is drawn to richly dressed
figures. Further away, couples sweep
across the ice, hand in hand, while some
gentlemen are playing kolf, a precursor
of modern ice hockey. The boots hung up
to dry on the fence in the right foreground
add a fine realistic note. Avercamp concentrated on faithfully rendering the landscape, with snow and ice to a large extent
determining the colours and the play of
light. He succeeded in depicting the light,
the sky and the atmosphere convincingly,
but never ventured to depict snowfall (see
pp. 36–37). The underdrawing has become
visible in some sections.

This painting by 'the Mute of Kampen'
was probably painted around 1610–1615,
when the deaf and dumb painter was
living in Kampen after his apprenticeship
in Amsterdam. It still reflects the influence
of the Flemish landscape tradition, which
had developed in Antwerp starting with
Pieter Bruegel the Elder (1520/25–1569).
Characteristic elements in this respect

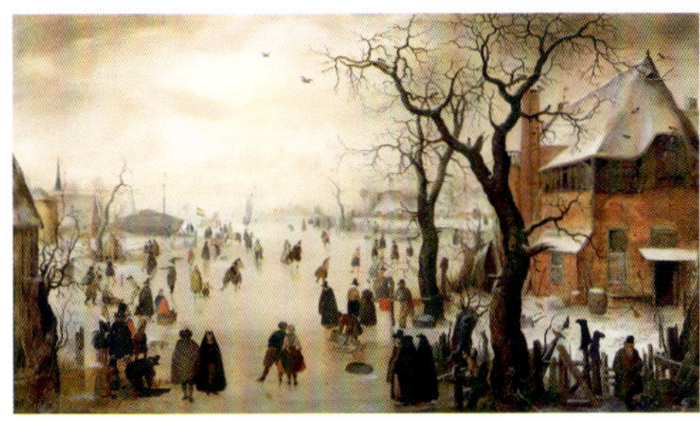

include the tall, decorative trees on the
right, and the house and tree in the left
foreground, serving as repoussoir, as well
as the stage-like composition, the many
colourful details and the anecdotal quality
of the scene. The theme of a winter landscape with skaters originates from the
sixteenth-century Flemish tradition of
depicting the months and the seasons.

The popularity of winter landscapes
in seventeenth-century painting was
directly related to the unusual climatic
conditions of the period.[15] From about
1550 to 1850 the whole of northwest
Europe passed through the Little Ice
Age, a period of extremely harsh winters
and relatively cool summers. In the
Netherlands, two-thirds of the winters
between 1600 and 1700 ranged from
cold to extremely severe. The country
endured long periods of frost and snow,
during which a thick layer of ice on
Holland's inland waterways made
navigation impossible and brought
part of public life to a standstill. It was
in the very period with the harshest
winters that Avercamp produced the
wintry landscapes that have come to
exemplify Dutch painting. As they
focused on producing realistic images

of their country, landscape painters
naturally documented these weather
conditions. Snow and ice alter the light
effects and colours in a landscape, and
artists saw it as a challenge to render the
light, sky and atmosphere true to life.
Recent technical research has revealed
Avercamp's astute use of the optical
properties of pigments to convey the wet,
icy cold convincingly in his paintings.[16]

Jan van Goyen
Winter Landscape with Skaters
1637

Jan van Goyen (1596–1656) belonged to
the first generation of painters to dedicate
themselves exclusively to depicting the
Dutch landscape. His ability to render
the atmosphere of the watery lands of
Holland was unparalleled. In the early
stages of his career, Van Goyen painted
dozens of Flemish-looking winter landscapes, largely populated with colourful
little figures. These pictures, many of
which were made as pendants for summer
landscapes, were greatly influenced by

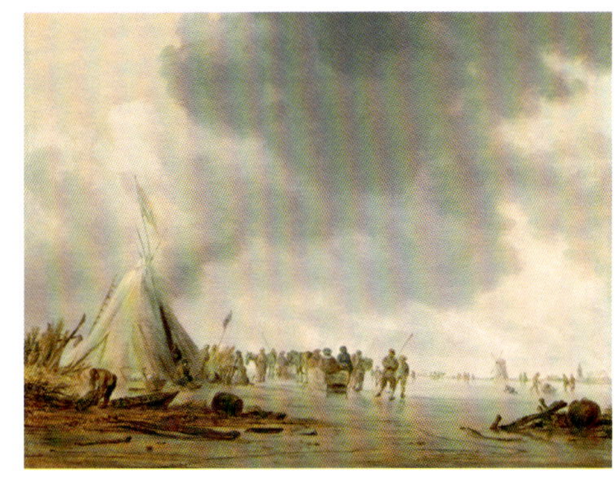

the work of his teacher, Esaias van de Velde (p. 65). From around 1630 Van Goyen reduced his palette to a limited number of earth colours. This predominantly monochrome quality would remain a constant factor in his paintings. *Winter Landscape with Skaters*, from 1637, is a separate winter landscape, in which the emphasis is on atmosphere. The horizon here is considerably lower than in the paintings from Van Goyen's early period. More than three-quarters of the painting is taken up by the sky. Dark clouds have gathered, which become lighter and less compact further into the distance.

Van Goyen worked rapidly and was a prolific artist: his extant oeuvre includes over 1,200 paintings. They include about 100 winter landscapes,[17] of which this painting is undoubtedly one of the most beautiful. On a wide expanse of ice, people are having fun skating or sledding. In the left foreground a fisherman is picking up a basket beside an icebound boat. The stall behind him, with a flag, is selling hot meals as well as other refreshments, judging from the smoke wafting from the tent. Diverse figures are depicted outside the tent, including a man smoking a pipe. On the horizon we see a windmill and a church tower. Here and there, subtle colour accents have been added to this otherwise monochrome painting, such as the red cap of the skater at the front. In this landscape, which was painted briskly, wet-on-wet, the brushstrokes are clearly visible. In some parts of the foreground, Van Goyen has allowed the underlying ground to glimmer through.

Jan Both
Italianate Landscape with Travellers
c.1645–1650

Jan Both (*c.*1615–1652) was one of the most gifted of the Italianates. After training in his home town of Utrecht, he went to Rome to join his brother Andries (*c.*1612–1641), who had been working as an artist there for some time. The brothers must have moved in the circles of the legendary fraternity of Dutch artists in Rome known as the Bentvueghels ('roost-fellows'). In 1639, Jan Both, who largely specialised in landscapes, received an important commission for the king of Spain's new summer palace in Madrid, Buon Retiro. Both spent the last ten years of his short life in Utrecht, where he died in 1652. Together with Jan Asselijn (*c.*1610–1652), also represented with a painting in the Van Otterloos' collection, Both is ranked among the most important and most influential artists of the second generation of Italianates. His sun-drenched southern landscapes were widely imitated.

The composition of this landscape is characteristic for Both: the image is bounded on one side by a massive rock face, while the other side opens up to reveal a panoramic vista. The most prominent motif is a winding road leading past a waterfall at the foot of the rock, which greatly enhances the diagonal effect of the composition. All the figures are either on or near this road: one is leading two donkeys along in the foreground, while further to the left is a small group of shepherds. More figures can be seen

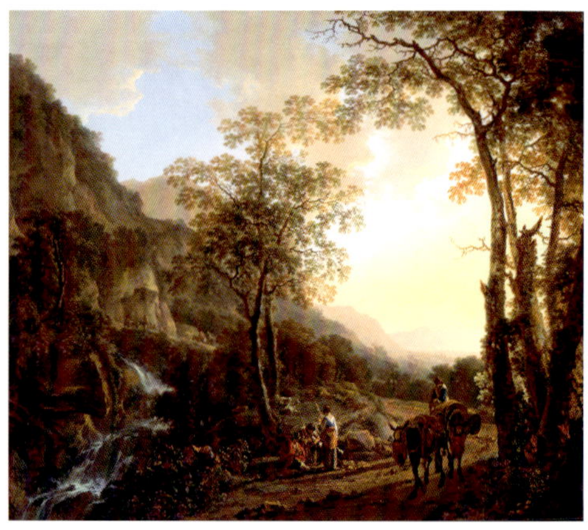

towards the background. The relatively simple structure of the composition does not immediately strike us because of the abundant greenery throughout, including the monumental trees in the foreground that are so characteristic of Both's work. Together with the hills they play an important role in enhancing the picture's depth and dominate the carefully balanced composition. The landscape bathes in a golden light, besides which it displays countless subtle nuances of colour. To achieve this, the artist made ingenious use of the light-coloured ground, which glimmers through the paint in places. Thanks to recent restoration, Both's refined use of colour can once again be admired to the full.

In general it is assumed that Both produced most of his paintings – over one hundred have been preserved – after his return to the Netherlands. Establishing a chronology for his oeuvre is difficult, since scarcely any dated landscapes are known. Judging from the relatively refined style of painting, the composition's pronounced three-dimensionality, and its warm palette, this painting can be dated to approximately 1645–1650. It is an excellent example of Both's later work.

This is the largest painting in the Van Otterloos' group of Dutch Italianates: measuring a remarkable 138 × 168 cm, it is one of the largest known works by Jan Both. But this superbly well-preserved painting is impressive not just for its size, but also for its strikingly high quality.

Paulus Potter
'The Rabbit Warren'
1647

This painting from 1647, which is signed in full, is one of the highlights in the oeuvre of Paulus Potter (1625–1654). That same year, the famous animal painter produced one of his best-known and largest paintings, *The Bull* (The Hague, Mauritshuis).[18] This work has the relatively small dimensions of what are known as 'cabinet paintings', which make up the majority of Potter's oeuvre. A group of animals is the main subject of this painting, which derives its title from the rabbit warren in the middle. Its occupant has just emerged. Around the warren from left to right, we see two donkeys (one is lying down, and is almost impossible to see among the thistles) and a goat with two kids. Another goat lies on the far right, while a third is approaching from behind the dune. Also visible is a young farmer's wife or shepherdess, who has appeared with a spindle. We are immediately struck

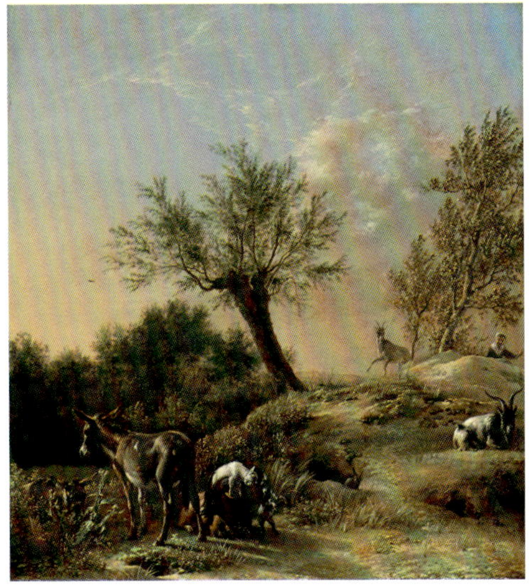

by the great liveliness of the scene. The sun bathes the scene in a warm glow, and the diverse shadows enhance the effect of depth. The characteristic light is caused by a low, late afternoon, slanting sun. The reflections of the sun's waning rays are rendered with an abundance of white highlights.

Potter undoubtedly studied the animals he depicted here in their natural surroundings. Nicolaes van Reenen, a son from the second marriage of Potter's widow, wrote in a letter to the artists' biographer Arnold Houbraken (1660–1719) that Potter habitually made drawings in the open countryside. No sketch or preliminary study can be identified for this painting, but the fact that certain motifs recur in other scenes by Potter indicates that it was based on studies from life. Potter had used the motif of little kids playing with their mother several years earlier, in a painting produced in 1643;[19]

only the coat of these creatures has a different colour. The standing donkey recurs in a painting from 1649.[20] The repetition of certain pictorial motifs is a characteristic aspect of Potter's oeuvre. In this scene, he has combined several preliminary studies of livestock observed in the meadows into a lively and convincing scene that never existed as such in reality. The animals' different positions recall the prints of Pieter van Laer (1599– after 1642), whose series of etchings depicting animals, produced in 1636, was a major influence on Potter and his contemporaries.

The animal painter's acute powers of observation are clear not only from the detailed rendering of the creatures themselves, whose diverse coats are elaborated with immense realism, but also from the representation of the landscape. The vegetation in the foreground is rendered in minute detail, while the landscape in the background is only cursorily indicated. The horizon is largely obscured from sight by the dune and the bushes. A crooked pollard willow stands out against the slightly overcast sky. The painting is based on a compositional scheme frequently used by this artist, in which a diagonal line marks the transition between the foreground and background of the landscape. It is not known whether Potter intended his picture to convey any deeper significance. Still, it is fair to assume that prosperous townspeople would have interpreted this idyllic scene as an image of the 'unspoilt' life in the countryside.

'We live with our collection.

This is our home'.

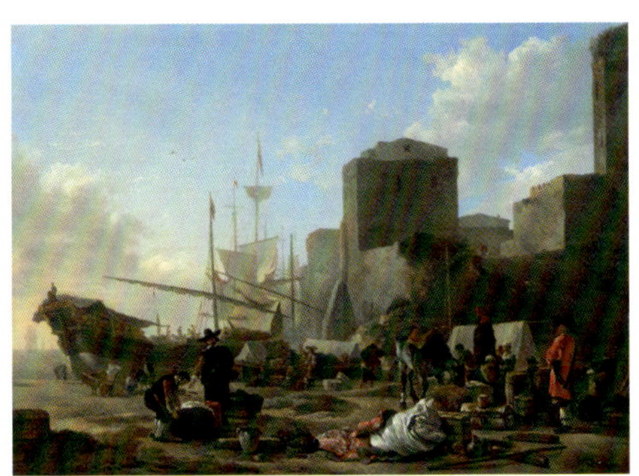

Adam Pijnacker
Harbour Scene
*c.*1650

Dutch painters of the Golden Age worked almost entirely for the open market; as a result, most of their paintings ended up in the hands of private individuals. This helps to explain how it can happen that paintings often resurface, even today, that are completely unknown even to leading experts. This previously unpublished painting by the Italianate Adam Pijnacker (1620/21–1673) languished in obscurity for many years, until it suddenly appeared at an auction in Cologne in 2000. It is therefore not included in the major monograph on this painter that was published in 1988.[21] In 2001 the painting was acquired by the Van Otterloos in the art trade. There has been a revival of interest in the Italianate painters of the Northern Netherlands since the Second World War. For years they were banished to the depots of Dutch museums, since they were branded 'un-Dutch'.

As one would expect of this artist, Pijnacker has not depicted the Dutch lowlands here but a harbour in the Mediterranean region. This theme was introduced into Dutch painting by artists such as Jan Asselijn (*c.*1610–1652), Jan Both (pp. 32–33) and most notably Jan Baptist Weenix (pp. 80–81), after which it was taken up by others such as Nicolaes Berchem (pp. 38–39), Johannes Lingelbach (1622–1674) and Pijnacker. It seems likely that the largely imaginary harbour views painted by the Antwerp-born artist Paul Bril (1554–1626) exercised considerable influence on the Italianate landscape painters of the Dutch Republic. Bril had emigrated to Italy as a young man, and spent the rest of his life there. It is interesting to note that the oldest Italian harbour scene, *View of Naples* of about 1558 in the Galleria Doria Pamphilj, Rome, was also painted by a Fleming, namely Pieter Bruegel the Elder (1520/25–1569), who pioneered numerous other motifs as well.

According to the artists' biographer Arnold Houbraken, Pijnacker spent three years in Italy: it is assumed that he lived there from about 1645 to 1648. This painting is generally dated to about 1650, in other words shortly after his return to the Dutch Republic. The busy harbour was drawn entirely from the painter's imagination, including the various buildings that are depicted, although Pijnacker must have based his motifs on impressions gained in Italy. On the quayside, merchants, workmen and travellers are shown amid miscellaneous merchandise. Standing in the distance are some Oriental figures wearing turbans. Behind the moored ships we can see the sea, with more ships. The sails of the three-master stand out in fine contrast against the blue sky of the sun-drenched scene: the warm golden sunlight is characteristic of Pijnacker. The bright red coat of the man on the right at the front and the colourful pieces of fabric in the foreground add lively accents to this painting, the colouring of which is otherwise quite subdued in tone. The harbour scene idealises the warmth and light of a summer afternoon.

Jacob van Ruisdael
Wooded Landscape
*c.*1655–1660

In 1650 the young Jacob van Ruisdael (1628–1682) decided to spend some time travelling. From his home city of Haarlem he journeyed to the Dutch-German border region, probably with his fellow townsman Nicolaes Berchem (pp. 38–39), to gain inspiration and to find motifs for landscapes. The two also visited Bentheim Castle, which was just over the border in

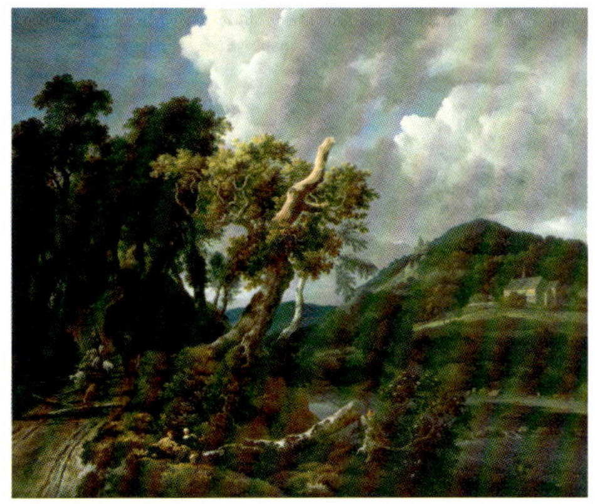

Westphalia. The castle must have made a
great impression on Van Ruisdael, since he
would use it as the primary motif for at least
a dozen of his paintings and include it less
prominently in several other scenes.[22] The
artist deliberately manipulated the situation he observed in Bentheim. Although
he has depicted the enormous castle fairly
accurately, by adopting an extremely low
vantage point for his composition he has
created the impression that the edifice
stands on a real mountain. By this device
he lent his scenes a striking monumentality. This manipulation of motifs would
become a key element of Van Ruisdael's
work. He usually combined it with a fairly
precise rendering of the buildings. In this
way he successfully endowed intrinsically
unassuming subjects such as watermills,
windmills, ruins, gravestones and coastal
beacons with a monumental quality. With
these innovations Van Ruisdael contrib-
uted significantly to the developments
that wholly transformed Dutch landscape
painting around 1650.

The change of course that took place
around 1650 was marked by an emphasis
on the dramatic nature of scenes, a
preference for larger formats, the use of
stronger colour contrasts, and a limpid
atmosphere. This phase of landscape
painting, which roughly spans the years
from 1650 to 1665, is known as the
'classical' period. This large wooded
landscape, which was not published until
2001,[23] is a textbook example of a landscape from this period. The painting,
which can be dated to around 1655–1660,
has been executed on a large canvas

measuring 109 × 142 cm, and is impressive
for that reason alone. The composition is
dominated by a large oak tree on the bank
of a river. The crown of the tree has been
felled by lightning or a windstorm. In
the foreground, a man and a woman are
resting at the roadside; the woman is
pointing to a large birch whose trunk
has snapped. While two men climb the
mountain in the distance, a shepherd
with a flock of sheep is walking down the
road, across which tree trunks have been
laid. In the right foreground we see two
fishermen hauling in their net.

In the mountainous landscape on the
far side of the river, buildings are depicted:
a complex with a little tower, the details
of which are based on the half-timbered
houses that Van Ruisdael had seen on his
trip to Westphalia, and a castle higher up
the mountain. Both these buildings and
the human figures appear insignificant
in comparison to the gigantic oak and
the snapped birch. The central subject of
this painting is the grandeur of nature.

Aert van der Neer
Figures in a Snowstorm
c.1655–1660

In the summer of 2008, the Van Otterloos
acquired this wonderful winter landscape
by Aert van der Neer (1603/4–1677) at an
auction. It made a perfect addition to
the winter landscapes that were already
present in their collection: a scene by the
'winter painter' Hendrick Avercamp from
around 1610–1615; a painting dated 1637

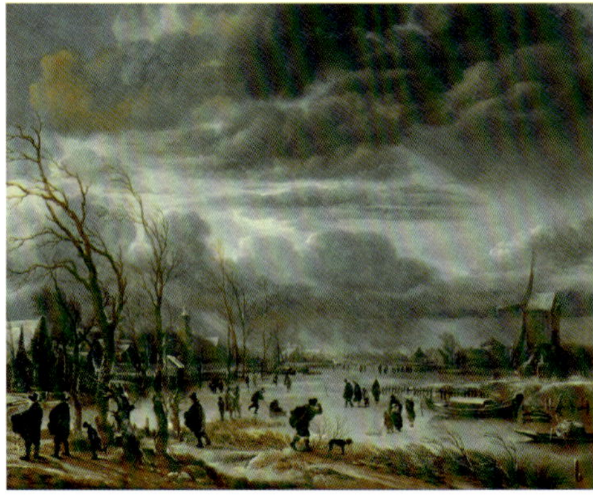

by the highly prolific Jan van Goyen, who
followed in Avercamp's footsteps; and one
dating from around 1675 by Jacob van
Ruisdael. Starting in 1642, the versatile
landscape painter Aert van der Neer too
turned his hand to a group of winter
scenes or *wintertjes*, of which this work,
from around 1655–1660, is one of the
highlights.

The painting depicts a snowstorm.
Falling snow is a fairly difficult motif, and
it is rarely depicted in seventeenth-century
Dutch painting: we find it only in work by
Van der Neer. We do see snowfall in older
Flemish paintings, by sixteenth-century
masters such as Pieter Bruegel the Elder
(1520/25–1569), the founder of the genre,
father and son Jacob (1525–1590) and Abel
Grimmer (c.1573–1619), and Lucas van
Valckenborch (1530–1597).[24] Van der Neer
was evidently familiar with the literature
of art, since he appears to be one of the
few artists to have followed the advice of
the well-known painter and theorist Karel
van Mander (1548–1606). In his influential
Grondt der edel vry schilderconst (1604), Van
Mander had urged fellow painters to

depict the 'gloomy winter days', days dominated by 'snow, hail, rainy squalls, frost, rime and impenetrable fog'.[25]

Van der Neer successfully rendered the visible features of winter: not just the ice, the snow on the ground and the frost, but also the biting wind sweeping across the land and the snow falling from the sky. The wind is visible in the foreground, for instance, where gusts are catching the coats and hats of people walking along. In the middle of the scene, a man steps off the bank with his dog onto the frozen river, which dominates the entire image and stretches into the distance, towards the horizon. The man holds onto his hat to keep it from blowing away. The leafless trees too are bending in the wind. The roofs of the village church and the neighbouring houses and farmhouses, as well as the windmill, are covered with snow. The falling snow was added after the rest of the painting was finished. Van der Neer added an incalculable number of white dots over the entire picture; they stand out particularly well against the dark clothing and the tree-trunks. In spite of the freezing weather, a strikingly large number of people are up and about on the ice: one is pushing a sledge, while others are skating, strolling, spearing eels through holes in the ice, or playing kolf.

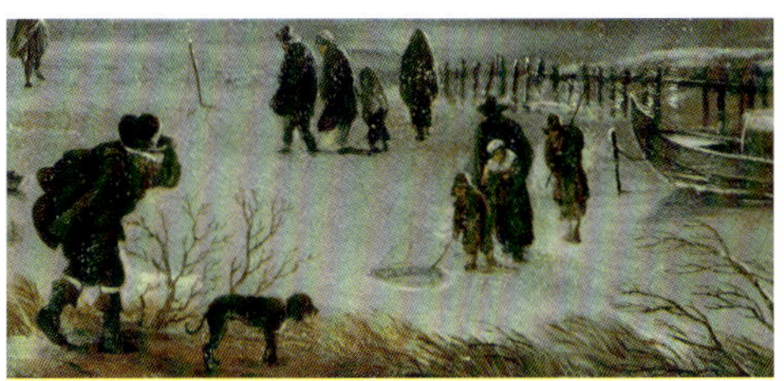

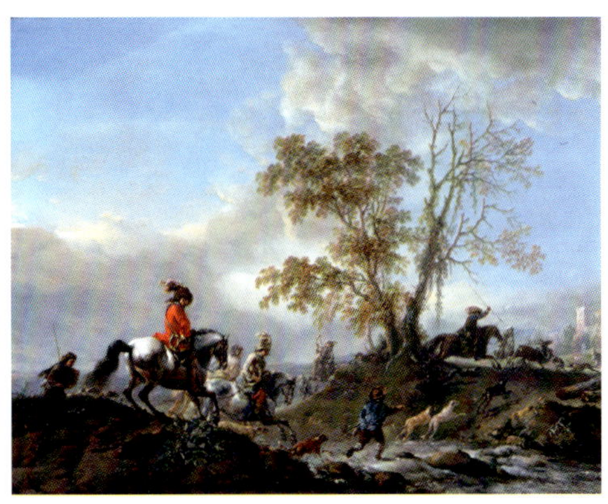

Philips Wouwerman
The Stag Hunt
c.1659–1660

Philips Wouwerman (1619–1668) is one of the most successful horse-painters in history. Depicting horses was his 'unique selling point'. Wouwerman's world consists of horses combined with equestrians, soldiers, stables, huntsmen and smiths. He was constantly finding new angles. A selection from Wouwerman's finest paintings and drawings was recently presented at the Mauritshuis in an exhibition dedicated to his work.[26]

More than any other Dutch artist from the Golden Age, he depicted various aspects of hunting. We encounter the motif in over 120 of his paintings.[27] The Haarlem painter always focused on a specific moment of the hunt: the preparations for departure, the pursuit of diverse kinds of hunting, a rest during the hunt, or the huntsmen's return home. This painting depicts a stag hunt: an elegant company with numerous hounds is heading for the place where

a stag is being attacked by hounds and huntsmen with spears. A huntsman behind a tree sounds his horn to signal that the hunt has begun. Although not all viewers will find the event itself palatable – we see an animal in its death throes – this is nonetheless an extremely attractive painting. The painter has clearly sought to achieve a dynamic scene, and the attitudes of the stylishly dressed horsemen and hurrying servants, with the numerous hounds, combine to suggest rapid movement.[28] To reach the stag, the group must ford a shallow brook. The viewer's attention is drawn to the horseman in the foreground, whose red coat provides a wonderfully vivid accent. That hunting was the prerogative of the upper classes is illustrated by the horsemen's costly apparel. The methodical arrangement of the composition, in which the figures and horses are partly cut off by low hills, enhances the convincing effect of depth, as does the beautifully elaborated cloudy sky.

The elegance and grace of this hunting scene are characteristic of Wouwerman's late work. In the final years before his death, we see a growing refinement in his scenes. It was in this period that Wouwerman made a number of paintings on copper, as in this scene from around 1659–1660.[29] The smooth surface of a copperplate was ideally suited to his fine technique.[30] Since copper is an extremely stable support, it allows for a better preservation of the paint layers – and hence the colours – than panels

or canvas, on which Wouwerman made
most of his paintings. This is partly why
this small painting has been so well
preserved. Its superb quality did not go
unnoticed, and the former owners of this
painting include famous collectors such
as the counts of Schönborn. The price it
fetched at auction in London in 2002
was a record for Wouwerman.[31]

Karel du Jardin
A Horseman at a River
1660

Although this landscape by Karel du
Jardin (1626–1678) was based on impressions gained in Italy, it was painted in
Amsterdam, in 1660, in the period when
the painter attained the heights of his
powers. We see a horseman urinating in
the water, while his horse drinks from
the river and a servant is occupied with
two dogs in the foreground. A third dog
barks at a goat that is walking through
the water. This animal, together with the
sheep, enhances the rural quality of the
surroundings. The atmosphere of the
landscape with its superb cloud formations – against which the mountain
peaks stand out in sharp contrast – has
been captured to fine effect. The clouds
are partly reflected in the water. The
young servant's red clothes and the
blue saddle produce colourful accents
in the painting, the palette of which is
otherwise confined to grey, brown, blue
and green tones. The landscape idealises
the warmth and light of a summer

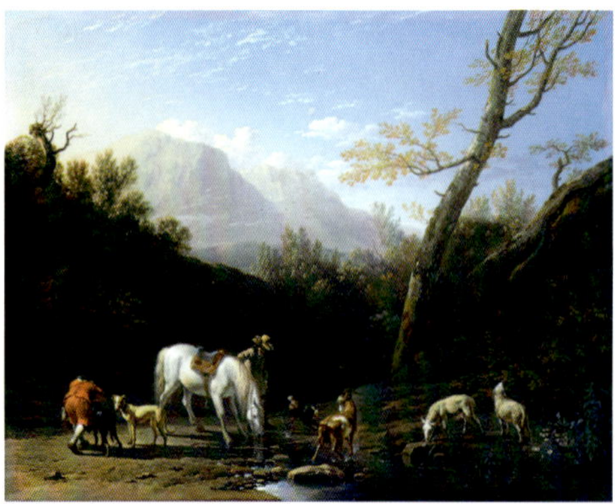

afternoon in the Italian countryside,
a typical feature of Du Jardin's work.

The whereabouts of this painting were
long unknown, until it recently reappeared in the Dutch art trade.[32] It was
greatly admired in the past, for instance
by the English art dealer John Smith,
who produced the first catalogue of Du
Jardin's work.[33] In the eighteenth century,
the painting belonged to the collection
of Pierre-Louis-Paul Randon de Boisset.
This famous collector was a great admirer
of Du Jardin, and owned four other
paintings by the artist. They included
the famous *'Le diamant'*, now in the Fitz-
william Museum, Cambridge, which is
still regarded as one of the painter's masterpieces and was produced in the same
period as the picture discussed here.

Besides Italianate landscapes like this
painting, Du Jardin also produced animal
paintings, genre scenes, history paintings
and portraits. This versatile and highly
prolific artist travelled on more than
one occasion to Italy, where he gained
inspiration for the painting described
here. The first of these trips was probably

in 1650; he then worked in Amsterdam
and subsequently in The Hague, after
which he left for Rome again in 1675.

Nicolaes Berchem
Landscape with a Stag Hunt
c.1660–1670

The Haarlem landscape painter Nicolaes
Berchem (1621/22–1683) is the son of
the still life painter Pieter Claesz (p. 51).
Aside from his father, the artists' biographer Arnold Houbraken (1660–1719)
lists five other artists as Berchem's successive teachers, including Jan van Goyen
(pp. 31–32). Berchem spent most of his
life in Haarlem, but in 1660 he is documented in Amsterdam, the city in which
he made his permanent home in 1677.
Berchem is one of the most important
painters of the so-called 'second generation' of Italianates. Even so, it is unlikely
that he ever actually went to Italy. He
derived the foreign elements of his
paintings primarily from the work of
artists who returned to Haarlem from

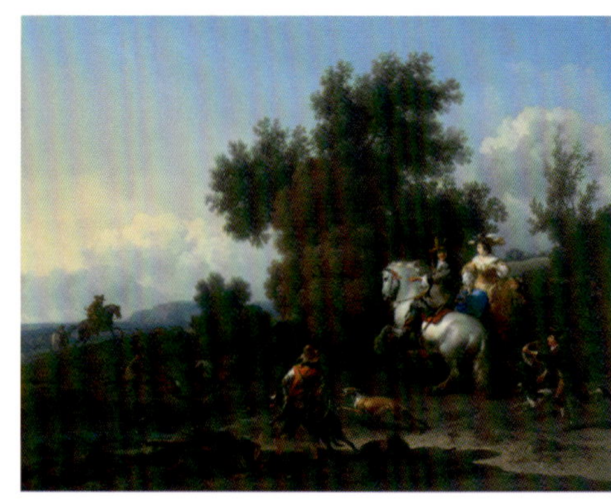

Italy, such as Pieter van Laer (1599–
after 1642) and Jan Both (pp. 32–33).

In this landscape with a hunting
party, the mountains at the back on the
left are the most conspicuously foreign
element. While other landscapes by
Berchem are completely sun-drenched,
here it is primarily the man and the
woman who are bathing in sunlight.
The man's white mount contrasts delightfully with the dark trees and the brown
horse behind him. That hunting was
the prerogative of the upper classes is
illustrated by the horsemen's costly
apparel. They are accompanied by two
boys who are providing assistance in
the hunt. The painting depicts the
climactic moment of the hunt: hounds
are pursuing stags, which are running
for their lives. But more huntsmen are
approaching from the left, so that the
creatures have little chance of escaping.
The spatial effect is enhanced by the
clouds in the blue sky and the landscape
that rises along an imaginary diagonal
line.[34]

For this and other hunting parties,
Berchem undoubtedly drew inspiration
from the work of Philips Wouwerman
(pp. 37–38), who depicted the diverse
facets of hunting in his landscapes more
than any other Dutch painter from the
Golden Age. Both Wouwerman and
Berchem were highly regarded in their
lifetimes, and their work fetched high
prices.

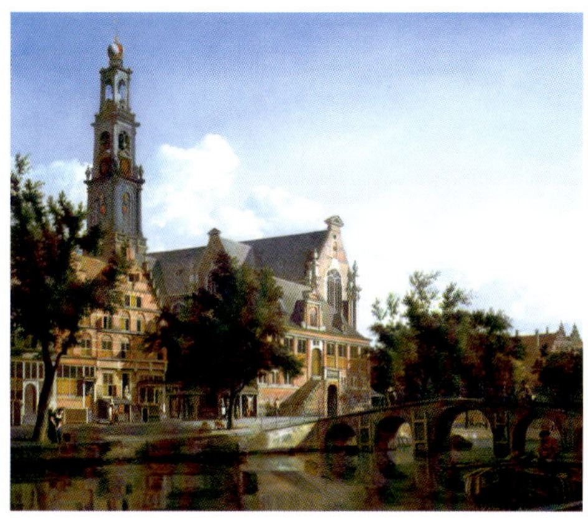

Jan van der Heyden
View of the Westerkerk in Amsterdam
c.1667–1670

The Westerkerk in Amsterdam is at the
heart of this cityscape by the famous
architectural painter Jan van der Heyden
(1637–1712). This church, which is still
impressive today, was built between 1620
and 1640 on a square between Keizers-
gracht, shown in the foreground, and
Prinsengracht. The church stands out in
sharp contrast against the blue sky. It was
long regarded as a unique building, as the
largest church built for Protestant worship
in the world. Many famous citizens of
Amsterdam lie buried in the Westerkerk,
including the painters Nicolaes Berchem
(pp. 38–39) and Rembrandt (pp. 79–80).
The building was designed by the famous
Amsterdam architect Hendrick de Keyser
(1565–1621). After his death, the project's
execution passed largely to his son Pieter
de Keyser (c.1595–1676), who designed
the tower, completed in 1639, in collaboration with the city carpenter Cornelis

Danckerts. For centuries, this 85-metre
tower was the highest in Amsterdam. It
was surmounted by the imperial crown
with which the later emperor Maximilian
had endowed Amsterdam in 1489 for its
city coat of arms. In the course of the
church's restoration in 2006–2007, the
original bright blue colour of the crown
was reinstated, partly on the basis of the
painting discussed here. In the painting,
the church is in part concealed behind the
Westerhal, the main guardhouse of the
militia, which was demolished in 1857.
The ground floor of the Westerhal was
used as a meat market, as is clear here
from the slaughtered pig being boned
by a butcher.

This cityscape is usually dated to
the period 1667–1670, when Van der
Heyden's career as a painter was in its
prime. In later years, he would focus more
on his work as an engineer and inventor.
While the painter took numerous liberties
in his other Amsterdam city scenes, here
he has evidently sought to produce a fairly
accurate image of reality. He did omit
from his scene the two higher dormer
windows of the Westerhal. Neither this
hall nor the stone bridge over the canal
exists today.[35] Van der Heyden would
repeat this composition in his *View of the
Westerkerk in Amsterdam* made around 1670,
which hangs in the Mauritshuis.[36]

The figures depicted in this painting
were probably added by Adriaen van de
Velde of Amsterdam (1636–1672), who
frequently collaborated with Van der
Heyden. In any case, the artist who
painted the figures forgot to add the

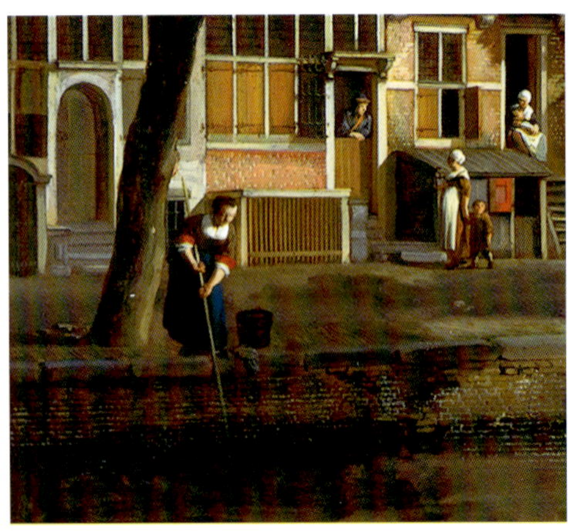

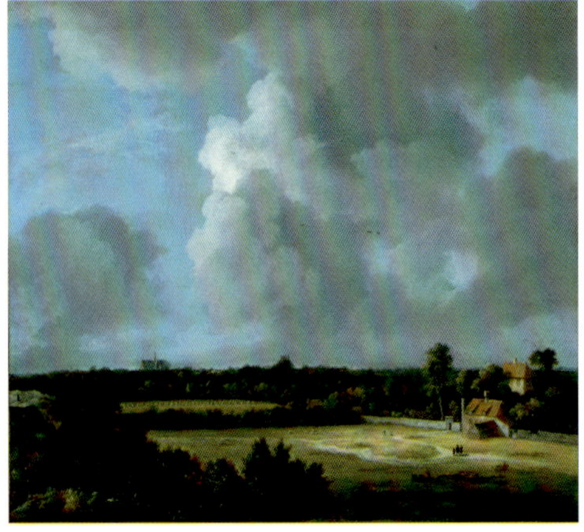

reflections in the water of those at the water's edge, such as the woman drawing water by the tree in the left foreground. This is particularly noticeable in the present painting, in which numerous other similar details are rendered meticulously. The painstaking detail of the stones of the façades and streets is characteristic of Van der Heyden, who probably used some kind of template to save time. Along with Gerrit Berckheyde (1638–1698), Van der Heyden was one of the pioneers of the cityscape as a distinct genre in the painting of the Northern Netherlands.

Jacob van Ruisdael
Landscape with a View of Haarlem
c.1670–1675

In seventeenth-century inventories, paintings such as this one were classified as *Haarlempjes* ('views of Haarlem'). In the 1670s, Jacob van Ruisdael (1628–1682) produced at least fifteen such panoramas of the picturesque landscape behind the

dunes around Haarlem and Alkmaar.[37] Van Ruisdael's *Haarlempjes* are among the highlights of his painted oeuvre. On the horizon is the Great or St Bavo's Church with its characteristic pointed central tower rising high above the city. To the right of this church, a large roof with four chimneys projects above a wood that extends across virtually the entire painting. To the right of this large house, which has not yet been identified, two windmills stand out against the dark sky.

Curiously absent from this picture are long strips of linen, lying bleaching in the fields, a motif that appears in most of the painter's other *Haarlempjes*. In contrast to these scenes, the city is not depicted here from the northwest but from the southwest, from the dunes near Heemstede. No preparatory study for this painting is known, although Van Ruisdael probably used drawings for this landscape, as for others. Dutch public collections possess a handful of preliminary studies for his other *Haarlempjes*, taken from his sketchbooks.

In spite of its modest size, the almost square image is an impressive scene. That is because Van Ruisdael has adopted a high vantage point, enabling him to keep the horizon low. As a result, the imposing cloud formations, which became the painter's trademark, fill more than two-thirds of the image and greatly enhance the effect of depth. White, grey and dark-grey clouds stand out clearly against a bright blue sky. Birds enliven the cloud patterns. The clouds give rise to alternating

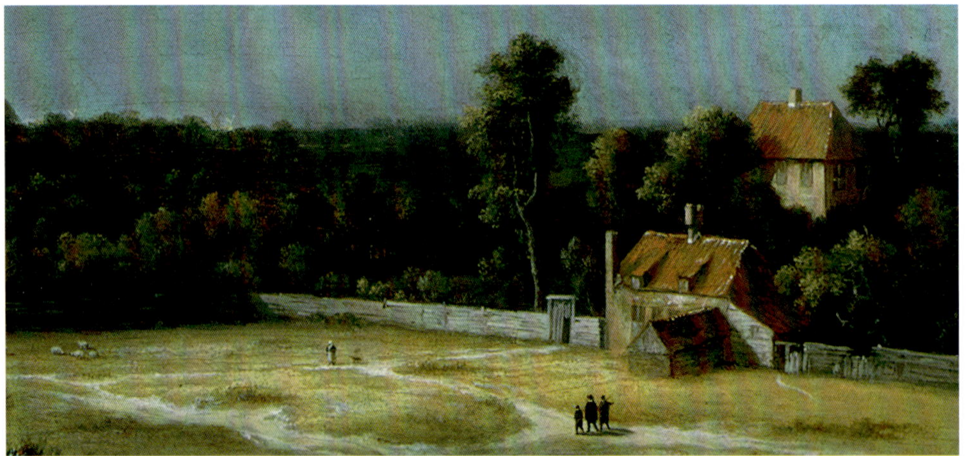

patches of sunny areas and shadows in the landscape. Van Ruisdael uses this effect subtly, to enhance the depth of the scene. Behind the dark-coloured bushes in the foreground, we see cattle grazing in a fenced pasture, the right part of which is illuminated by sunlight. Several figures are walking along the footpaths leading in front of the country house and the farmhouse: a woman with a dog, and a group of three men. In the background, sheaves of corn stand beside a second farmhouse.

Jacob van Ruisdael
Winter Landscape with Windmills
c.1675

This painting, produced around 1675 by Jacob van Ruisdael (1628–1682), splendidly completes the group of winter landscapes in the collection. It belongs to the relatively small group of around 30 winter landscapes produced by Van Ruisdael.[38] None of these paintings is dated, but most appear to have been made after 1660. In the main, they are of modest dimensions and display a relatively simple choice of motifs: a group of buildings with a few trees and bushes at the side of a frozen canal. The painting discussed here is one of a group of winter landscapes that are generally dated to around 1675, in each of which the primary motif is one or more windmills. In Van Ruisdael's day, a variety of windmills stood in the polders around Amsterdam, where the painter made his home in 1657. These characteristic

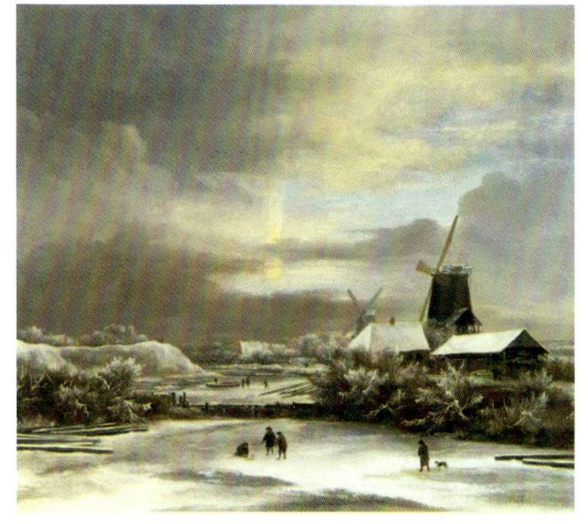

structures are featured most notably in his early work. Around 1670 the painter revisited this motif to depict it in a remarkably monumental form in *The Windmill at Wijk bij Duurstede* (Amsterdam, Rijksmuseum). In the painting discussed here, windmills stand at the centre of a group of houses on the bank of a frozen waterway. Behind the sawmill with a house and storehouse stands a second windmill, a little further away. Tree-trunks lie around the ice in several places, some sawn and others waiting to be sawn, providing horizontal and diagonal accents in the image.

The composition makes an impression of remarkable spaciousness. The distinctly diagonal structure of the winter landscapes from the 1660s has been replaced here by a more horizontal structure. Since there are no strong accents in the foreground, the flat landscape can stretch freely towards the horizon. The primary motif is seen from a greater distance, as a result of which it appears less monumental. The muted grey tones

and the colours in the sky are in total harmony with the snow-covered land-scape. The slightly cloudy sky evokes the mood of a bright winter's day on which the sun breaks through the clouds. In this respect, the painting contrasts greatly with several of Van Ruisdael's other winter landscapes, which are conspicuous for their remarkably gloomy atmosphere.

Notwithstanding this contrast, the atmosphere conveyed here is still a far cry from the merry scenes by painters such as Hendrick Avercamp or Jan van Goyen showing people having fun on the ice. The diminutive figures appear more than anything else to emphasise the vastness of the landscape. They are scattered around the entire landscape: in the foreground, two kolf players are waiting for their companion, who is tying on his skates, and on the right, a man is walking with his dog. In the background we see some skaters beside an icebound boat.

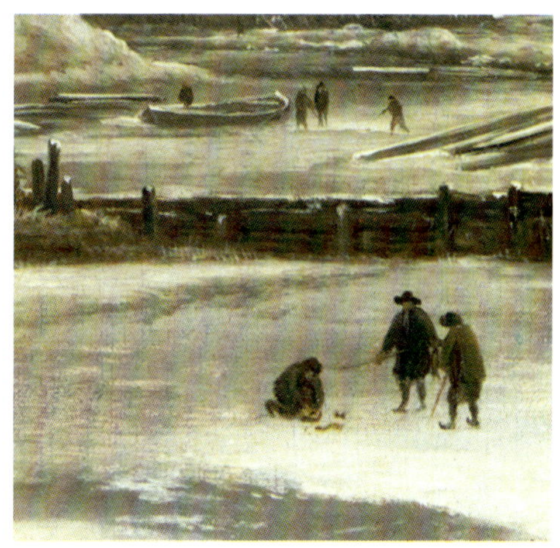

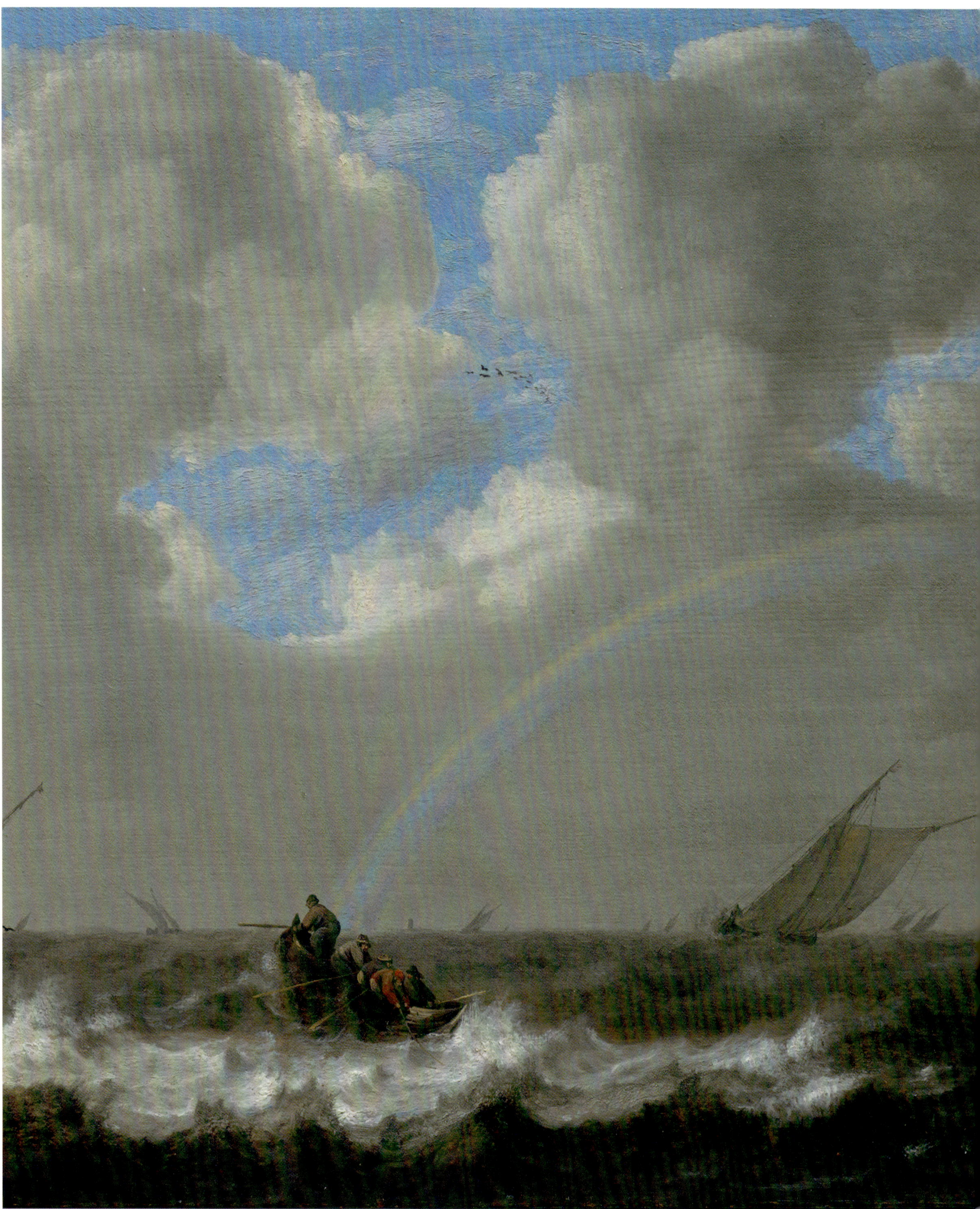

Seascapes

Jan Porcellis
Boats on a Choppy Sea
c.1631

Jan Porcellis (1583/84–1632) is one of
the first painters who made the transition
from colourful, narrative seascapes to a
type that emphasised mood. With his
atmospheric scenes, he made a major
contribution to marine painting. Porcellis
was one of the most innovative painters
of his day, and was praised by his contemporaries. His work was extremely popular
with other artists: Rubens owned a
painting by him, and Rembrandt had as
many as six. Porcellis's relatively small
oeuvre consists of sixty-odd paintings,
thirty drawings and a series of etchings.

This seascape from around 1631,
with its fairly subdued palette, is one of
the last works painted by Porcellis and
depicts a sea in stormy weather.[39] Most
of the image is taken up by an impressive
cloud mass. The only indication of land
is a tower in the middle of the horizon.
Sailing-ships are trying to navigate the
turbulent waves. Most of these vessels
are only faintly visible on the horizon.
In the foreground, fishermen are getting
ready to put to sea in their little boat:
one hauls a net in, while three others
are already manning the oars. The foam
and spraying waves convey the strength
of the wind. The sea is built up almost
in the manner of a stage set: a strip
illuminated by sunlight is depicted
between two strips of dark waves, which
significantly enhances the effect of depth.
The blue sky behind the dark clouds

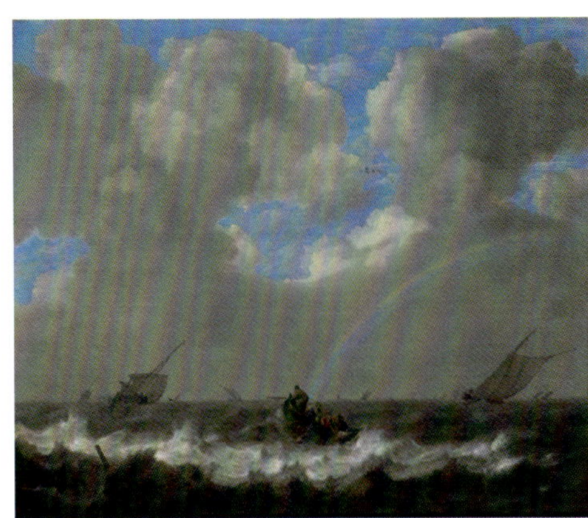

adds to this effect. Here and there, the
bright blue of the sky is reflected in the
sunlit strip.

It has just been raining, as is clear
from the rainbow. This draws our attention to the fishing-boat and is itself a
striking detail in this scene. Curiously,
Porcellis used only blue and yellow for
his rainbow. This natural phenomenon
is seldom depicted in Dutch landscapes.
One of the best-known examples is in
a painting dating from 1614 by Adriaen
van de Venne (1589–1662), *Fishing for
Souls*,[40] in which the large rainbow pos-
sesses symbolic significance and does not
constitute a landscape motif as it does
here. This marine by Porcellis is one of
the earliest Dutch landscapes depicting
a rainbow. Only later, with artists such
as Jan van Goyen and Jacob van Ruisdael,
do we find paintings in which rainbows
play a prominent role. In the Southern
Netherlands, where Porcellis was born,
examples of works featuring this fairly
uncommon motif include landscapes
by Rubens.

Willem van de Velde the Elder
*The Brederode Setting Sail from Vlieland,
9 June 1645*
c.1645

This uncoloured scene by Willem van
de Velde the Elder (1611–1693) is what is
known as a pen painting. This rather old-
fashioned technique involved painting
with a pen on a prepared canvas or panel
– in this case the latter. The artist was
evidently insufficiently skilled in the art
of painting, a shortcoming that would be
amply outweighed by the prowess of his
son, Willem van de Velde the Younger (see
p. 47). Father and son shared a studio in
Amsterdam. In or after the 'Year of Disaster'
of 1672 they moved to England, where King
Charles II (1630–1685) placed a studio at
their disposal in Queen's House, Greenwich. In 1674, the king even offered them
both a permanent salary: in the case of
Willem van de Velde the Elder 'for taking
and making draughts of sea fights', and for
his son 'for putting the said draughts into
colour for our particular use'. This probably
reflects the customary division of labour

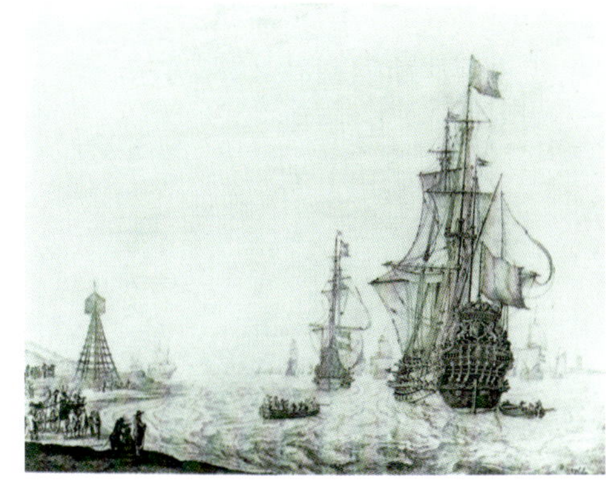

"

in the studio. The Van de Veldes would spend the rest of their lives in England.

This pen painting dates from the years in which Van de Velde the Elder was still working in the Dutch Republic. He used to accompany the fleet on all manner of occasions as a kind of draughtsman-reporter. The subject of this painting is the departure of a large merchant fleet: on 9 June 1645 some 300 ships sailed from the island of Vlieland to the Baltic.[41] To afford protection from privateers, as well as from Swedish and Danish warships, this impressive fleet was escorted by 47 warships. The Brederode, the flagship of Admiral Witte de With, was accorded a prominent role. It was one of the largest Dutch warships of its day, and was equipped with no fewer than 59 cannons. Clearly visible here are the sculpted escutcheon with the coat of arms of Stadholder Frederik Hendrik, held by two lions, and beneath it the name of the ship: 'BRE DE RO DE'. Here we witness the moment at which the fleet set sail for Scandinavia. A sloop is on its way to the flagship, and the flag above the escutcheon is giving the signal to weigh anchor. Diverse onlookers have gathered to watch the fleet leave. On the left we see a large beacon on the beach of Vlieland. On the far right we can just make out the island of Terschelling, with Brandaris lighthouse.

That Van de Velde was present on the beach of Vlieland in 1645 when the fleet set sail is clear from a series of drawings in which he documented the event. He used these drawings, most notably a large one that is preserved in Museum Boijmans Van Beuningen in Rotterdam, for this painting,

which was probably made shortly after the fleet's departure. Later on he would make two larger pen paintings with the same motif.[42] But in no other work did the Brederode receive as much emphasis as in this small painting.

Simon de Vlieger
Sailing Ships in a Breeze
c.1648–1649

Simon de Vlieger (1600/1–1653), who was probably born in Rotterdam, moved in 1643 and settled in Amsterdam, where his star soon rose. For several years, he lived next-door to the famous marine painters Willem van de Velde the Elder and his son, Willem van de Velde the Younger (see pp. 43 and 47). While the Van de Veldes took a particular interest in portraying ships, De Vlieger devoted himself to making atmospheric paintings of the beach and the sea.[43] His oeuvre consists largely of seascapes and beach scenes, although he also produced land-scapes. In his early work, which frequently depicts shipwrecks amid towering waves,

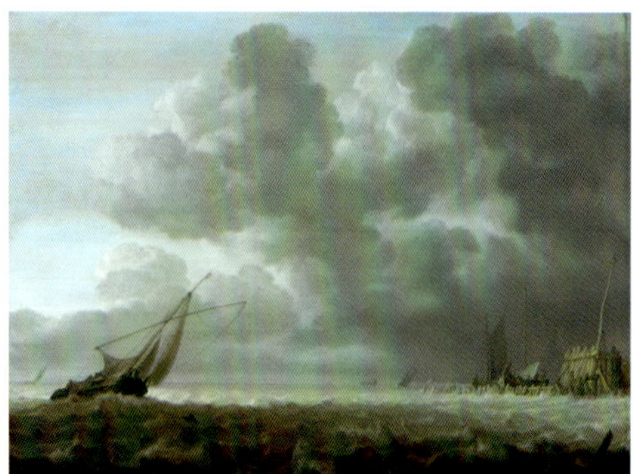

the influence of Hendrick Vroom (1566–1640) is clearly discernible.

It is generally assumed that De Vlieger drew his inspiration largely from the seascapes of Jan Porcellis (see p. 43) with their low horizons. While in a painting by Porcellis from around 1631 the sea is casting up turbulent waves (see p. 122, fig. 29), the swell in this painting by De Vlieger is less powerful. The seascape is dominated by an impressive cloud mass that takes up the majority of the painting. Small boats are out at sea, many of them only faintly visible on the horizon. In the left foreground we see a fishing vessel that is on its way to a wooden breakwater or groyne with a beacon, where two ships have already moored.[44] This painting does not show a beach, an element frequently depicted by De Vlieger. It is a lively representation of everyday life in coastal waters, where human life and the natural world are closely entwined. The composition is extremely balanced and refined: the dark waves in the foreground merge subtly into a sunlit strip, which produces an effect of great depth. The combination of dark and light clouds, too, produces an enormous sense of space. The sailing-boat in the left foreground contrasts delightfully with the cloudy sky. For the rest, this painting's appeal is determined by the muted colouring and broad, strikingly confident brushstrokes. De Vlieger placed his signature on a floating piece of driftwood on the right of the picture, prominently in the foreground. Many seventeenth-century painters signed their seascapes in this way.

De Vlieger is regarded as one of the most prominent marine painters of his day. The late work of this painter, who died in 1653, was particularly influential: Willem van de Velde the Younger (p. 47), who probably studied under De Vlieger, and Jan van de Cappelle (pp. 45–46), were among those who drew inspiration from these paintings. Van de Cappelle, whose work was unmistakeably influenced by De Vlieger, owned as many as nine paintings and over a thousand drawings by this artist. This painting belonged for many years to the collection of Michael and Renata Hornstein in Montreal. The Van Otterloos acquired it from a Dutch art dealer in 1999.

Jan van de Cappelle
Boats in a Calm
1651

The Amsterdam artist Jan van de Cappelle (1626–1679) occupies a unique place in the marine painting of his day. In his best works, he attained a monumentality and serenity that are characteristic of what is called the 'classical period' of Dutch landscape painting. Around 1650, painters such as Jacob van Ruisdael (pp. 35–36) and Meindert Hobbema (1638–1709) were striving to achieve a similar monumentality in their paintings. In marine painting, Van de Cappelle occupies a place between Simon de Vlieger (pp. 44–45) and Willem van de Velde the Younger (p. 47), who was the most influential painter in the final decades of the seventeenth century.

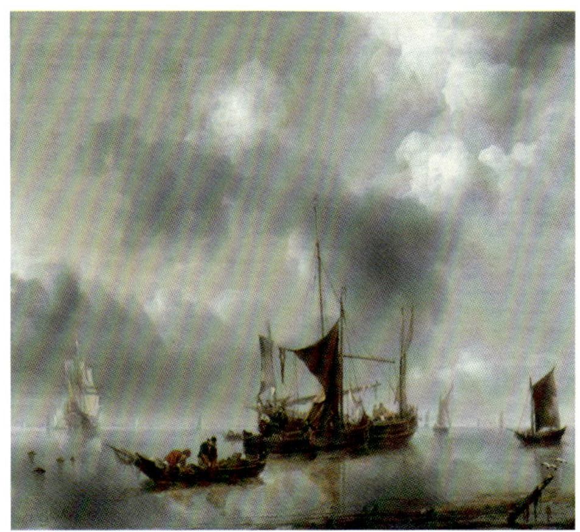

Van de Cappelle is one of the most important Dutch marine painters of the Golden Age, but he was probably productive only for a short time: some 75 seascapes by his hand are known today, as well as ten winter landscapes. The few paintings he dated were made between 1649 and 1663. The recent restoration of this painting clearly revealed both the signature and the year, '1651' (see also p. 20).[45]

This scene displays several characteristic features of Van de Cappelle's work. One is its modest palette: he used predominantly cool, silvery-grey hues for the sea and sky and brown hues for the ships. The composition displays ships of different types and size, which are lying at anchor in groups amid calm waters. The ships and clouds are subtly reflected in the smooth surface of the water. The monumental cloudy sky and calm sea are linked, as it were, by an almost tangible vapour, a recurrent feature of Van de Cappelle's paintings. There is a breeze, nonetheless, since the sails are certainly not hanging limply. The placing of the ships with their

conspicuous sails creates a strong effect of depth. In spite of the emphasis on the overall impression of the scene, the painter has also taken care to render the ships and the activity on them. Sailors are busily attending to their ships and cargoes or talking to each other. Their clothes add modest colour accents to the atmospheric scene. A strikingly large number of paintings by Van de Cappelle have declined in quality because of deteriorating condition. In this respect, the painting shown here is a happy exception to the rule, since it has been well preserved.

Van de Cappelle did not enjoy any formal training as a painter – he was trained as a dyer, and was to have taken over the family's flourishing crimson dyeworks after his father's death – but he must have been highly familiar with the seascapes of De Vlieger, and may have spent some time in his studio. Several of the paintings that Van de Cappelle painted around 1650, including the seascape discussed here, were to a large extent inspired by De Vlieger's scenes. The paintings made by Jan Porcellis (p. 43), who died in 1632, also influenced Van de Cappelle, who incorporated as many as 16 paintings by this marine painter into his large art collection. We are well informed about this collection by a probate inventory drawn up after Van de Cappelle's death in December 1679. From this we learn that he left a large fortune, besides six houses, plots of land, the dyeworks and a 'pleasure yacht'. His large art collection consisted of almost two hundred paintings and some six thousand drawings, including work by Rembrandt and Jan van Goyen as well as Porcellis and De Vlieger.

Salomon van Ruysdael
River Landscape with a Sailing-Boat
1655?

Salomon van Ruysdael (1600/3–1670) was the painter *par excellence* of the Dutch lowlands with their characteristic rivers and lakes, polders and church towers. In his long career, spanning almost fifty years, he created a large oeuvre that displays the polder landscape in all its facets and in every season. The Naarden-born Van Ruysdael enrolled in the painters' guild in Haarlem in 1623 and continued to work in this city until his death in 1670. He was an uncle, and one of the teachers, of the Haarlem landscape painter Jacob van Ruisdael (see pp. 35–36, 40–41), who spelled his name 'Ruisdael' in his signature to distinguish himself from his prolific uncle.

This river landscape comes from the collection of Wilhelm von Bode

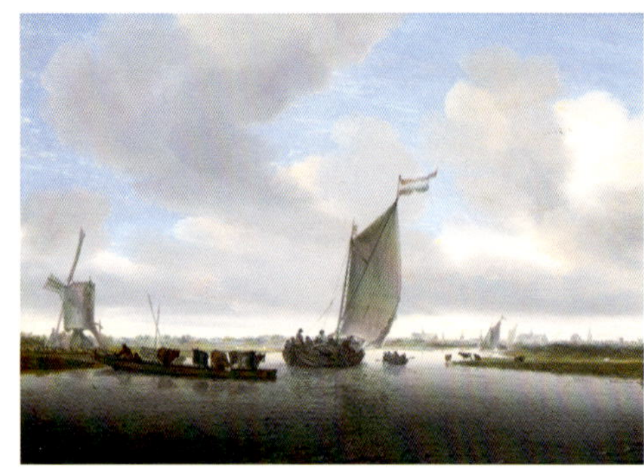

(1845–1929), who was one of the greatest authorities on seventeenth-century Dutch painting in his day.[46] Von Bode must have delighted in this well-preserved painting, which demonstrates the painter's great talent. The scene has been delineated rapidly in confident brushstrokes, using only a limited palette. The ground has been left partly visible, and plays a prominent part in the painting's tonality. River landscapes of this kind with ferries, dominated by clouds and water, were Van Ruysdael's favourite subject. The Van Otterloos own two paintings with this central motif: one dating from 1649 (see p. 21, fig. 3) and this far smaller one, which

displays a poorly legible date, possibly 1655. The entire foreground is taken up by the rippling water. The light-grey clouds, which occupy almost two-thirds of the painting, are reflected in it. Van Ruysdael enhanced the effect of depth by enveloping the foreground in shade, and by depicting the water from a relatively low viewpoint. As a result of all these 'devices', the painting radiates an air of monumentality in spite of its modest dimensions. The ferry with its passengers that appears to be heading for a city on the horizon leads the viewer's gaze into the picture's depths. Beside the ferry is a small rowing-boat, and on the horizon we see two sailing vessels. The composition is bounded on the left by a windmill, near which a ferry with five cows is mooring. More cows appear on the strip of land to the right, with a flock of birds in the sky. The fluttering of the red, white and blue flag on the ferry suggests that there is a light breeze.

The city on the horizon of this painting has sometimes been tentatively identified as Leiden. It is supposedly depicted from the north-east, with two churches: the Hooglandse Kerk and Pieterskerk. But this theory is less than convincing, certainly when we compare the buildings in this painting with images of the city by contemporaries such as Jan van Goyen. The buildings in Van Ruysdael's paintings can seldom be identified. All the evidence suggests that the painter's aim was not to record topography but to evoke the atmosphere of the Dutch polderland.

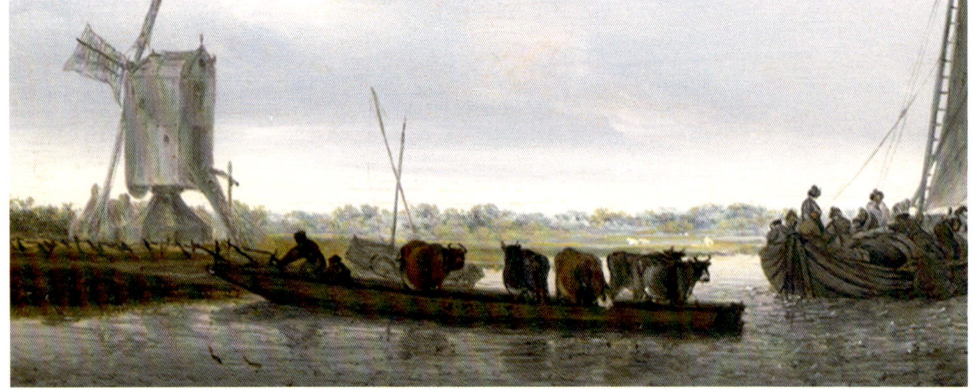

Willem van de Velde the Younger
Fishing Boats by the Shore
*c.*1660–1665

Like his father (see pp. 43–44), Willem van de Velde the Younger (1633–1707) devoted his entire career to producing images of ships and maritime subjects. He undoubt-edly received his first instruction in this field from his father. The family had moved to Amsterdam shortly before young Willem's birth, but in or around 1648 he was sent to Weesp to serve an apprenticeship with Simon de Vlieger, an artist who is also represented in the Van Otterloos' collec-tion (see pp. 44–45). This seascape by Willem van de Velde the Younger shows a calm sea with fishing boats on a day with barely a breath of wind. Near a sandbank or spit of land lies a fishing-boat, probably a flat-bottomed vessel. In the foreground lies one of the anchors, while a second anchor hangs over the rail. To the left, a small rowing-boat with two men is making fast. The captain of the fishing-vessel has probably run his boat aground deliberately – a common practice with flat-bottomed vessels of this kind. Judging by the white flag with the red cross of St George flying from the mast, this can be assumed to be an English boat. Behind it are three men outside a simple tent; one of them is busying himself at a cooking-pot from which rise large clouds of smoke. On the left we can also see several sailing-vessels, one of which, on the far left, is flying the Dutch flag. A little rowing-boat is moving along beside this group of ships. On the horizon, very faint indications of more ships and a

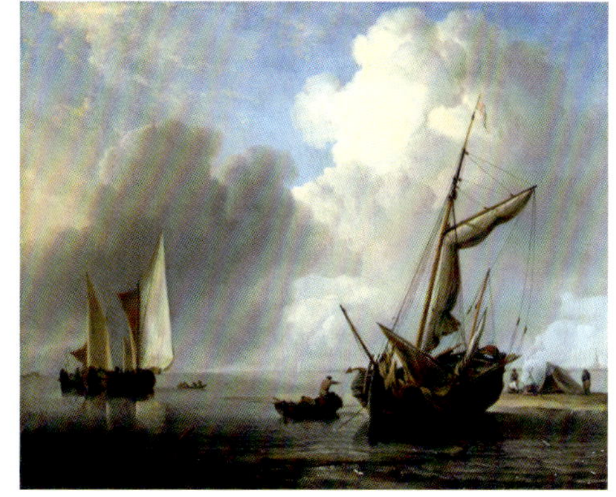

few buildings can just be made out. This painting was produced in the rough period 1660–1665, at the height of Van de Velde's career.[47] Much of his oeuvre is

characterised by the choice of an almost serene seascape, in which the weather and the sea are calm. Over half of the image is taken up by the cloudy sky. This endows the scene with great depth, with its overlapping dark and lighter clouds, set against a blue sky. Especially in the foreground, the play of light and dark is executed very subtly, with the light sandbank or spit of land contrasting with the dark fishing-boat. Similarly, the mast with its furled sails stands out against the clouds. The painter's keen eye for such details is also clear from the reflection of the white sails of the ships in the dark water in the left foreground.

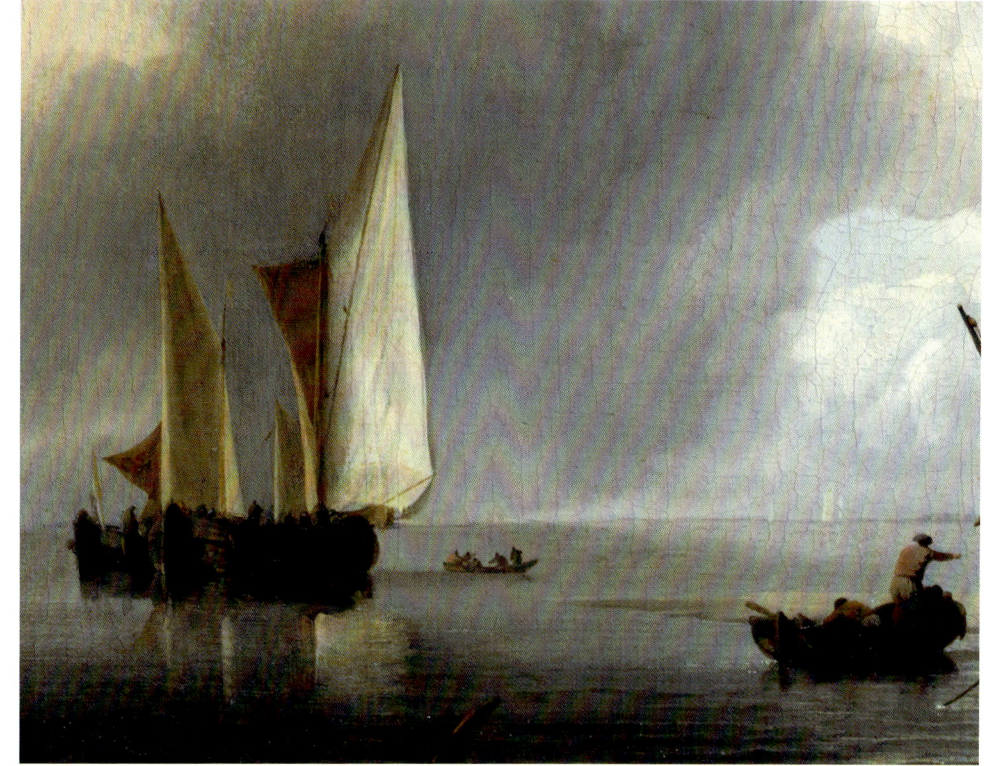

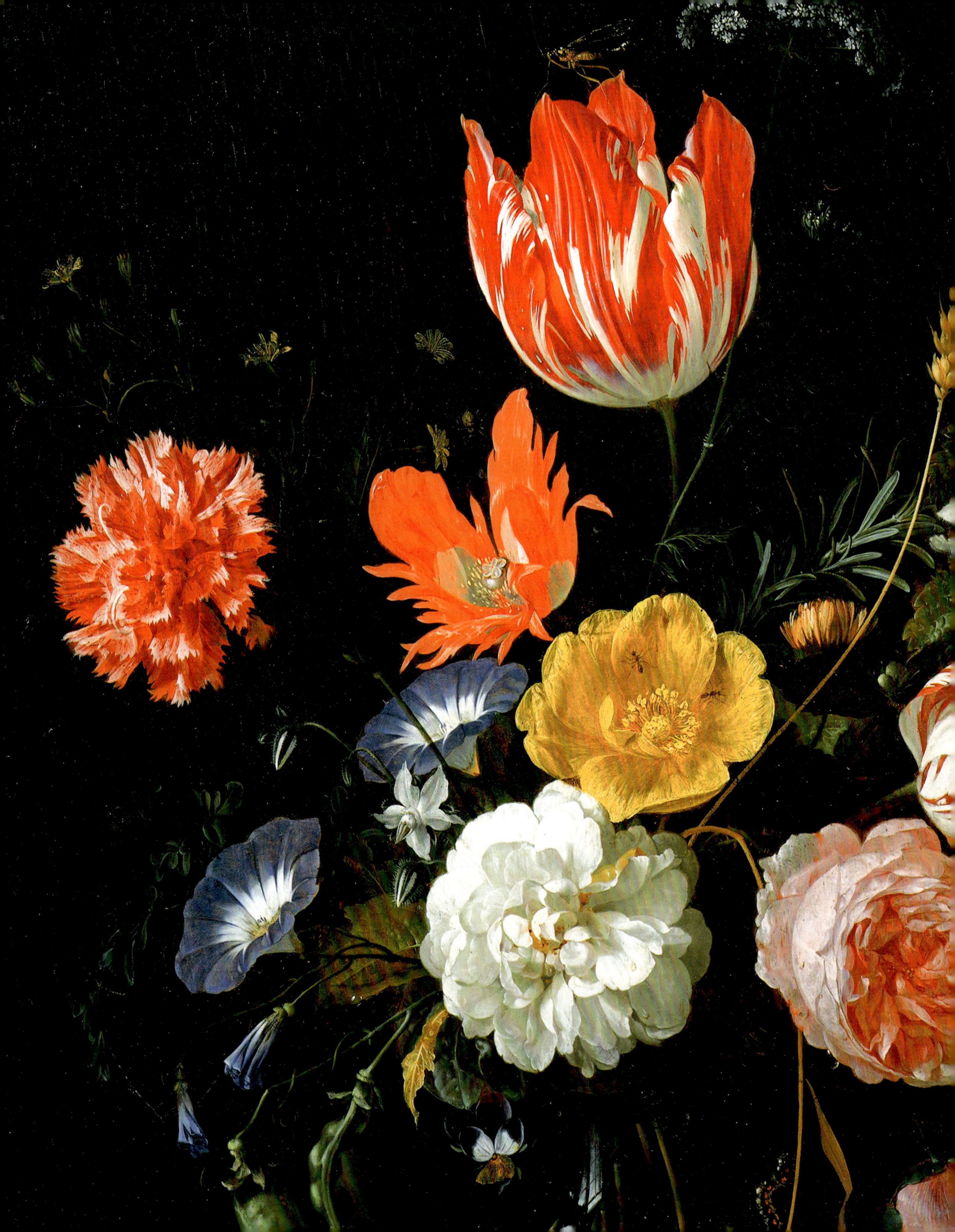

Still Lifes

As many painters produced still-life paintings, they became highly specialised in order to distinguish themselves from others. Many produced flower and fruit still lifes, while some confined themselves to one highly specific kind of still life. Such sub-genres include kitchen and market scenes, banquet and breakfast pieces, tobacco pieces (with diverse smoking materials), sumptuous still lifes (*pronkstillevens*), and scenes featuring only fish or poultry. The phrase 'still life' first occurs around 1650, and only much later did it become the general term for this category. Like other genres, the still life had its origins in the Southern Netherlands, after which it flourished in the Northern Netherlands in the seventeenth century. A clear stylistic development is discernible in the Golden Age. In the early years, artists produced paintings in which the flowers, fruit and other items of food are clearly visible. With the passage of time, the compositions became somewhat looser and more refined, with more attention being paid to light and dark; in consequence, painters tended to opt more frequently for a dark background.

Merchants and explorers brought exotic objects, products and plants to the Dutch Republic from abroad. One example is the tulip, today one of the Netherlands' leading export products, which was first imported from Turkey in 1593. Soon the country was in the throes of a veritable 'tulip mania': not only were fortunes invested in the cultivation of new tulip species, but people also invested in tulip bulbs themselves, in some cases leading to financial ruin. The widespread interest in plants and flowers produced a boom in flower still lifes. Many artists painted flowers together that actually bloom in different months. Painters did not depict existing bouquets; they produced paintings based on studies made in different seasons. So just as in the case of genre scenes, the apparent realism of flower pieces is an illusion.

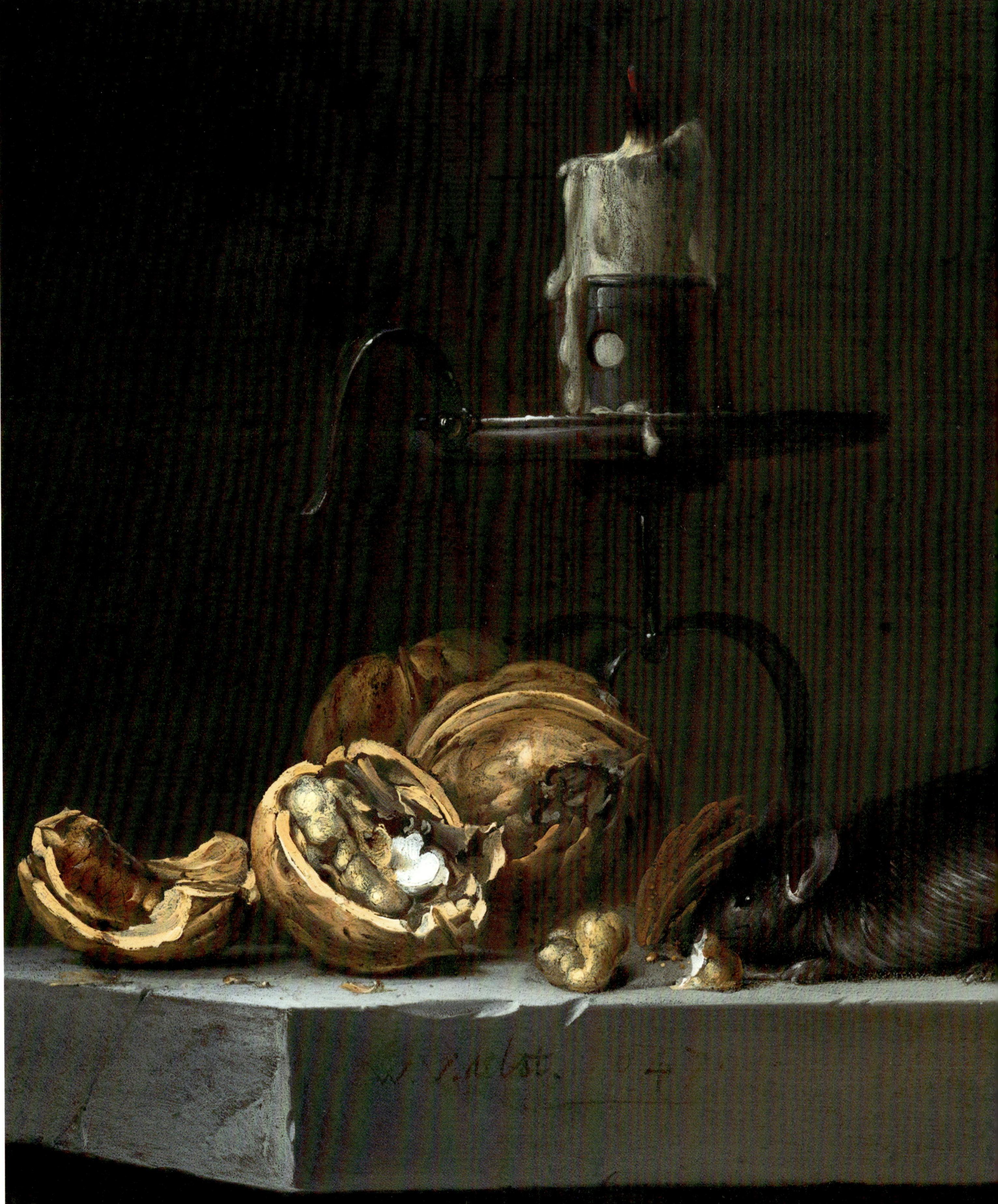

Still Lifes

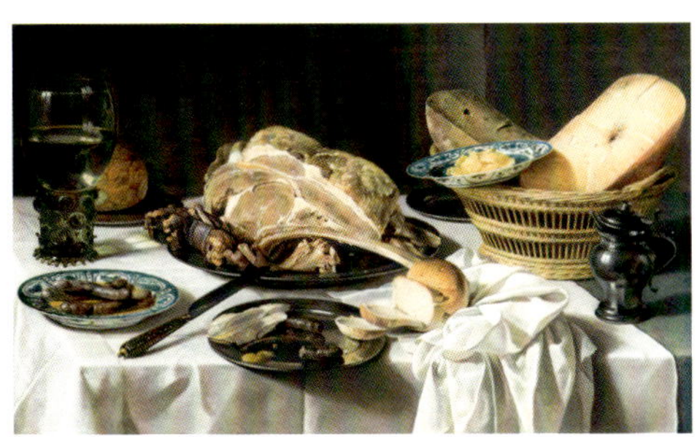

Pieter Claesz
Still Life with a Ham and Cheeses
*c.*1627–1628

This painting, which the Van Otterloos managed to acquire for their collection in December 2009, is a fine example of the 'banquet scenes' to which Pieter Claesz (1596/97–1660) owes his fame: a still life on a laid table, painted in a limited palette.[48] Along with his slightly older contemporary Willem Heda (pp. 51–52), Claesz is ranked among the foremost still life painters of the first half of the seventeenth century. Around 1630, these two artists, both of whom were active in Haarlem, introduced the monochrome still life featuring objects arranged in a quasi-casual manner on the corner of a table. They engaged in an artistic dialogue: both repeatedly depicted the same silver tazza and a more common-place roemer in their paintings.

In this still life by Claesz, we see a large roemer filled with white wine, set against a neutral background. The table is in front of a niche or recess in a plastered wall. Aside from the wine, the viewer's atten-tion is drawn mainly to a variety of food items: plates of sausages, a large ham, buns, and a basket containing cheeses.

Perched on the basket with cheeses – food that was eaten with almost every meal in this period but that is remarkably infrequent in Claesz's work – is a dish with butter curls. It brings to mind the seventeenth-century saying to the effect that 'Dairy on dairy is the devil's work', meaning that adding cheese to butter on your bread was excessive. To the right of the starched linen tablecloth – the folds are still clearly visible – stands a small tin pot, probably containing mustard. Claesz signed the painting in his usual way: he placed his monogram, 'PC' in ligature, on the blade of the knife, which has a beautifully carved handle.

By confining his palette to a limited number of hues, mainly dominated by grey, brown, yellow and green tones, Claesz has succeeded in creating a remarkably atmospheric scene. The nuanced illumina-tion, in which the shadows are convinc-ingly elaborated on the white cloth, is enhanced by effective little highlights, most notably on the mustard-pot. An-other delightful detail is the rendering of the surface structures, ranging from the smooth skin of the sausages to the grainy structure of the cheeses and the buns.

Numerous writers have speculated about the possible significance of such scenes. According to one interpretation, the perishable food items are indicative of a vanitas symbolism. In the course of Claesz's career, symbolism seems to become less prominent; the emphasis shifts to the poetic character of his serene compositions. This also applies to the present undated still life, although it

appears to be a fairly early work, probably dating from 1627 or 1628. With his pains-taking, silvery illumination and sublime rendering of textures, Claesz has endowed his everyday subject with enchanting beauty.

Willem Heda
Still Life with a Tazza
1633

Together with his somewhat younger contemporary Pieter Claesz (p. 51), Willem Heda (1594–1680) is ranked among the foremost still-life painters of the first half of the seventeenth century. These two artists worked in Haarlem, and around 1630 both started painting still lifes featuring objects that do not appear to have been arranged in any orderly way. In fact, these painters devoted considerable thought to such compositions. Again and again they succeeded in devising new compositions with virtually identical objects. The silver tazza and the large green roemer recur repeatedly in the paintings of both artists, who were apparently very familiar with each other's work. It was probably Heda

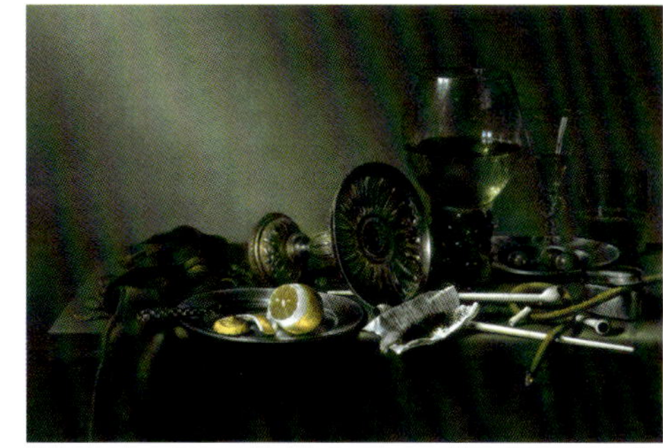

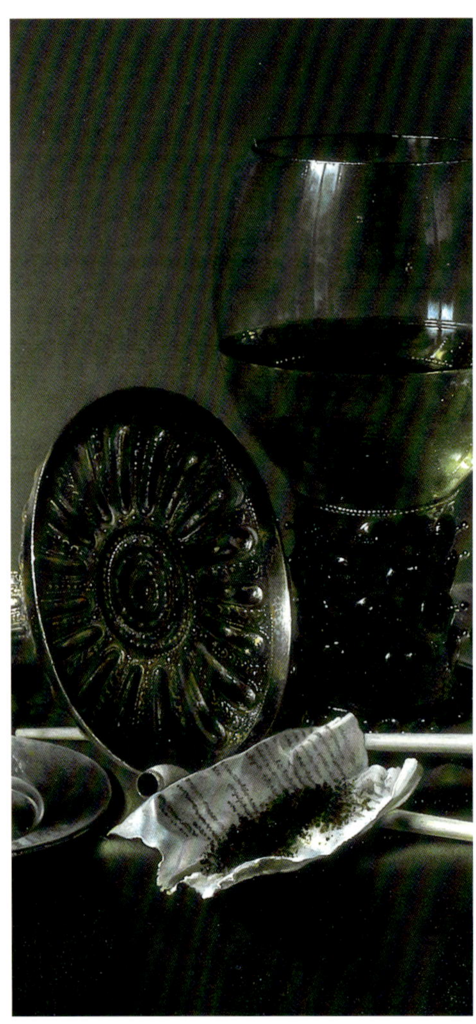

with drink. On the dark tablecloth, we see in the left foreground a partly peeled lemon on a tin plate. The knife, the handle of which is richly inlaid with whalebone and mother-of-pearl, stands out in sharp contrast against the cloth. Several nuts lie around the plate. Our attention is particularly drawn to the smoking items in the right foreground: one of the three Gouda pipes is broken. To fill the pipe, tobacco from the silver tobacco box has been scattered on some old printed paper. The smouldering taper was used to light it.

The still life, which is dated 1633, appeared on the New York art market only recently, in 1996. It is one of the highlights of Heda's oeuvre. The colours are subtly attuned to each other, creating a truly harmonious whole. The yellow of the lemon provides a striking accent among the otherwise extremely muted tones. As usual with Heda, the rendering of textures is superbly accomplished. The different materials are all depicted convincingly, from 'smooth' objects such as plates and the glass to the more grainy skin of the lemon. This painting, like Claesz's slightly earlier *Still Life with a Ham and Cheeses*, exemplifies the brilliance of the Haarlem still life painters of the Golden Age.

who originally introduced the motifs, after which Claesz adopted them. Who actually owned the precious tazza at that time is unknown.

Other items of glassware are depicted on the table in addition to the roemer of wine: behind the little plate of olives stands a glass decorated *à la façon-de-Venise* and a simple beer glass, both also filled

Willem van Aelst
Still Life with a Candle, Walnuts and a Mouse
1647

This still life, painted on a copperplate, is a product of the early career of Willem van Aelst (1627–after 1683). He signed and

dated it at about 20 years of age: '.W.V. aelst. [16]47'. From this year it may be deduced that the picture was produced not in Delft, the painter's home town, but in France. For that is where Van Aelst lived between 1645 and 1649, before he left for Italy to work as court painter to the Grand Duke of Tuscany, Ferdinando II de' Medici (1610–1670). From 1657 onwards he worked in Amsterdam, but used only the Italian variant of his signature, 'Guill[el] mo van Aelst'. Here the painter was still inscribing his initials in Dutch.

While in his later work Van Aelst would have a preference for elegant still lifes with a bright and varied palette, this is a relatively simple scene. On a stone table we see a candlestick with the stump of a candle, a handful of walnuts and a mouse that is nibbling the contents of an open nut. The relatively low viewpoint endows the mundane objects with an air of monumentality. The simplicity of this composition reflects the prevailing tradition of painting in Haarlem and Amsterdam, where artists had started producing plain still lifes in small formats

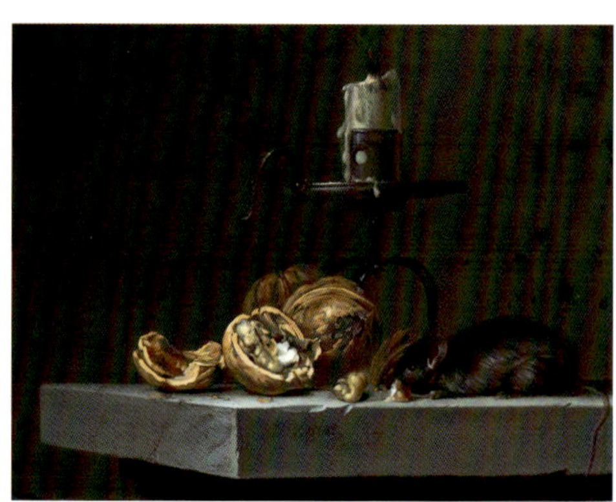

earlier in the century. The pioneers of this genre were the Haarlem still-life painters Pieter Claesz and Willem Heda, who are mainly known for their breakfast pieces (*ontbijtjes*) and richly laid tables (see pp. 51–52). But from about 1627 onwards they also produced a number of sober still lifes with a small number of objects on a stone table. Both Van Aelst's simple composition and the muted palette of browns and greys recall the work of the two Haarlem painters. Van Aelst deliberately allowed the reddish-brown ground to glimmer through the paint layer to create a warm effect.

Many of the still lifes produced in the Golden Age also convey a deeper significance. Here, the recently extinguished candle, in particular, can be interpreted as a vanitas motif, and the same may apply to the gnawed walnuts and cracked tabletop. The combination of walnuts, a candlestick with an extinguished candle and a mouse is extremely unusual. Even so, we find the same combination of motifs in a drawing dating from 1594 by the Antwerp artist Joris Hoefnagel (1542–1601?). In this small drawing in the Rijksmuseum, Amsterdam, a mouse is sitting on a table near an open walnut and a half-burned candle, while a second mouse pokes its head through a hole in the table.[49] The drawing contains a variety of intellectual references relating to the dedication to a friend of Hoefnagel's, Johann Muizenhol [=‘mouse-hole’]. This name explains the drawing's subject. We do not know who may have commissioned Van Aelst's still life; its provenance is as yet a complete mystery.

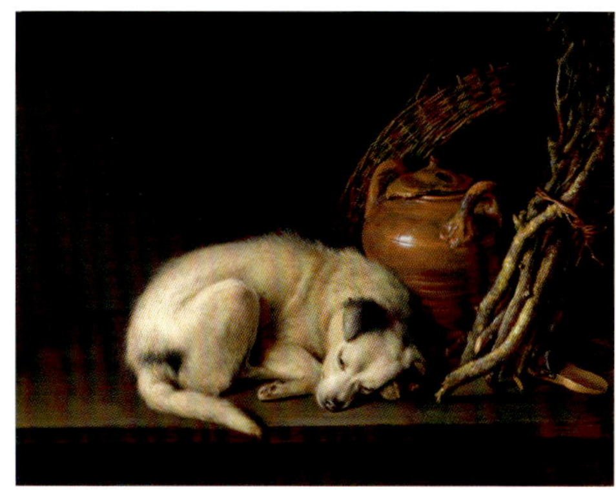

Gerrit Dou
A Resting Dog
1650

After an apprenticeship with a copper engraver and a glass engraver, Gerrit Dou (1613–1675) worked in the Leiden studio of his father, himself a glassmaker and glass engraver. In February 1628 he started as an apprentice with the 22-year-old Rembrandt (1606–1669), and stayed with him for three years. When Rembrandt left for Amsterdam, Dou set up business as an independent painter in Leiden, where he would live and work for the rest of his life. The painter Philips Angel (c.1618–after 1664) eulogised Dou in a festive address published in 1642 as *Lof der Schilderkunst* ('In Praise of Painting'). The great renown that Dou enjoyed in his lifetime is clear from the high prices fetched by the small paintings he made, as well as the commissions he received from prominent figures. One of Dou's specialties was depicting scenes with a feeble light source in a dim interior, a type of picture that he devised himself and that became a great success.

His introduction of 'invisible brushstrokes' and the minute detail of his works have earned the painter the title of 'father of the Leiden *fijnschilders*' (fine painters). Numerous painters, including Frans van Mieris the Elder (pp. 69–70), trained with him.

Dou is best known for his figurative pieces and portraits, but he sometimes made still lifes as well. The meticulously smooth finish of this painting from 1650 is characteristic of Dou's technique. No other painter was able to depict such a large variety of materials in such a realistic, almost illusionist style. Diverse types of materials are depicted highly convincingly: the glazed earthenware pot with the damaged lid, the branches of firewood tied together, the wooden slipper below them, and the wicker basket in the background. The little dog itself is a true *tour de force*: its image is remarkably lifelike, from its coat to its wet nose and the soft pads of its paws. Its tail sticks out over the edge of the table. A splendidly observed detail is the gaze in the dog's open eye. People were just as attached to their pets in the seventeenth century as they are today. In fact the famous poet Constantijn Huygens wrote a poem to his little dog Gekkie on 25 October 1682, after the creature's death, at his country-house of Hofwijck in Voorburg.[50]

Dou had depicted the motif of a dog resting beside an earthenware pot once before, in *The Prayer of the Spinner*, from around 1645, in the Alte Pinakothek, Munich. *A Resting Dog* can be seen as one of the highlights of Dou's oeuvre.

'A good friend gave us that skeleton-shaped shell. We usually display it on an antique cabinet near the painting'.

The little painting's whereabouts were completely unknown for years, until it suddenly appeared at an auction in 2005. The price it fetched there was a world record for this painter.[51]

Adriaen Coorte
Still Life with Shells
1698

The still lifes produced by the artist Adriaen Coorte (active *c.*1683–1707), whose life is still shrouded in mystery, constitute a striking group in the paintings produced around 1700. Fewer specialist still-life painters were working in the Northern Netherlands at this time than before. While his fellow artists delighted in depicting abundance in their still lifes (p. 61), Coorte found his strength precisely in simple scenes. In this respect, he can be linked to the early seventeenth-century tradition of still-life painting (see pp. 51–52).

Coorte's sober compositions contain a number of recurrent motifs. His most characteristic works present a stone table with one or more kinds of vegetables, fruit, nuts, or – as here – shells. This little painting was executed on paper that was later pasted to a panel, a common practice with Coorte. Here the painter has grouped together exotic shells that differ widely in terms of shape, colour, surface structure and format. To render all these aspects as clearly and true to life as possible, he chose to place the shells separately from one another, with very little overlap.

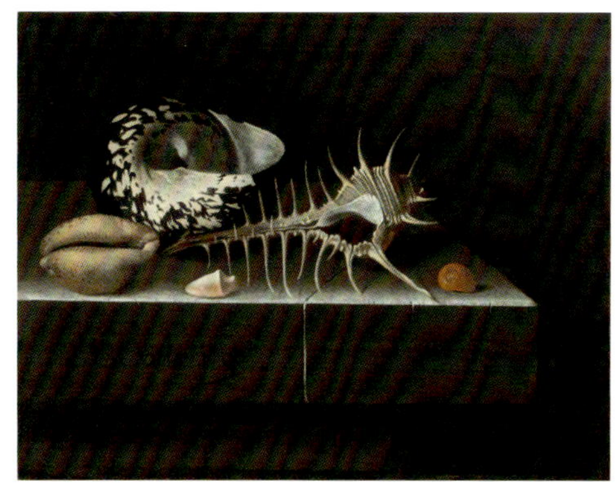

The extremely spiky contours of the *Murex tribulus*, the skeleton-shaped shell, contrasts with the two smooth, coloured little shells in front of and beside it.[52] The shells have been placed against a dark background. The bright illumination endows the still life with an unrealistic, almost magical quality. Since only the top of the stone table is illuminated, its edges stand out sharply. In one of these edges, a deep join is visible. Coorte's main concerns were atmosphere and detail.

This painting, which is dated 1698, is one of a small group of shell still lifes that Coorte produced in a short space of time. The Musée du Louvre, in Paris, has two small paintings from 1696 which mirror each other's composition and were made as companion-pieces. Coorte produced two more shell still lifes the following year. The year after that, 1698, he created the painting discussed here, along with a second one with five shells, in a horizontal format. All these paintings have now been acquired by different private collections.[53] Exotic shells of this kind, which Coorte usually depicted life-sized, were brought

to the Netherlands in ships belonging to the Dutch East India and West India Companies. Middelburg, the city in which Coorte most probably worked, was for many years the second port after Amsterdam in the United Provinces.

In the seventeenth century, shells were sold to collectors for large sums of money. These collectors may have purchased pictures of such naturalia to decorate their cabinets of curiosities or *Kunstkamers*. Four paintings with shells by Coorte, probably including the one discussed here, were incorporated into the collection of one Gerardus Beljard of Middelburg a hundred years after they were made.[54] It was not until 1969 that they parted company and ended up in different collections.[55]

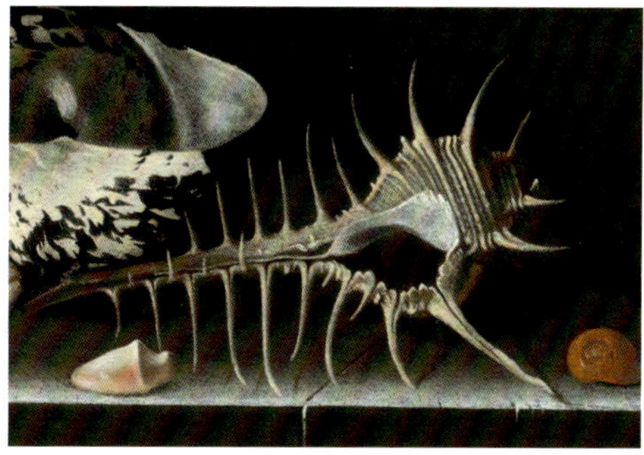

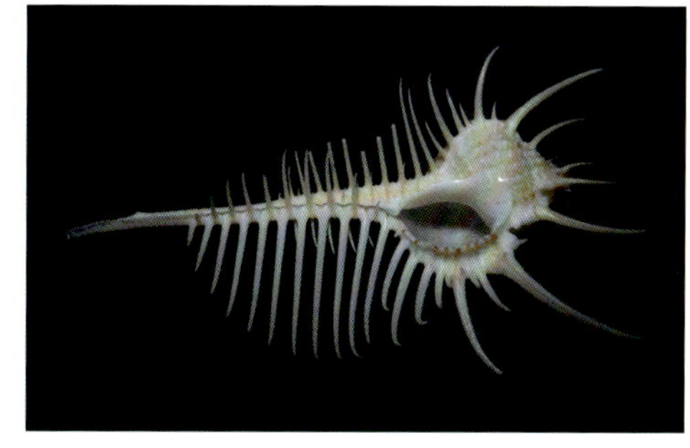

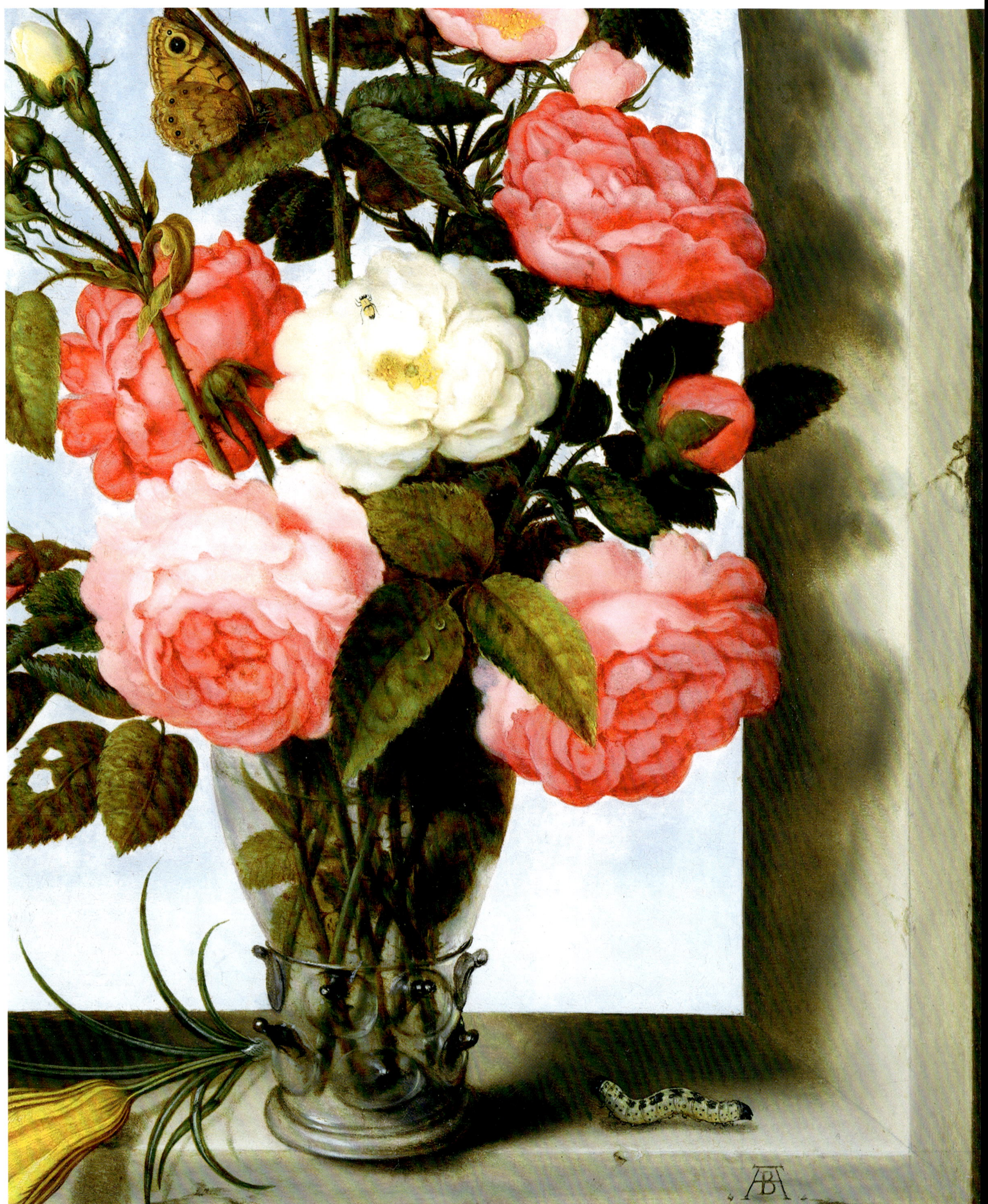

Flower Still Lifes

Ambrosius Bosschaert the Elder
Still Life with Roses in a Glass Vase
*c.*1619

Ambrosius Bosschaert (1573–1621) was born in Antwerp, but around 1587 his parents moved to Middelburg for religious reasons. It was here that this founder of the floral still life would spend most of his life. In 1604 he married Maria van der Ast, the sister of the still-life painter Balthasar van der Ast (pp. 57–59), one of his many pupils. The painting discussed here first reappeared in 1992. It displays Bosschaert's specialty: a bouquet in which the flowers are depicted true to life and scarcely overlap. A meticulous observer of nature, this artist felt a sense of kinship with Albrecht Dürer, whose famous monogram ('AD') he adapted by way of paraphrase in the lower right corner: 'AB'. Bosschaert placed the glass vase of roses in a stone window-frame, which is rendered in *trompe l'oeil* style. The effects of light and shade have been studied with great care. Thus, even the yellow crocus casts its shadow on the stone. As a true *fijnschilder*, Bosschaert has done his utmost to make the brushstrokes invisible. There is no expansive landscape vista such as those we encounter in other works, such as his well-known still life in the Mauritshuis.[56] But we do see here the creatures that are so characteristic of Bosschaert's work: a caterpillar, a butterfly, a dragon-fly and a fly.

The great popularity of floral still-life paintings in the first few decades of the seventeenth century was probably related to the growing interest in botany among scholars and laymen alike. In 1592, Carolus

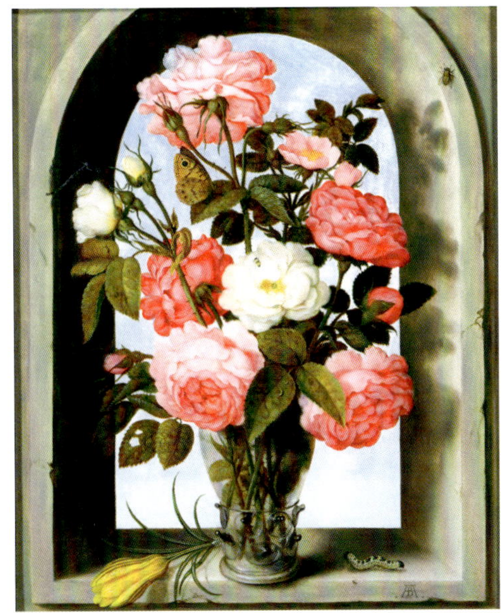

Clusius was appointed director of the botanical gardens in Leiden, and a start was made on the scientific study of flowers and plants. Clusius also became the key authority to deal with questions from amateur botanists, and he distributed seeds and bulbs, some imported and others he cultivated himself. Lay enthusiasts became more and more conscious of the remarkable aspects of the extraordinary plant world all around them. Thus, the Middelburg plant lover Johan Somer sent Clusius a *conterfeytsel* (portrait) of a yellow fritillary (*Fritillaria latifolia*) in 1597, noting proudly that it had bloomed in his garden the previous summer. It is tempting to surmise that this *conterfeytsel* may have been painted by Bosschaert. This is not inconceivable, since yellow fritillaries occur in many of his still lifes. Middelburg had a sizeable population

of affluent amateur botanists, who undoubtedly formed a lucrative clientele for Bosschaert. In any case, his paintings were extremely popular and were sold for quite large sums of money.

It is striking that one of the leaves in the foreground has been gnawed by insects; the holes stand out sharply against the blue sky. This is probably a reference to the brevity of life: in the seventeenth century, a bouquet was not only an extremely attractive subject, but also a vanitas symbol. Thus, a print by Jan Theodoor de Bry after a flower piece by Jacob Kempener, in 1604, bore the caption: 'Flos speculum vitae modo vernat et interit aura' ('The flower is a mirror of life, she blossoms but perishes in the wind'). It was Bosschaert's achievement to package this idea subtly in the form of a beautifully painted bouquet.

Balthasar van der Ast
Flower Still Life
*c.*1630

Balthasar van der Ast (1593/94–1657) was one of the most productive still life painters of the first half of the seventeenth century. He started off living and working in Middelburg, after which he was active in Utrecht from 1619 to 1632, and subsequently in Delft. His oeuvre is impressive in its variety. He painted large, complex bouquets and baskets of flowers, but he also produced compositions with only a few flowers or shells, in some cases just a single one. In his early period in Middel-

'Rose-Marie hesitated for a long time before deciding she wanted to buy it, only to discover that it had just been sold. And who was the buyer? I was! I had bought it as a present for her 50th birthday'.

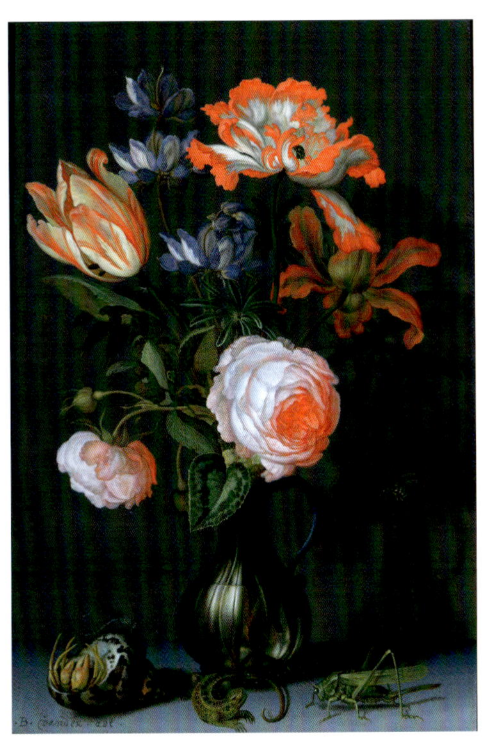

Elder (p. 57). Around 1630, when he must have painted this flower still life, which is almost unknown in the literature, the composition of his bouquets became significantly looser. The dark backgrounds gradually gave way to lighter ones. Here, the shadow cast by the bouquet on the wall has been rendered superbly.

Here Van der Ast presents a fairly loose flower arrangement in a glass vase with an elegant handle. That this bouquet was certainly not painted from life is clear from the combination of tulips with roses, flowers that bloom in different seasons. Van der Ast's bouquets occasionally feature identical flowers, sometimes after an interval of several years. Like his teacher Bosschaert, the painter evidently worked on the basis of drawn or painted studies that he made in different seasons.

In the foreground, Van der Ast displays his virtuosity in depicting shells and small creatures that enliven the otherwise 'still' life painting. The shell on the left contains a hermit crab, besides which are a sand

lizard and in the right foreground a bush cricket. A damselfly is depicted on the shell, and a wasp hovers on the right. There is a ladybird on one of the rose-petals. Shells were among the most popular and most precious collectors' items in the seventeenth century. They were sold for exorbitant prices (see also p. 55). The shell's inclusion emphasises that few could afford a bouquet such as this one.

Jan Davidsz de Heem
A Glass Vase with Flowers
c.1655–1660

Jan Davidsz de Heem (1606–1683/84) was one of the most versatile still-life painters of the seventeenth century. He started his career in Leiden, where he produced sober still lifes in muted colours. From the first half of the 1630s onwards, he worked in Antwerp, where he initially focused primarily on painting 'sumptuous' still lifes. His style changed dramatically in this period.

burg he was influenced by the austere, symmetrical bouquets of his brother-in-law and teacher Ambrosius Bosschaert the

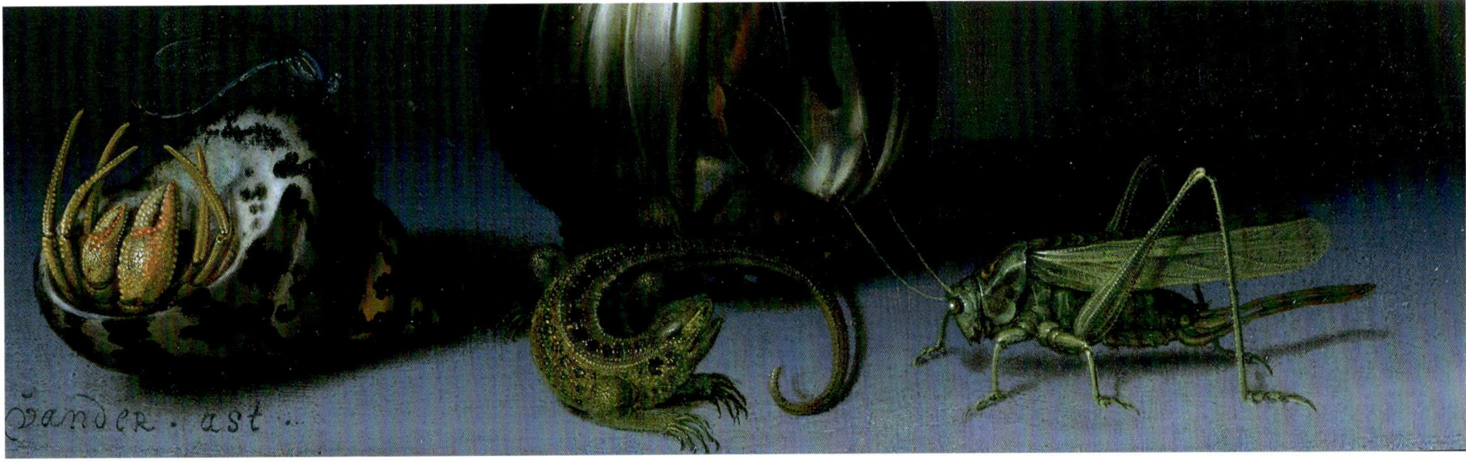

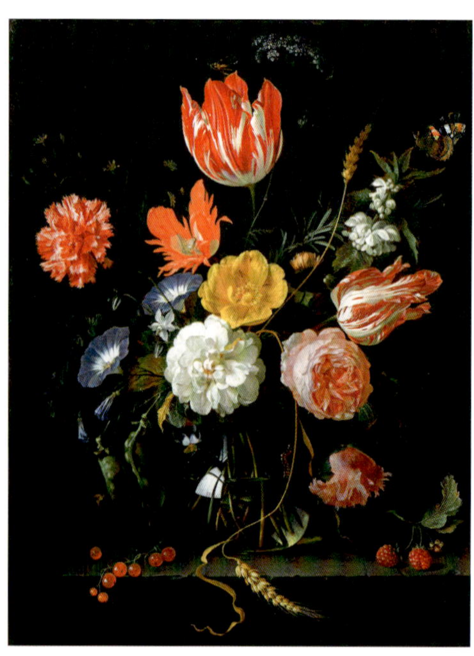

His compositions became more complex, with a pyramid or slanting heap of fruits, fish, shellfish and flowers. His palette, too, became much more exuberant.

Around 1650, he began to devote himself to flower paintings, perhaps inspired by the colourful, lavish bouquets and festoons of the Antwerp Jesuit brother Daniel Seghers (1590–1661). De Heem was responsible for several innovations: most importantly, he allowed his bouquets to hang over the edge of the vase in a seemingly loose and carefree manner, and in this way filled the picture plane with flowers. He also reintroduced the colourful palette that had been so typical of Flemish flower pieces in the days of Jan Brueghel the Elder (1568–1625).

This particular painting was probably made around 1655–1660, when De Heem was still living and working in Antwerp. Reflected in the glass vase is a stained-glass window, probably the window of the artist's studio, complete with cloudy sky. De Heem's brilliant technique is discernible not just in the marvellous array of flowers, but also in less conspicuous details such as the caterpillar climbing the snapped ear of corn in the foreground and other creatures such as a butterfly and even a few ants. Dewdrops enliven the bouquet, which consists of a wide range of flowers: diverse roses (white, pink and yellow), to their left, the blue and white flowers of the convolvulus, above this a poppy, and in the upper left corner a carnation and a white borage (starflower, *Borage officinalis*). A little violet can be seen beneath the roses. The still life is surmounted by a red and white flamed tulip (a flower that blooms in a different season than the rose), cow parsley, and

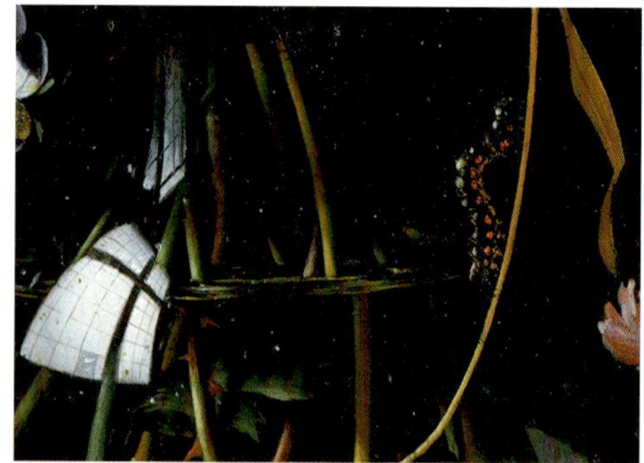

to the right of this a marigold, dead nettle, a second flamed tulip and at bottom right a pinkish-red poppy. Hanging at bottom left, rather curiously, are some peapods, which we should scarcely be likely to include in a bouquet of flowers today. Lying on the stone table are a sprig of redcurrants and a sprig of blackberries, to which the painter has added subtle highlights to denote reflected light. The composition of the still life is extremely measured: the flowers are arranged such they scarcely overlap, if at all. The magnificent colours of the bouquet stand out particularly well against the dark background.

De Heem later divided his time between Antwerp and Utrecht. This enabled him to serve as a *trait d'union*

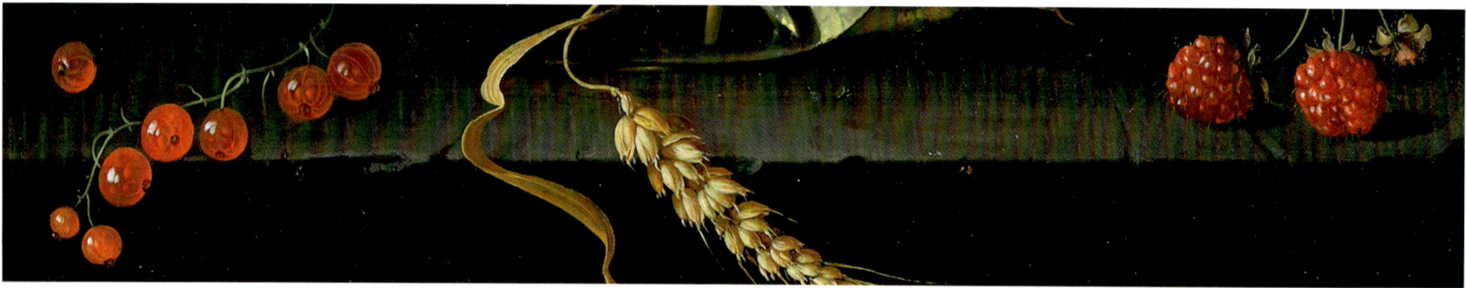

between the rather sober still life painting of the north and the more exuberant type practised in the south. Although he produced a large oeuvre of still lifes, only twenty of his flower pieces are known today.

Rachel Ruysch
Flower Still Life
1709

Rachel Ruysch (1664–1750) was something of a phenomenon in the Dutch Republic of the seventeenth and eighteenth centuries. She was not only a gifted painter, but also brought ten children into the world. She continued to work until an advanced age, and was still making floral still lifes when she was eighty. Ruysch had been trained in her youth by Willem van Aelst (see pp. 52–53). In addition, her father, Frederik Ruysch (1638–1731), the famous Amsterdam professor of anatomy and botany, must have played a key role in her life. He was not only an amateur painter, but from 1685 onwards he was in charge of Amsterdam's botanical gardens. Rachel Ruysch was related on her mother's side to the architect and painter Pieter Post (1608–1669), one of the most important architects of the Golden Age. She herself also built up a great reputation, particularly after 1708, when she and her husband, the portrait painter Jurriaen Pool (1666–1745), were appointed court painters to Johann Wilhelm, Elector Palatine (1658–1716). The collection of paintings that Johann Wilhelm built up in Düsseldorf was one of the most

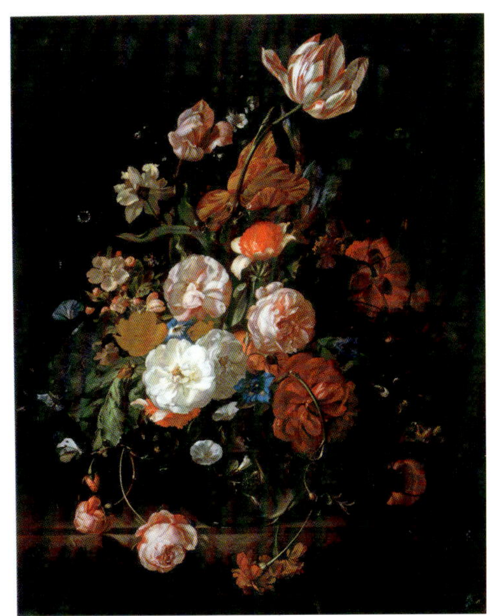

beautiful in Europe, with work by Italian, Flemish and Dutch painters. All the paintings that Ruysch made from 1708 onwards were produced for him. The flower still life discussed here, dating from 1709, belongs in this group. The painting belonged to diverse notable princely and museum collections, until it was sold by the Alte Pinakothek in Munich in 1937.[57] In 2007, the Van Otterloos purchased it in the art trade.

With this floral still life, Ruysch appealed wholly to eighteenth-century taste. As in the work of contemporaries such as Jan van Huysum (1682–1749), the emphasis here is on the decorative effect. There seems to be no moralistic message, such as one will find in many seventeenth-century still lifes, but the composition of the bouquet – just as in those paintings – sprang from the artist's imagination.

This is obvious, since the flowers, which have been painted with great care, bloom in different seasons. At the top are three tulips and a double daffodil; in the middle we see a double anemone, different-coloured roses, a white convolvulus and a blue gentian; on the right are two poppies and a sprig of honeysuckle, while on the left are a small sprig of apple blossom and a blue convolvulus. The flowers are placed in a glass vase on a marble tabletop. The round vase is wreathed, as it were, by the pink rose and the broken stem of a marigold. The curved and round shapes lend the composition a remarkably harmonious air. The subtly illuminated flowers and the white butterfly in the lower left corner stand out in delightful contrast against the dark background.

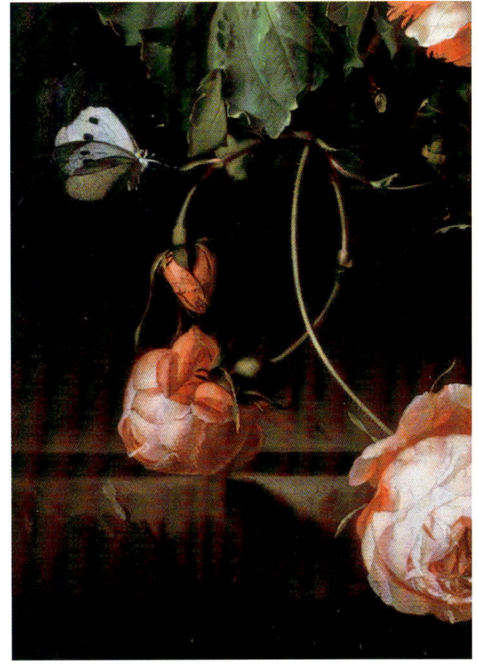

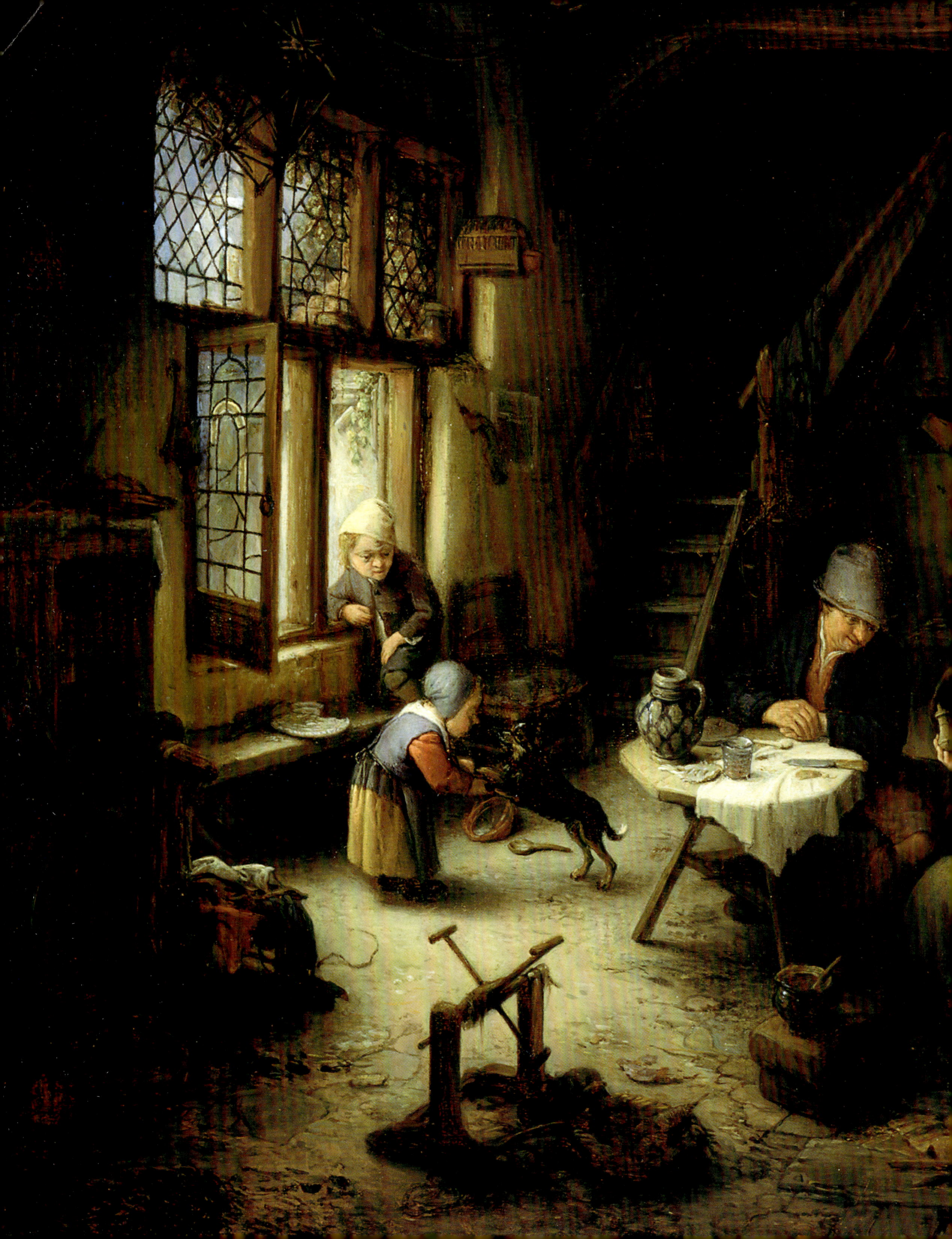

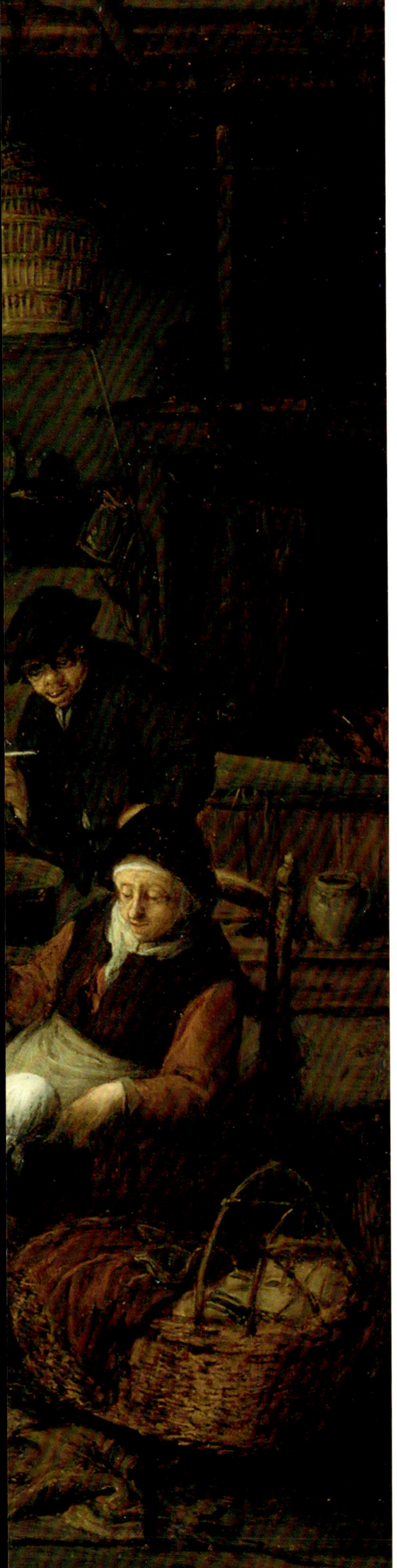

Genre Pieces &
Church Interiors

Genre pieces are scenes that appear to show a slice of life, with anonymous figures. Paintings of this kind display immense variety, ranging from simple peasants in an inn to elegant figures in a luxurious interior. The motif of everyday life was introduced into the Dutch Republic by Flemish immigrants and was soon adopted by others. Art historians long regarded scenes of this kind simply as realistic images of everyday life in the seventeenth century. But since the exhibition *Tot lering en vermaak* ('For instruction and delight') in the Rijksmuseum, Amsterdam (1976), it has been generally accepted that numerous genre scenes possess a deeper, frequently moralistic, significance. In interpreting these paintings, prints from the sixteenth and seventeenth centuries are often an indispensable aid, since their captions provide comments on the images taken from everyday life. They frequently urged people to live virtuous, chaste lives. This message is sometimes depicted quite explicitly, but more commonly it is somewhat veiled. In later periods, the deeper significance of the scenes was often forgotten. One must be cautious about seeking to interpret every detail, however, since not every genre scene contains concealed symbolism.

The Golden Age was also known for many paintings of church interiors, related motifs and in some cases completely imaginary church interiors. These pictures frequently include human figures: people visiting the buildings or attending services. Around 1650, Gerard Houckgeest introduced some major changes: a diagonal perspective, a more colourful palette, and a more prominent role for the light streaming in. Besides Houckgeest, Hendrick van Vliet (1611/12–1675) and Emanuel de Witte are also regarded as key innovators of the Dutch church interior.

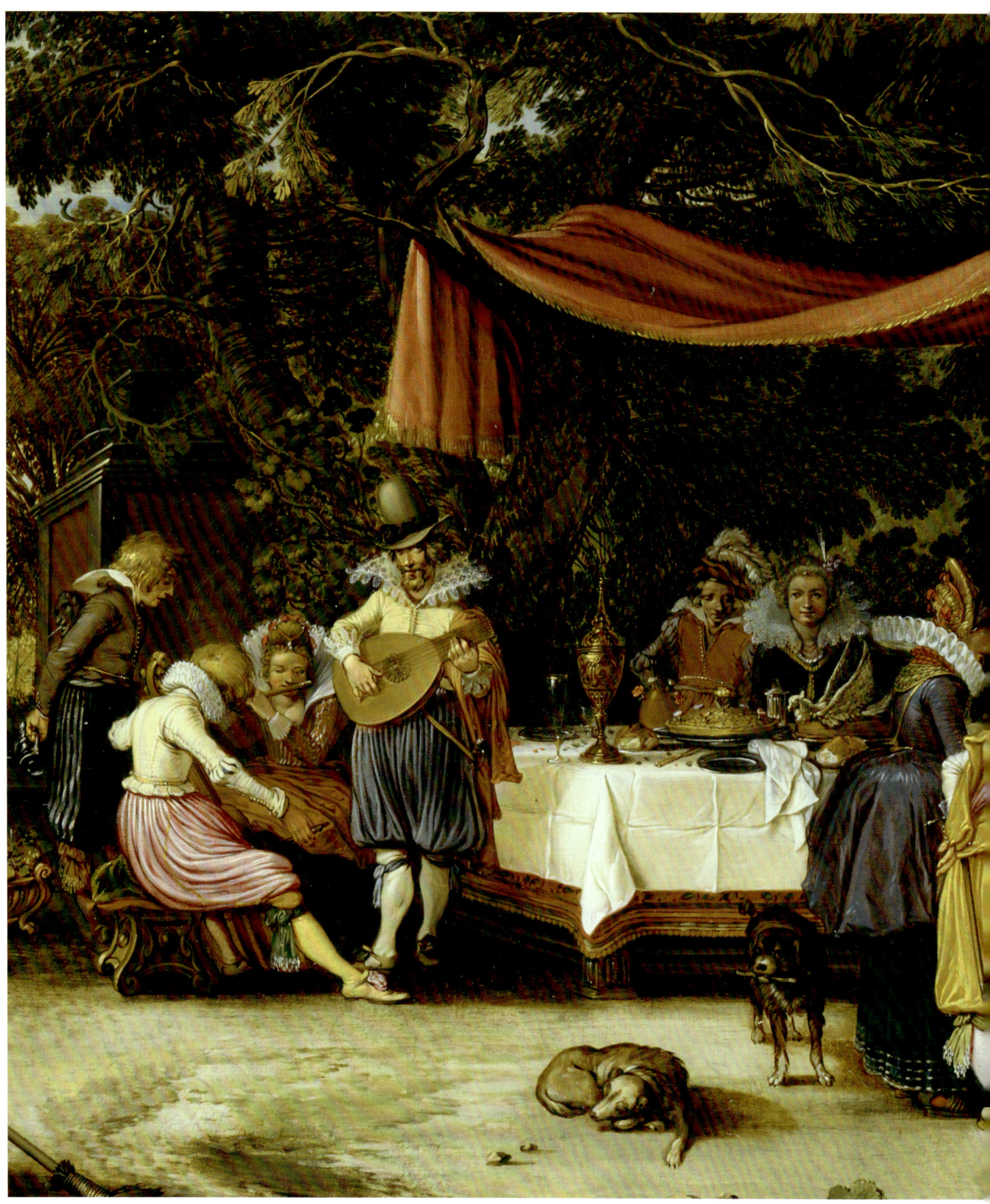

Genre Pieces

Esaias van de Velde
An Elegant Company in a Garden
1614

Esaias van de Velde (1587–1630) was one of the great innovators of Dutch landscape painting. But he also produced a small cluster of some twelve paintings of garden parties. This recently rediscovered painting from 1614 is one of the earliest and most ambitious examples of these 'merry companies'.[58] Paintings of this kind were very popular in the seventeenth century. We see a group of extremely stylish figures enjoying themselves at a party. The young people are dressed in the latest fashion, with extravagant, ample sleeves, costly lace collars and top hats decorated with ribbons and feathers. They are in the garden of a country estate, many of them seated beneath a large piece of fabric that has been hung between the trees. They are enjoying each other's company while music is being played. The table is full of food and drink, and to its right we see a temporary structure on which richly decorated dishes and flagons have been placed. An animated conversation is going on in the right foreground, while the couple behind the table are sitting in serene repose. People are making music in lively fashion to the left of the table, and on the far left, a young servant is preparing oysters. Other servants are pouring drinks from a wine cooler.

This painting, along with another picture of a garden party in the Mauritshuis, also dating from 1614, is one of the earliest dated works by Van de Velde

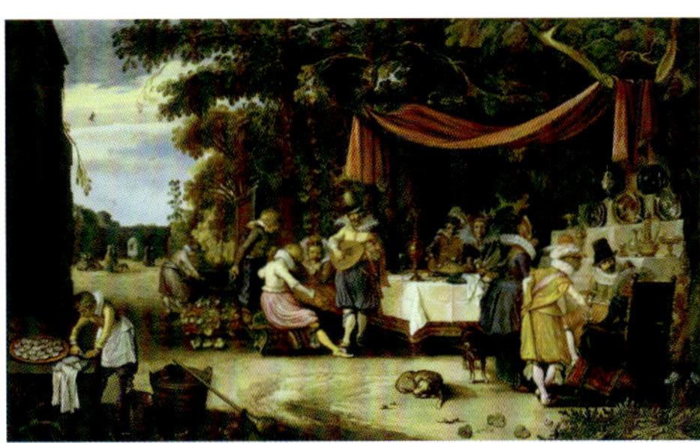

that is still known today. The painter probably drew inspiration for scenes of this kind from the work of David Vinckboons (1576–c.1632), who was probably his teacher. Vinckboons painted similar scenes of garden parties around 1610, also showing elegantly-dressed figures in parklike surroundings. Vinckboons's work often contains a deeper significance; he sometimes even included allusions to the iconography of the prodigal son. Such references warn against the consequences of compulsive gambling or rash behaviour. In Van de Velde's work, however, there seems to be no trace of any explicit deeper significance. Rather, attention appears to focus on the amorous adventures of the elegant figures with their fashionable clothing and their lavish fare and tableware. Even so, such scenes always have moralistic overtones, to the effect that 'too much of ought is good for nought'.

Isaack Koedijck
A Barber Surgeon Tending a Man's Foot
c.1649–1650

The Van Otterloos' collection also contains paintings by artists who are virtually

unknown today. This is one such work. At first sight, one might think that the painting was made by the well-known Leiden artist Gerrit Dou (see p. 53), but it is clearly signed on the table 'I Koedijk'. Isaack Koedijck (1617/18–1668) was rescued from oblivion in articles appearing from 1909 onwards by Wilhelm Martin, Abraham Bredius and Cornelis Hofstede de Groot, all of them art historians who worked in the Mauritshuis. Thanks to their research, we are quite well informed about Koedijck's life. Probably in response to unremitting financial problems, Koedijck and his wife decided to try their luck outside the Dutch Republic. In 1651 they arrived in Jakarta, then known as Batavia. At the request of the Dutch East India Company (VOC) they then journeyed to Agra in northern India, where Koedijck was to be appointed

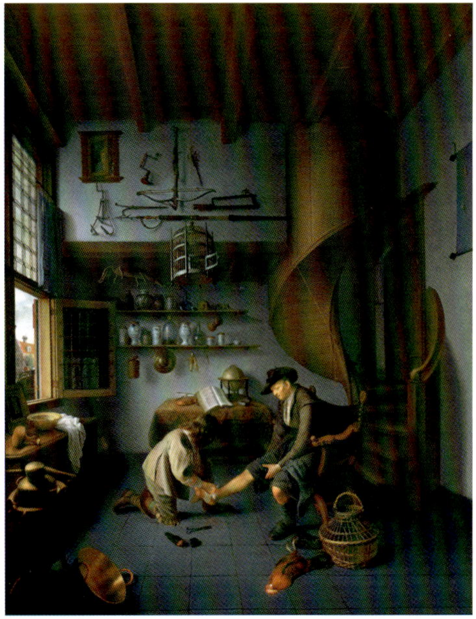

court painter to the 'Great Mogul' Shah Jahan (1592–1662). These plans foundered, however, and Koedijck set up as a merchant instead, initially in Ahmadabad and later in Surat, an important trading post of the VOC. In 1659 the couple returned to the United Provinces. The painted oeuvre of the merchant and keen traveller Koedijck, who also worked as a jewellery dealer, is quite small, and consists largely of genre pieces that are extremely similar to Dou's. Nothing is known about any contacts between the two, but Koedijck must have been very familiar with Dou's early work.[59]

This painting, which must have been made before Koedijck's departure for Jakarta, displays a barber surgeon who is bandaging the foot of a simply-dressed man. The patient is holding his leg with both hands. On the ground lies a case with instruments, with a separate pair of scissors to one side. The prominently-

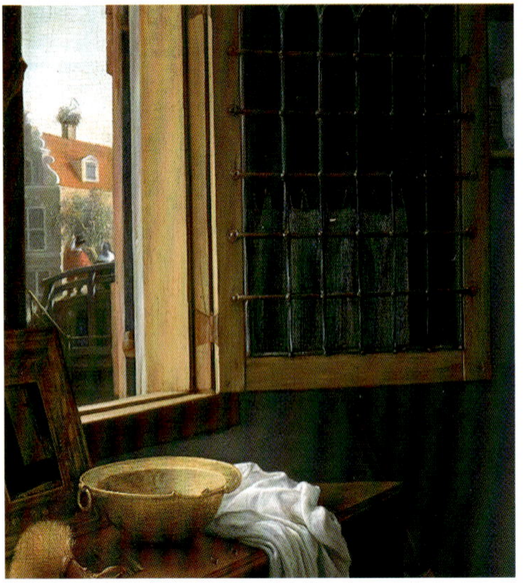

displayed dead rooster may be the man's payment for his treatment. While the patient's face is depicted in fine detail, with the somewhat fixed gaze that accompanies pain, the face of the barber surgeon is completely concealed behind his long hair. Countless objects around the room refer to the diverse activities of this barber surgeon, who was certainly not a quack. There were two kinds of physicians in the Golden Age: university-trained *doctores medicinae* and surgeons. While the former concerned themselves mainly with internal diseases, surgeons, most of whom had acquired their knowledge from practical experience, focused on treating wounds, abscesses and boils. They also performed bloodletting, which was part of the treatment of many diseases at the time. In most cities, the surgeons belonged to guilds, which oversaw compliance with their regulations. It was common for surgeons to combine this work with the occupation of barber, as here. Lying on the cupboard by the window is everything a barber needed for his occupation: in front of the mirror are a shaving brush, a comb, a brass shaving basin and a towel. The Van Otterloos acquired a basin identical to this for their collection; it is usually displayed in the vicinity of the painting. In the foreground are other metal objects – a distilling apparatus with a basin – near some branches from a tree.

The rear wall of the room, in particular, is filled with objects from top to bottom. The stuffed crocodile hanging near the window defines the location, since this

was a standard item in every pharmacist or surgeon's workplace. On the tablecloth is a still life of a violin, a globe, an open silver tobacco-box and two books, one of which lies open. On the left-hand page we can read the words 'Maurits van Nassau' (Maurice of Nassau), the name of Stadholder Maurits, Prince of Orange, who died in 1625. Whether Koedijck intended this to convey some specific meaning is unclear. The shelves above the table are full of various apothecary jars and bottles, some of which are labelled. On the top shelf are a human skull and the skeleton of a small animal, while from the bottom shelf hang a wicker basket, a second brass shaving basin, a cob of corn, and a scissor-shaped pair of forceps. Above the shelves is a rather intimidating ensemble of medical instruments and implements such as a *speculum matricis*, used in difficult deliveries, a skull drill, and a saw used for amputations. Added to these items are a few weapons, such as a crossbow and a harpoon. A woman who appears high up behind a little window adds a lively note to the wall. A striking element in this room is the spiral staircase that leads to another room half-way up. Attached to this staircase is the rope of a pulley, the empty cage of which is hanging from the ceiling. Through the window on the left we glimpse something of life in the outside world. Standing on the bridge is a man wearing a red coat, who is drawing the attention of a woman dressed in black to a stork's nest.

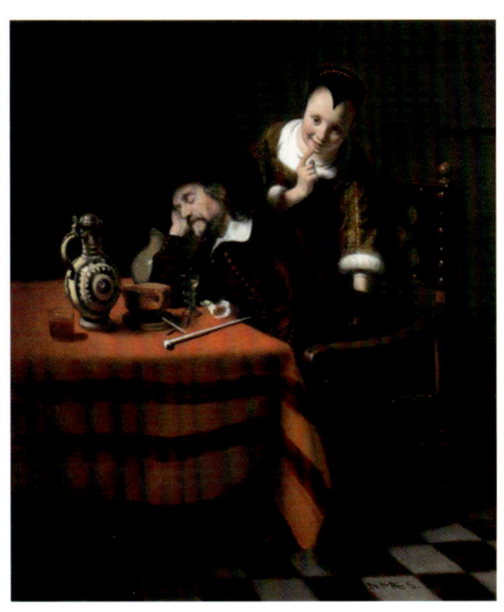

Nicolaes Maes
A Young Woman Picking the Pocket of a Sleeping Man
c.1655

Nicolaes Maes (1634–1693) was one of Rembrandt's most important pupils. He was apprenticed to the famous painter in Amsterdam around 1650. By the end of 1653, Maes was back in his native city of Dordrecht, where his paintings earned him only a modest income. This may explain why he moved to Amsterdam in 1673, since this was still the city where painters could expect to win the largest number of commissions. He would spend the rest of his life there. Maes started out painting biblical scenes, the large size and warm palette of which, in red and brown tones, reflect the strong influence of his teacher, Rembrandt. In the period 1655–1660 he concentrated on depicting domestic scenes with one or two figures, such as women making bobbin lace or spinning, girls peeling potatoes, and eavesdropping maidservants. At the same time, he also gradually ventured into portraiture, and from 1660 he devoted himself entirely to painting elegant portraits. Although in his day Maes achieved his greatest success with his portraits, nowadays it is his genre scenes that are most greatly admired, because with these small, intimate scenes he struck off down a new path, becoming a major source of inspiration for painters such as Pieter de Hooch (1629–1684) and Johannes Vermeer (1632–1675).

Only thirty genre pieces by Maes are known. *A Young Woman Picking the Pocket of a Sleeping Man* was probably painted around 1655, the period in which he produced his finest genre scenes. We witness a young woman picking the pocket of a man who has fallen asleep in his armchair at a table. His drowsiness may come from tobacco and alcohol. On the table we see a full roemer and a beer glass near an earthenware jug, as well as stone pipes and a scrap of paper with some tobacco. Beside the earthenware bowl containing red-hot coals are some matchsticks to light the pipe. Maes has left it unclear whether the second glass belongs to the thief or to a guest who has already left. Nor do we know the identity of the woman, who is richly dressed, with a fur-trimmed jacket. Perhaps she is the sleeping man's wife, and has hit on a playful way of warning him of the consequences of the excessive consumption of alcohol and tobacco. An alternative explanation is that she is a guest who is taking advantage of the situation.

The woman gazes at the viewer and gestures with her finger, admonishing silence. In this way, the viewer is drawn into the scene, as it were, and almost made privy to a secret. This resembles other scenes by Maes, in which the protagonist makes similar gestures urging the viewer to be quiet or to keep a secret. The painting discussed here seems to be among the earliest of this group. Maes derived the motif of the figure exhorting others to be silent from the little-known artist Isaack Koedijck (see pp. 65–66). Koedijck painted the scene in Amsterdam around 1650, the time when Maes was training with Rembrandt.[60]

Maes shows little of the room in which this incident takes place – only the tiled floor and a map on the wall. By focusing

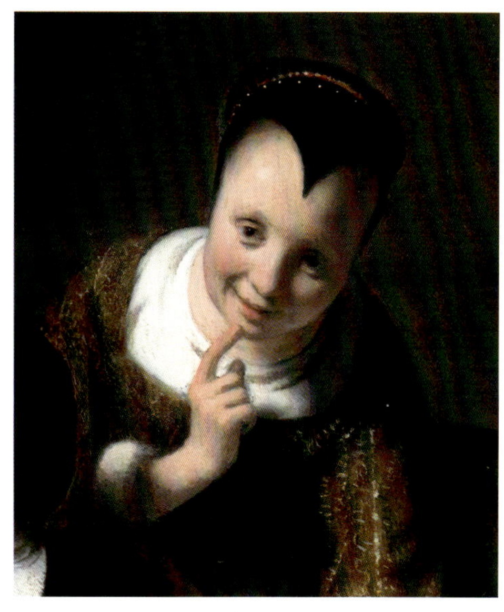

on the man and the woman, he creates
an intimate scene. This intimate quality
is strengthened by the relatively subdued
palette of warm reds and browns, with
accents in black and white. The rendering
of the different textures – earthenware,
glass and various fabrics – is highly
convincing. For a long time, this attractive painting led a hidden existence, as
part of the collection of paintings at
Penrhyn Castle in Wales.[61] In 2002 the
Van Otterloos were able to acquire it in
the art trade.

Gabriel Metsu
An Old Woman Eating Porridge
c. 1657

This scene is one of the early highlights
in the work of Gabriel Metsu (1629–1667).
In the seventeenth century, besides 'merry
companies', depicting affluent burghers as
characters making music, writing letters
or eating oysters, artists also produced
genre pieces featuring 'ordinary' burghers
engaged in less exalted activities. For
instance, genre painters documented
the everyday sale of fish, meat, poultry
or fruit and the cleaning, preparation or
consumption of food. This painting
focuses on the latter motif: an old woman
eating porridge. She is eating from a
glazed earthenware pot that she is holding
on her lap. To cool the hot food, she blows
on her spoon, spilling a bit of porridge.
The woman, whose only companion is a
cat, is completely absorbed in her meal.
More food is depicted on the table: a dish

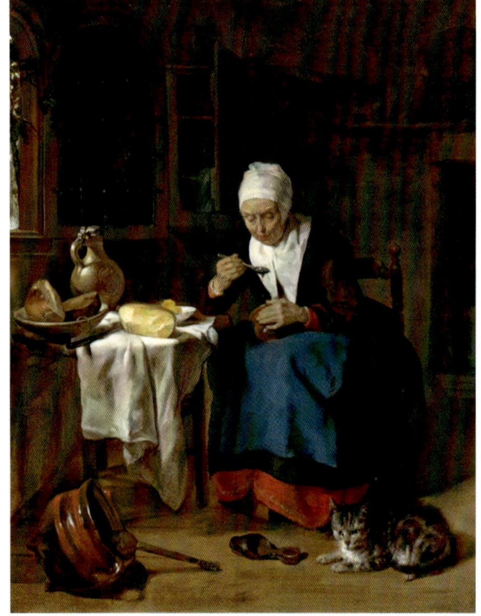

with loaves of bread, a cheese, and an
earthenware beer jug.

The simple interior looks a little
chaotic. In the foreground, for instance,
we see a cooking-pot lying on its side
(laid there to spoon out the last remnants
of porridge?) and in the background an
open cupboard door and a rather cluttered
shelf. The worn-down sandal on the

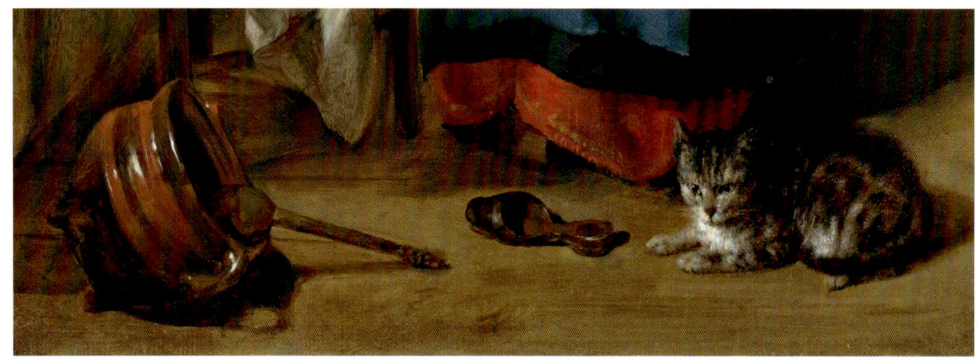

ground was added by the painter as a
mundane detail; he painted out a second
one. Rooms of this kind, with an open
window on the left and a passage to
another room on the right, were frequently depicted by the Leiden painter Gerrit
Dou (see p. 53). It was also Dou who had
introduced the theme of a woman eating
porridge in the 1630s. Many of his Leiden
followers adopted it from him, such as
Dominicus van Tol (1635–1676) and
Quiringh van Brekelenkam (after 1622–
c.1669). For the painter's contemporaries,
scenes of this kind with aged women
had a variety of associations. The women
– often widows – with their simple meals
symbolised virtuous qualities such as
sobriety and modesty. At the same time
they allude to the transience of life.[62]

This small painting by the Leiden-
born Metsu was probably made around
1657, when the artist had already been
living and working in Amsterdam for
several years. Metsu displays a confident
technique in this picture. The play of
light on the objects on the table creates
an attractive spectacle. The woman's
colourful garments – a white cap and

collar, a blue apron and a red petticoat –
immediately strike the eye in the scene,
which is otherwise a fairly monochrome
scene.

This painting probably belonged
to a collection in Amsterdam in the
seventeenth century. A document dating
from 1684 refers to 'An old woman eating
porridge by Gabriel Metsu', which is
probably this painting. After changing
hands several times, in 1889 it was incorporated into the renowned collection of
Edward Guinness (1847–1927), the later
Earl of Iveagh. Under his leadership, the
brewery that bore his name would go
from strength to unprecedented strength.
Guinness's collection can still be seen
today at Kenwood House in London,
He bequeathed it to the city, but his
heirs sold this painting. In 2009 the Van
Otterloos purchased it through the art
trade.

Frans van Mieris the Elder
The Old Fiddler
1660

Frans van Mieris the Elder (1635–1681)
is regarded as the best of the Dutch
fijnschilders, artists who endeavoured, in
their smoothly executed and precise
images, to achieve a perfect rendering of
textures. He was peerless in his ability to
depict with paint, convincingly and true
to life, materials as diverse as velvet, silk
and glass. But Van Mieris was more than
just a craftsman: his scenes from everyday
life frequently possess a narrative quality

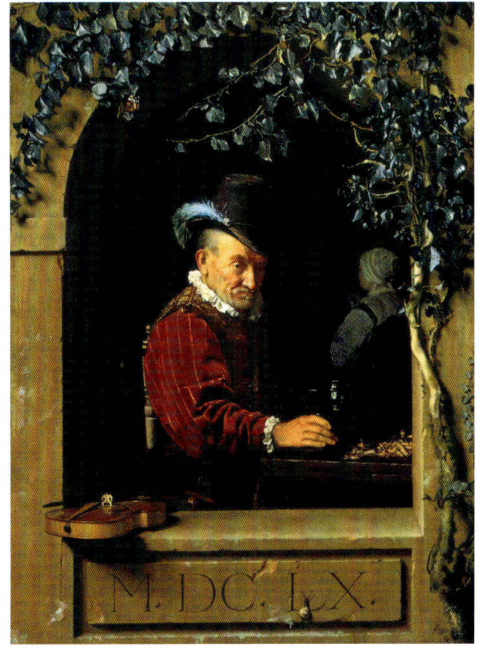

and sometimes convey a deeper significance. Few seventeenth-century painters
were so popular – and so well paid – as
Van Mieris. Until the early nineteenth
century his delicate little paintings were
among the highlights of numerous
collections. Then tastes changed, and they
were frequently dismissed as smooth and
uninspired. But there has been a revival
of appreciation for Van Mieris's work over
the past few decades. Interest initially
focused mainly on his representation of
everyday life, but soon his unparalleled
technique, too, started to command
growing admiration.

Here Van Mieris shows an old fiddler
sitting at a small table, seen through a
stone window-frame. This characteristic
compositional form can be traced to the

work of his most influential teacher,
Gerrit Dou (see p. 53). The musician is
dressed in a costume with a red velvet
doublet, a brown jerkin, and a plumed
hat. He has put his violin and bow down
on the windowsill beside him. On the
table is a prunted beaker, and beside it a
snack in the form of some shrimps. A snail
crawls up the wall through the date of
the painting – 1660, carved out in Roman
numerals – and a butterfly has alighted on
one of the leaves of the ivy growing around
the window. At the back of the drinking
establishment is a barmaid, with her back
turned to the fiddler. She has a blackboard
on which to keep a tally of her customers'
drinks. The man appears to have been
sitting here for some time. Recent restoration work exposed an earlier version of the
chair, so that now not one but two backs
of the chair are visible behind him.

The motif of a figure tallying drinks
also occurs in a print showing a drinking
philosopher in Vondel's *Gulden winckel*. In
the accompanying lines of verse, Vondel
urges moderation in drinking: 'Here sits
the Wise man, he'll have no more than
three modest-sized drafts / Tapped for
him before the noonday repast'.[63] And
the print indeed shows only three small
wineglasses on the man's table. Van Mieris
appears to be using the motif of the
woman as a silent comment on the old
fiddler's drinking.

It was recently discovered that Van
Mieris initially conceived this scene
without the painted window that serves as
frame.[64] Only later did he enlarge the panel
and transform it into a 'niche piece'. In a

different version, which is in the Pushkin Museum in Moscow – possibly executed by a studio assistant – a panel large enough to accommodate the window was chosen straight away.[65] The window was also retained in ten later copies.[66] In Van Mieris's *Man Filling a Pipe* from 1658 in the Brukenthal Museum, Sibiu, the figure was painted on a small plank of wood that was subsequently inlaid in a larger panel, as here.[67] But in that case the smaller plank was sunk into the larger one, so that part of the window was actually furnished with relief!

Jan Steen
The Drawing Lesson
c.1660–1665

Jan Steen (1626–1679), famous for scenes of high comedy, shows a more serious side in this work. We see a painter bending over his pupil to correct a drawing on blue paper with a piece of charcoal. Judging by the palette and the brushes in the painter's other hand, he has briefly interrupted his own work to fulfil his teaching obligations. His attentive pupil – he looks a little like

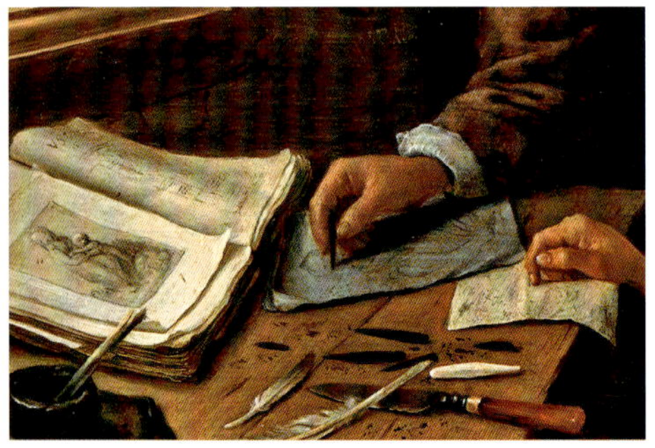

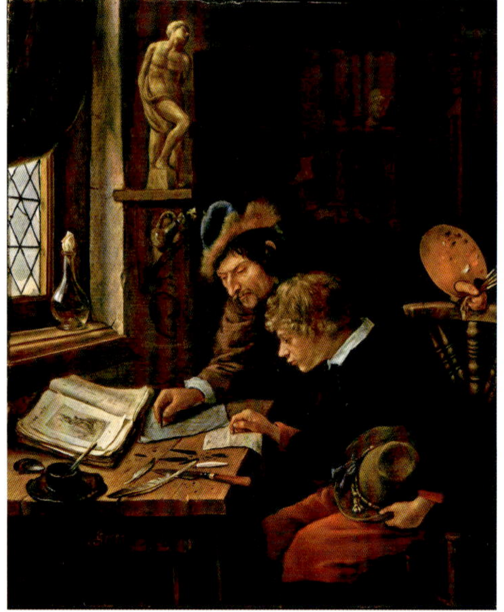

Steen's son Thaddeus, who would also become a painter – has probably made a copy of the picture of the Madonna and Child in the style of Raphael that can be seen in the book lying open on the table. Steen's contemporaries saw draughtsman-ship as the basis of all the arts. It seems a curious turn of fate that although Jan Steen was an extremely prolific artist, remarkably few of his drawings have been preserved.

The scene tells us about studio practice in the seventeenth century. Diverse drawing materials lie around the table, such as charcoal, white chalk, quills, and an inkpot. There is a knife for sharpening quills and rough paper on which to practice drawing. The bottle on the window-sill probably contains varnish or oil that has been left to stand there to become clear; to its right hangs a small

jug. On the basis of style and technique, this scene is usually dated to around 1660–1665.

It was probably somewhat earlier that Steen painted a similar studio scene, with a female pupil as the central figure. In this larger painting, in the J. Paul Getty Museum in Los Angeles, we again see a painter with a palette in one hand making corrections to his pupil's drawing.[68] In this work, a second pupil watches on, from behind a lectern. An aspect that is missing from both these scenes is drawing from live models. But Steen does display important aspects of the artist's training in these two paintings: copying drawings and prints, and drawing from plaster casts of famous sculptures. In the version discussed here we see a plaster copy of *The Slave*, Michelangelo's famous statue in the Musée du Louvre, Paris. Hanging from a shelf at the back are a plaster foot and a mask. As symbols of deception, masks were the invariable attribute of Pictura, the female figure who personifies the art of painting.

Adriaen van Ostade
A Peasant Family in a Cottage Interior
1661

Adriaen van Ostade (1610–1685) depicted Dutch peasant life in a totally individual way. This peaceful scene from village life is a typical example of the kind of paintings that made him famous. A peasant family is depicted in an interior. The man and his wife are sitting at a table with some food

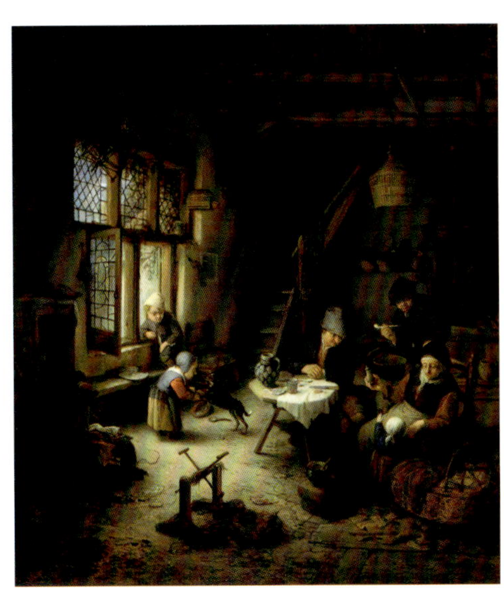

In his scenes of village life, Van Ostade was continuing a tradition that can be traced back to Pieter Bruegel the Elder (1520/25–1569) and his followers. Scenes of this kind, in which peasants are often depicted as extremely ignorant or boorish, were known in the seventeenth century as *grillen* or *grollitjes* (burlesques). Adriaen Brouwer (1605/6–1638) was a major exponent of this genre and had a decisive influence on Van Ostade's development. Both these artists worked in Haarlem. From around 1640 onwards, Van Ostade's work changed in character and his view of peasant life became milder and more poetic. The static and peaceful nature of this scene, dated 1661 – a good example of his more mature work – is quite different from his early paintings, which depict the peasants in all their supposed ignorance and boorishness in farcical scenes of fighting, drinking or prattling.

From 1650 onwards Van Ostade's technique became more and more refined, with more emphasis on details. While his early work is fairly monochrome, his use of colour gradually became somewhat warmer, as we see in this painting. The subtle treatment of light is exemplified

by the sunlight streaming through the window. The clothes provide occasional accents in the scene, most notably the colourful outfit of the little girl playing with the dog.

and drink. We see an earthenware jug, a beer glass and a dried fish. Behind the couple, a labourer stands smoking a pipe. Besides the three adults, there are also three children in the room: the woman is concerning herself with the youngest child, next to a wicker crib, while a small boy at the window watches a girl playing with a dog. The facial expressions and body language of all the figures have been captured well, as has the humble interior. Diverse objects convey the impression of disorder, such as a broken plate on the windowsill and a spoon lying near it on the floor. An elementary spinning-wheel is depicted quite prominently in the foreground, further emphasising the plainness of the surroundings. The expensive stained-glass windows contrast somewhat with the sober details of the dwelling, such as its earthen floor rather than tiles or wooden planks.

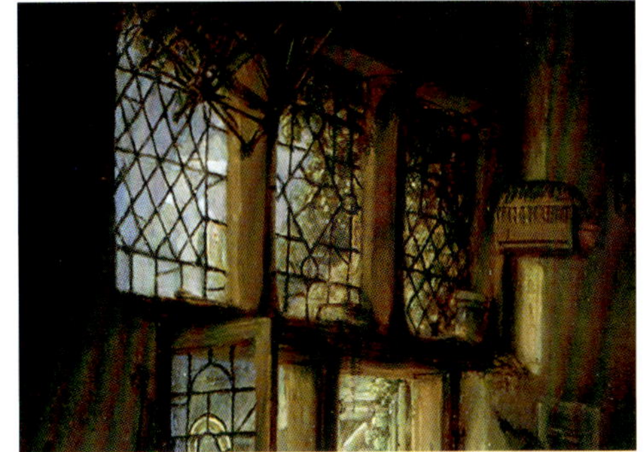

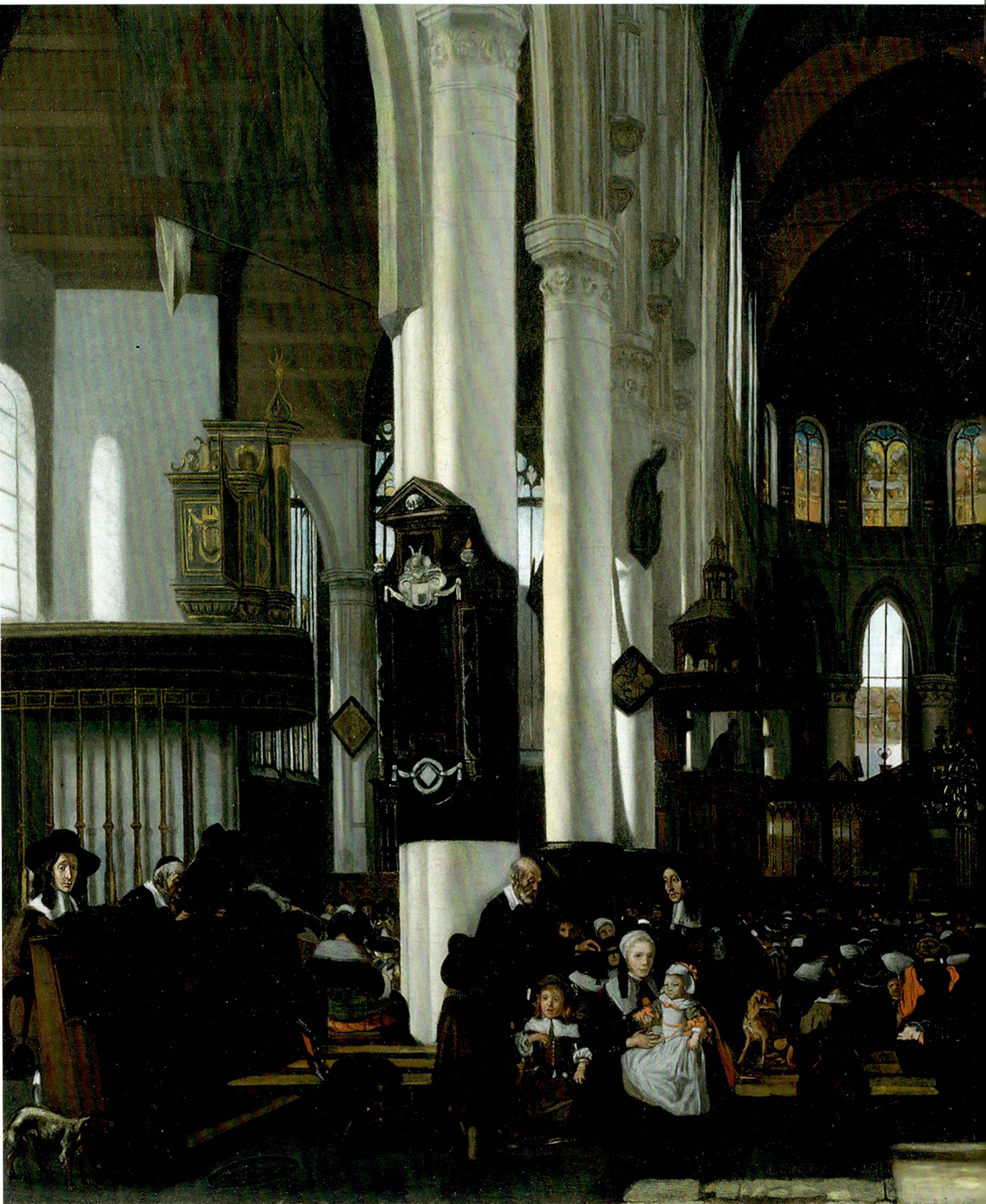

Church Interiors

Gerard Houckgeest
*The Nieuwe Kerk in Delft with the Tomb of
William the Silent*
c.1651–1652

The assassination of William of Orange (or
William the Silent) in Delft in 1584 was the
darkest hour in the Netherlands' struggle
for liberty against the Spanish overlords.
After the Twelve Years' Truce came into
effect in 1609, greatly improving the situation in the Northern Netherlands, the States-
General decided to honour the 'Father of the
Nation' with a monumental tomb in the
Nieuwe Kerk, Delft. The commission was
entrusted to the leading sculptor of the day,
the Amsterdam master Hendrick de Keyser
(1565–1621; see also p. 39). The monument
was completed about a year after his death
by his studio, which had been taken over
by his son Pieter de Keyser (c.1595–1676).[69]
From 1650 on, Gerard Houckgeest (1600–
1661) produced various paintings of the
Nieuwe Kerk with the mausoleum – not
coincidentally two years after the conclusion
of the Treaty of Münster that brought the
Eighty Years War to an end and signified
the recognition of the Dutch Republic as
an independent state. This painting is a
variant by the artist's own hand of the
painting dated 1651 in the Mauritshuis,
and was probably made quite soon after it.[70]
Judging by the costumes, the figures standing around the tomb were added later,
apparently by a different hand. Here and
there, an underdrawing has become visible.
For instance, the artist evidently intended
to paint a child to the left of the woman –
exactly as in the painting in The Hague.

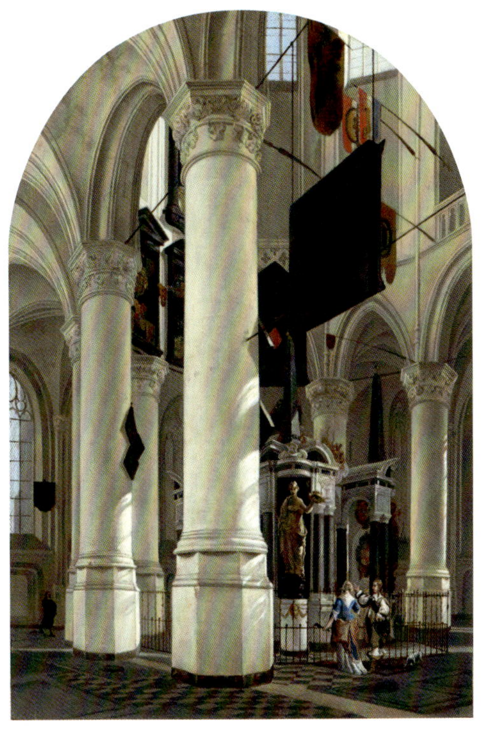

For the people of the newly independent
republic, the mausoleum must have
possessed great emotional and symbolic
significance. That is presumably why
Houckgeest chose to depict this side of
the tomb, with the statue of Liberty, for
his painting. At the other corners of the
tomb stand statues representing Strength,
Religion and Justice.[71] We can just make
out half of this latter statue on the right,
with its gilded scales. The iconography
of the tomb as a whole alludes to the
foundations of the young state. In the
middle, beneath the canopy, are two
effigies of William of Orange: seated and
recumbent, living and dead. Houckgeest's
largely lifelike paintings of the mauso-

leum were probably commissioned by a
relative or supporter of the Orange-Nassau
family. To date, it has not been possible to
trace the earliest provenance of this
painting beyond the nineteenth century.

Houckgeest produced only a small
oeuvre, but he played an important part
in the development of the painted church
interior of the Northern Netherlands.
Until 1650 he had primarily devoted
himself to imaginary architecture in the
style of Bartholomeus van Bassen (c.1590–
1652), who was probably his teacher. The
innovations he introduced around 1650
included a shift to a diagonal perspective,
a penchant for painting ostensibly random
little corners of the church, a more colourful palette than in the past, and a greater
emphasis on the sunlight streaming in.
With these features, all of which are in
evidence in the painting discussed here,
he clearly distinguished himself from that
other great painter of church interiors,
the Haarlem painter Pieter Saenredam
(1593–1665).[72]

By placing the column in the foreground very close to the viewer, Houckgeest achieved a marked effect of depth.
Our gaze is automatically drawn inwards
and above all upwards, to the top, where
the bright daylight streams in through the
choir windows. The large black plaques
high up on the walls are commemorative
plaques for members of the House of
Orange, nine of whom already lay buried
in the Nieuwe Kerk in 1651. Aside from
William of Orange these included the
princes Maurits and Frederik Hendrik, as
well as Willem II, who had died in 1650.

Around 1800, during the French occupation, these plaques were removed, including the one that is seen here only from the back, hanging between columns in the foreground. The painter has deliberately left out the column that should have been depicted on the far right, in order to enhance the effect of depth. In a far larger interior of the Nieuwe Kerk, which Houckgeest completed in 1650, he did include this column.[73]

Emanuel de Witte
Interior of the Oude Kerk in Amsterdam c.1660–1665

This painting by Emanuel de Witte (1616/18–1691/92) depicts the interior of the Oude Kerk in Amsterdam. This church was one of the painter's favourite subjects. After he moved to Amsterdam, in 1651 or 1652, he made some thirty paintings of this Late Gothic building. The Oude Kerk lent itself perfectly to the atmospheric paintings that De Witte liked to make. That his main concern was the atmosphere of the monumental building is clear from the liberties he took with its interior. For instance, here he has lengthened the columns somewhat and moved the church furniture to enhance the effect of spaciousness. In two other paintings he depicted the church from roughly the same vantage point.[74] All three were produced in the same period, somewhere between 1660 and 1665.

The architectural history of the Oude Kerk, which is dedicated to St Nicholas,

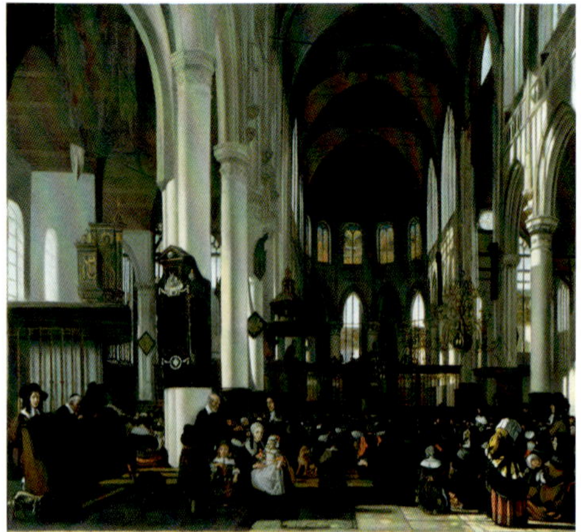

the patron saint of Amsterdam, dates from the fourteenth century. In the sixteenth century the hall church was converted into a cruciform basilica to accommodate a larger congregation. Since this conversion was never completed, the church's interior has a somewhat capricious structure. Here De Witte depicts the central nave and the choir during a service. In the centre is the minister at his pulpit. A large congregation of men, women and children has gathered in the church, although not everyone is entirely focused on the matter at hand. The mother with her child on her lap is actually sitting with her back to the pulpit, while the figures around her also scarcely seem to be taking in much of the service. The man behind the woman is giving an older man a contribution for the offertory. Judging by the individual facial features of this group, these may be portraits of the person who commissioned the painting and his family. This is certainly not an implausible hypothesis, since several other church interiors by De Witte undoubtedly contain portraits

of those who commissioned them. The memorial on the foremost column on the left is so close to the group of figures that it may be construed as a reference to the family. Unfortunately it has not yet been identified. A number of other figures in the right foreground belong to the painter's standard repertoire: the girl with her back to us, the woman, likewise depicted from behind, the seated woman with a child, and the man standing behind her. These four figures recur, though grouped differently, in a painting in London, where De Witte placed them in the same church.[75]

The alternation of light and darker sections gives rise to a highly atmospheric painting. It is apparently a cloudless day, since light is streaming in from all sides of the monumental building. The high and light windows bathe the architecture in an attractive illumination. The shadows, which are meticulously elaborated, define the architecture. In the choir, the darkest part of the building, the rich colours of the stained-glass windows are conspicuous.

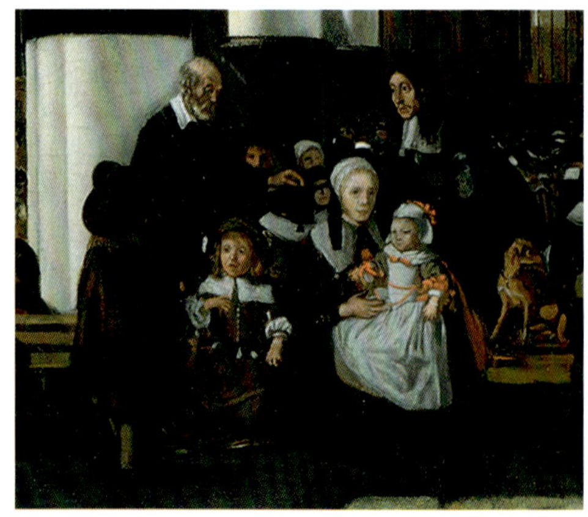

'This painting?

Love at first sight!'

Portraits & Tronies

Portraiture of the Dutch Golden Age is a fascinating phenomenon. Never before had so many portraits been painted, at the same time, of people from all walks of life. These works are characterised by pronounced realism, great diversity, and above all superb quality. The vast output of portraits in the seventeenth century is directly linked to the phenomenal economic success of the Dutch Republic, which was one of Europe's superpowers. While power in other countries was concentrated in the courts and the landed nobility, in the Republic of the United Provinces it was the bourgeoisie who gradually became the leading decision-makers. The growing economic importance of prominent merchants and entrepreneurs enabled them to rise to high-ranking positions in local authorities and civic institutions. The increasing power of these regents restricted the influence of the court and the aristocracy in The Hague, the republic's political heart, fostering the genesis of a new, bourgeois society. With their new social status and growing self-assurance, affluent Dutch citizens soon acquired the habit of commissioning portraits of themselves. These commissions were often related to some special event: an engagement or a wedding, the birth of a child, or an honourable appointment. In other words, the membership of the civic guard or an appointment to an administrative position frequently led to a portrait commission. It was not uncommon to have several portraits made of yourself during your lifetime. All these portrait commissions gave artists opportunities to devise new types and compositions to satisfy their clients. The diversity of portraits was unprecedented.

Although throughout the seventeenth century portraiture was one of the two most frequently practised genres of painting – along with landscapes – the art critics of the day treated it with disdain. In 1604, the painter and art theorist Karel van Mander (1548–1606) described portraiture in his *Schilder-Boeck* as a 'side-road of the arts', to which painters resorted merely to assure themselves of an income.

Tronies, or studies of heads, constitute a separate category in portrait painting, since they are images of anonymous models. In such heads, or busts, the point was not to achieve a likeness of the model – in some cases the artist himself – but to produce studies of specific facial expressions or characters.

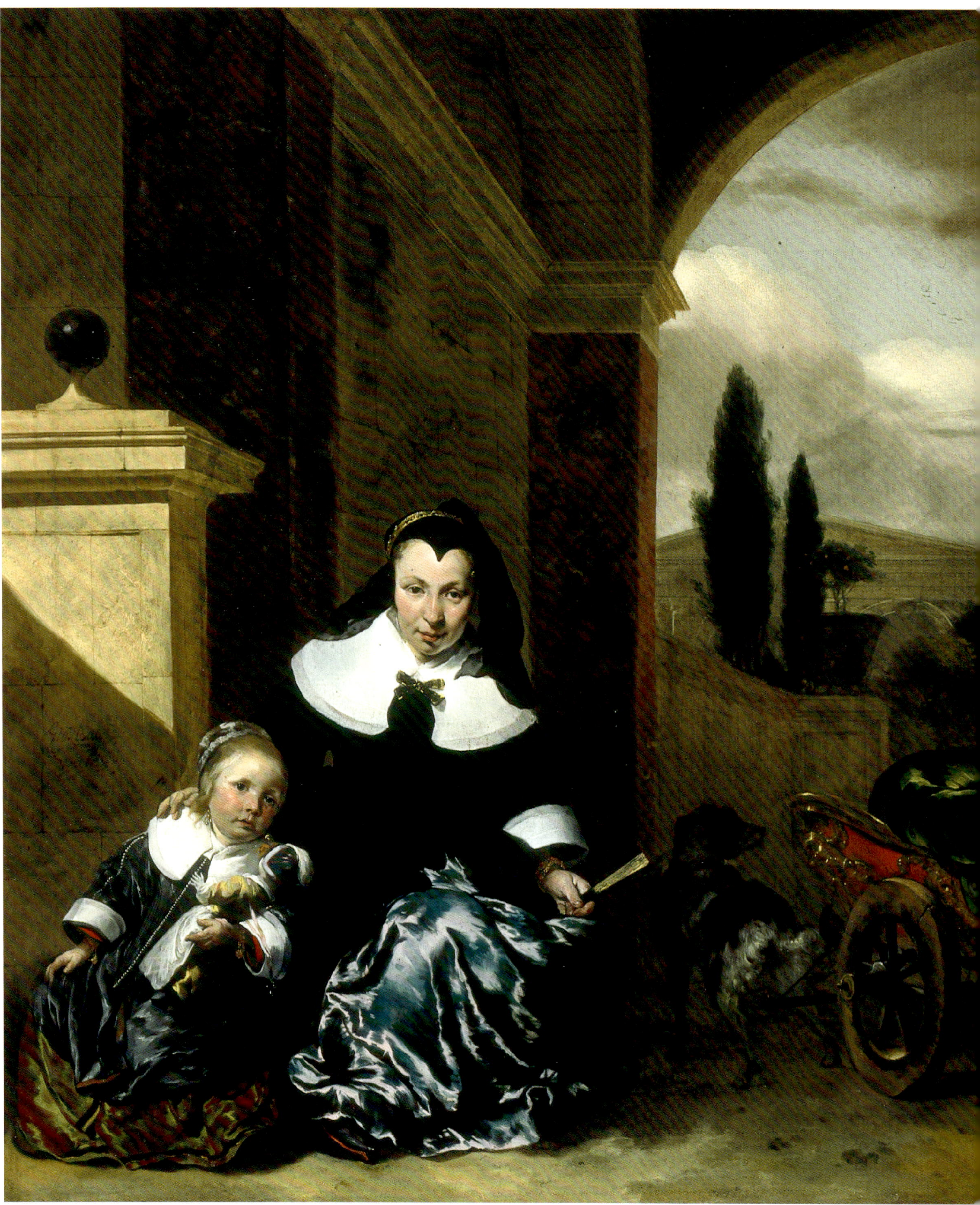

Portraits

Rembrandt
Portrait of Aeltje Uylenburgh
1632

This delightful painting from 1632 is characteristic of the portraits produced by Rembrandt (1606–1669) in his first year in Amsterdam.[76] It also sheds light on his personal life. For in 2000 it became clear that Rembrandt had depicted here a member of his future family. The Amsterdam researcher Jaap van der Veen succeeded in identifying the woman – who was 62 years of age according to the inscription in the upper left corner ('Æ 62') – as Aeltje Pietersdr Uylenburgh (1570–1644),[77] the wife of the Reformed Protestant minister Johannes Sylvius (1564–1638). The couple witnessed the baptism of several of Rembrandt's children. Aeltje belonged to Rembrandt's circle of intimates. She was a cousin not only of the Amsterdam art dealer Hendrick Uylenburgh (c.1584/89–1661), in whose house Rembrandt was lodging at the time, but also of the far younger Saskia Uylenburgh (1612–1642), who would become the painter's wife in 1634. The fathers of Hendrick, Saskia and Aeltje were brothers.

Van der Veen discovered a will dating from 1681 that had been drawn up by Cornelis Sylvius, the son of Aeltje and Johannes, which includes descriptions of portraits of the couple by Rembrandt: 'two portraits of his late father and mother painted by Rembrandt van Rijn' (in translation). The portrait of Sylvius has probably been lost. We know his facial

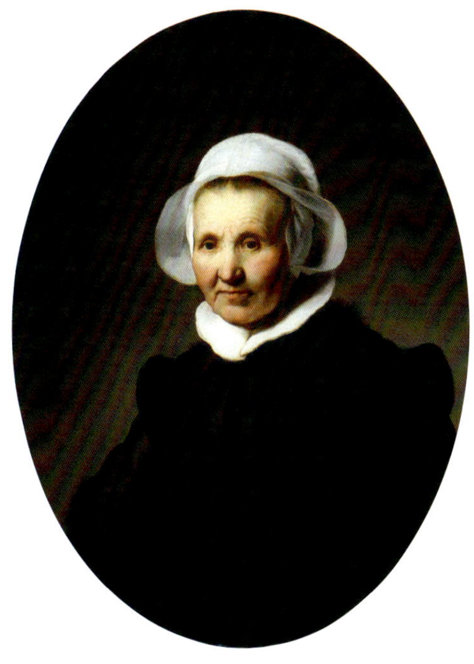

features from works including two etchings by Rembrandt, one of which was made in 1633. The composition of the painted portrait of Sylvius, made to be hung to the left of Aeltje's, can largely be reconstructed on the basis of a portrait of a man by Rembrandt also dating from 1632, which was painted on an oval panel of the same dimensions.[78] In this portrait, the sitter is represented – like Aeltje – to the waist, and gazes directly at the viewer.

For many years *Portrait of Aeltje Uylenburgh* was not exhibited in public. Until 2000, when the painting was sold at auction in London and fetched a record price for a work by Rembrandt,[79] it belonged to the collection of Baroness Bathsheva de Rothschild (for this and the earlier provenance of the painting, see pp. 90–91). This descendant of the famous family of

bankers lived in Tel Aviv. When members of the Rembrandt Research Project went to study the portrait there in 1978, the image was covered with a thick layer of yellowed varnish. Not until the portrait, which has been preserved superbly, was cleaned and restored in 2000, did the beauty of its execution become apparent. The woman's clothing has been painted in varied hues of black and grey. Her face is depicted in minute detail, down to the wrinkles in the soft skin around her mouth and eyes. The face appears lifelike thanks to an ingenious combination of opaque and translucent layers of paint, and derives added vitality from a short line of white paint under the right eye. Set against a virtually plain background without shadows, the face is framed by the white cap and collar with their subtle light reflections. Rembrandt has had some difficulty deciding how to place the seated woman in the portrait. This time he decided against including the back of the chair, as he had done in the past.[80] We know from X-radiographical analysis that he twice reworked the contours of the figure; the right shoulder was initially higher.

Rembrandt turned 26 in the year in which he produced Aeltje's portrait. At the end of 1631 he had moved from his home town of Leiden to Amsterdam, where he built up a special relationship with the Uylenburgh family. He took lodgings with Hendrick Uylenburgh, who ran a thriving art gallery in which young painters were trained. Rembrandt worked there, mainly on portrait commissions for prominent townspeople. In 1634, when he joined Amsterdam's guild of painters, he married Saskia. Rembrandt was still living in the house of her far older cousin at the time, and it was here that he must have produced the portrait of Aeltje. Besides other members of the family, Rembrandt also depicted many merchants, senior officials and Church ministers while he was living here. This likeness of Aeltje Uylenburgh is one of the most beautiful portraits that Rembrandt made in this period.

Jan Baptist Weenix
Portrait of the De Kempenaer Family
*c.*1653

In Holland's Golden Age, countless portraits of private individuals were produced, to be hung in their homes. The majority were likenesses of adult men and women. Married couples were usually depicted in separate paintings, composed as pendants. Numerous children's portraits are also known. Occasionally, entire families were

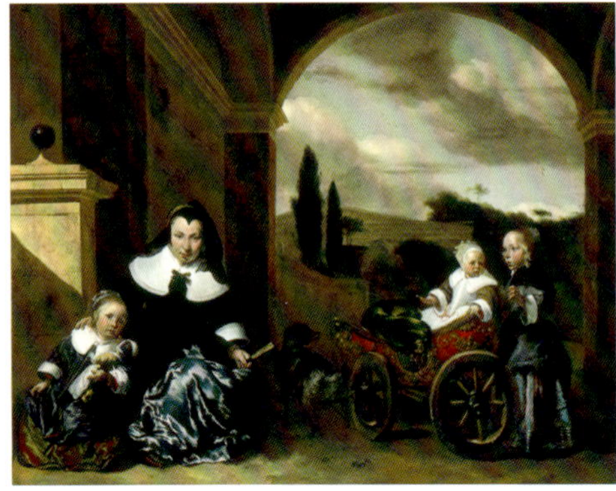

depicted in a single painting. In the varied repertoire of types and sorts, this group portrait of the De Kempenaer family is remarkable in many ways. It was made by Jan Baptist Weenix (1621–1659), an artist who was chiefly known as a landscape painter. Another singular note is the absence of the father: this is a portrait of a widow with her three children.

Weenix is known for his Italianate landscapes, and the setting he has chosen for the mother and her daughters has a distinctly Italian ambience. With this landscape setting, the portrait almost has the air of a genre piece. The architecture, with its classical design and cypresses, recalls the painter's many years in Italy – a period of which he was so proud that he Italianised his name, Jan Baptist, as we see in the signature, applied prominently on the balustrade: *Gio[vanni]: Batt[ist]a. / Weenix fe*. The Italian setting, which also occurs frequently in Weenix's genre pieces, appears not to have any deeper significance. It simply presents a fine background for the figures. Only the woman makes eye contact with the viewer. While in most seventeenth-century family portraits the parents are depicted standing, here Weenix has portrayed the mother seated, with one hand resting on the shoulder of her middle daughter and the other holding a fan. This lends the portrait a certain informality and intimacy.

The mother and her daughters have been identified on the basis of an old label that was once on the back of the painting and some supplementary research in the Utrecht archives.[81] The black-clad widow

is Christina Lepper (1624–1683), who had married the Utrecht merchant Jacobus de Kempenaer (1619–1652) on 6 December 1644. At his death on 28 June 1652, only two of their six children were still living; when their seventh child was born, the father himself was already in his grave. Christina (1647–1683), the eldest daughter, is depicted on the far right. Posing in the richly-decorated dog-drawn pram – a prop from the painter's studio – is her younger sister Jacoba, born in 1652 or 1653. In her right hand she holds a jingling gold bell, at the end of which is a semi-precious stone. The bell, which is fastened around her waist with a gold chain, served as a charm to ward off disease and misfortune, no frivolous accessory given the high rate of child mortality in this period. Depicted with her mother on the far left is the middle daughter, Margaretha (1649–1726, also known as Margrieta). She is holding a doll with its own rattle hanging from a pink ribbon. Like her elder sister she wears gold brain bracelets around her wrists. Given the children's ages, the painting must have been made around 1653, about one year after the birth of the youngest child. The family were still in mourning for the father, as is clear from Christina Lepper's black outer garments and headscarf, the grey dresses of the two older girls, and the black scarf of the eldest daughter.[82] Christina would remarry in 1657; her second husband was the widower Pieter de Visscher.

This painting remained in the family's possession well into the twentieth century. Margaretha inherited it after her mother's death in 1683. Since the painting was repeatedly handed down (with a few interruptions) – to women bearing the name of Margaretha, it is also known as 'the Margaretha portrait'.[83] This long family tradition came to an end in 1994, when the last Margaretha put the family portrait up for auction. Two years later, the painting, with its remarkable provenance, was acquired by the Van Otterloos.

Frans Hals
Portrait of a Preacher
c.1660

Notwithstanding its simplicity and modest dimensions, this portrait by Frans Hals (1582/83–1666) makes a strong impression.[84] A man is depicted as a half-figure, set against a plain background. He wears a black doublet cut in a conservative style, with an unassuming white collar. His skull-cap has led to the traditional assumption that he was a preacher. Although other occupational groups too wore skull-caps in the seventeenth-century Dutch Republic, it can nonetheless be inferred from the man's short hair and austere clothing that he was indeed a minister of the Church. He appears to be holding a Bible in one hand. This pose, with the other hand concealed behind the black cloak, is characteristic of Hals's portraits of preachers, such as that of the influential Church minister Herman Langelius of Amsterdam, made around 1660.[85]

Almost simultaneously with the portrait discussed here, Hals produced

two other likenesses of men in sober attire, including a portrait in the Mauritshuis that is painted on a somewhat smaller panel.[86] The collar of the man in the latter portrait is embellished with small tassels (*akertjes*), a rather unusual adornment for a preacher. In addition, he does not wear a skull-cap. None of the men depicted by Hals in these small portraits has been convincingly identified to date. In 1680, Arnold Moonen wrote a poem about Hals's portrait of the Haarlem minister Jan Ruyll.[87] The text of this poem does not, unfortunately, reveal any of the details of this image. Moonen emphasised in his verse tribute that Hals could convey the man's appearance but not the wise lessons from his 'golden mouth'. In the past, the poem has been linked – probably wrongly – to the portrait described here.[88]

The atmospheric character of the portrait and the intense observation of the sitter are qualities that also characterise the large regent pieces that Hals would produce later, around 1664.[89] The free painting technique of this small portrait likewise corresponds to that of the famous works. The loose brushwork in the man's face and hand is characteristic of the Haarlem painter's late work. The portrait was probably made around 1660, when Hals was in his late seventies but still at the height of his powers. The facial expression of the man, who is looking at the viewer, has been captured extraordinarily well. All the emphasis is on his face, since the background has been kept plain. This background has been painted quickly, with ingenious use of the lighter ground, which glimmers through it. The doublet, too, is painted very thinly in places. The face, on the other hand, is elaborated so meticulously that in spite of the apparently loose brushwork, it seems to have required more than one session. It stands out superbly against the dark background.

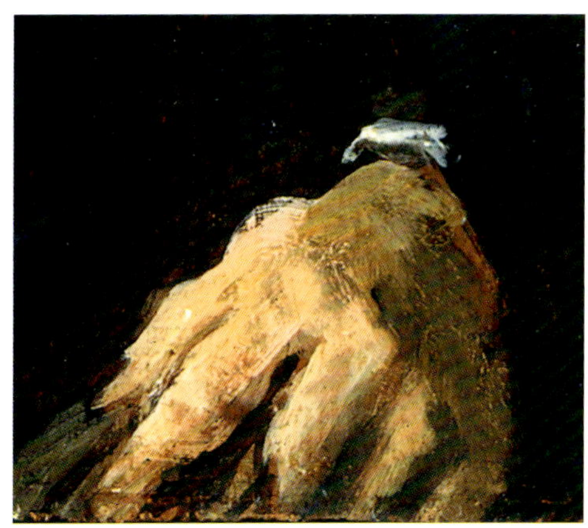

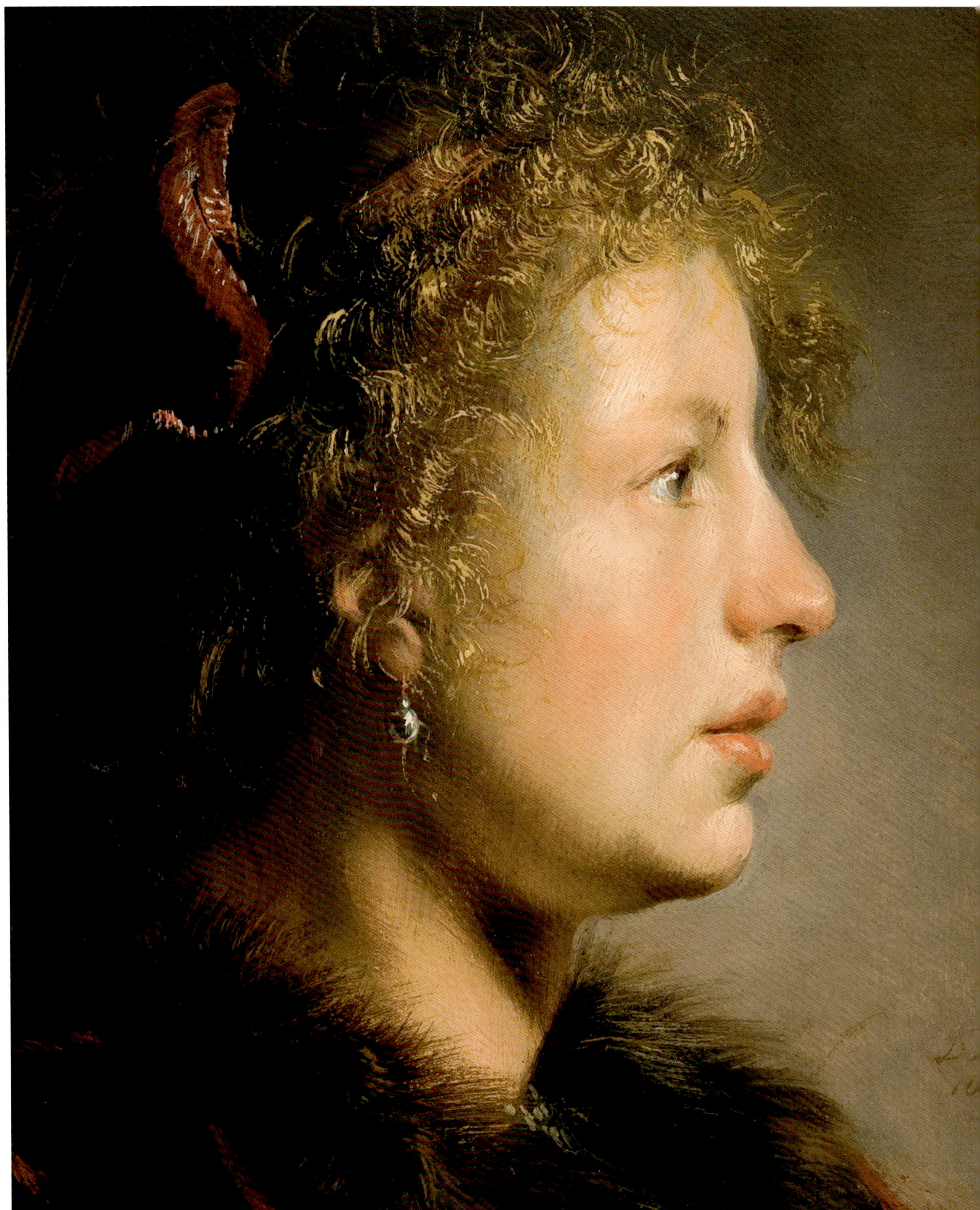

Tronies

Jan Lievens (1607–1674) is known today mainly for his early work, which he produced in the spirit of artistic rivalry with the young Rembrandt (1606–1669). In 1625, Rembrandt had returned to Leiden after a five-month stay in the studio of Pieter Lastman (1583–1633) in Amsterdam, who had previously taught Lievens. In the period from 1625 onwards, reciprocal influences are discernible in the work of these two artists, in choice of subject as well as in composition and technique. One of the first authors to recognise the talents of the young Lievens was the poet and art lover Constantijn Huygens (1596–1687). In his unfinished autobiography, which he started between 1629 and 1631, he praised Lievens in the same breath as Rembrandt. In 1631 the paths of the two artists diverged: Rembrandt moved to Amsterdam, while Lievens left for England in 1632, and artistically too entered different spheres. In England he was greatly impressed by the work of Anthony van Dyck (1599–1641), who worked for King Charles I and his court. When Lievens left England again in 1635, he did not return to the United Provinces but settled in Antwerp, where he enrolled in the St Luke's Guild and married a daughter of the sculptor Andries Colyn de Nole (1540–1636). In 1644 financial distress compelled him to move the family to Amsterdam. At a later stage

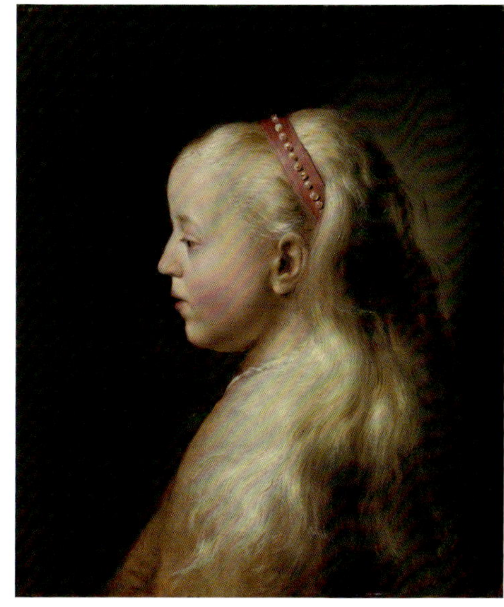

of his career, he achieved prominence with his history paintings, besides which he was much in demand in upper-class circles as a portraitist.

Lievens was first and foremost a painter of figurative pieces, of *tronies* and half-figures, as well as biblical and mythological scenes. *Bust of a Young Girl* was painted around 1631–1632, shortly before he left Leiden. It is a study head, or *tronie*, to use the seventeenth-century term. Although the sitter is anonymous, Lievens depicted her on several occasions. She is probably depicted in an etching that Lievens produced in the rough period from 1629 to 1631.[90] In addition, a painting in the Museum der bildenden Künste in Leipzig, made at the same time as the work discussed here, certainly shows the same girl.[91] In that work, however, she is depicted not in profile

but from the front, her head turned slightly to one side. As early as in 1641, the German painting was described as a *tronie*, which again emphasises that these are not portraits. In both images we are struck by the long, radiant blonde hair, which Lievens has depicted very strikingly and which appears to be the actual subject of the two paintings. In the *tronie* in the Van Otterloos' collection, we see scratches here and there around the forehead; these have been added with the tip of the paintbrush to create a stronger suggestion of relief. Like the hair, the pearls on the girl's headband have been painted very vigorously and convincingly. Since the girl is depicted here in profile, against a largely dark background, all the emphasis is on her face and hair, in which two tones prevail: the blonde of the hair and the pink and red of her lips, cheeks and headband.

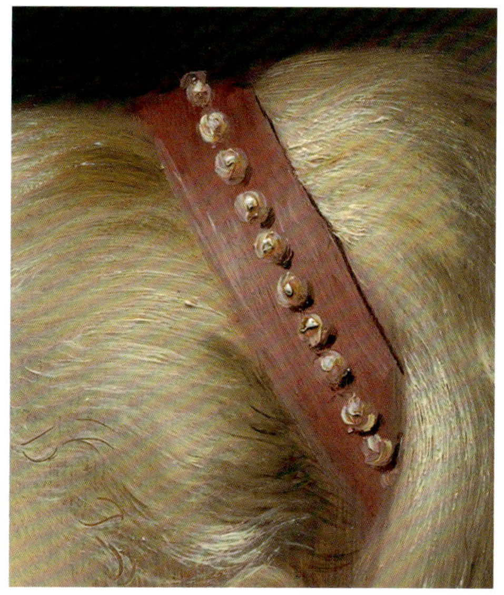

From the beginning of his career, and most notably in his Leiden period from 1625 to 1632, Lievens had always taken a great interest in study heads. Like his friend Rembrandt, with whom he may have shared a studio, he painted, drew and etched *tronies*. As early as around 1635, he published a series of etched heads or *tronikens*.[92] As far as his painted oeuvre is concerned, the portrait discussed here is undoubtedly among the finest in this genre.

Salomon de Bray
Bust of a Young Woman in Profile
1636

The Haarlem artist Salomon de Bray (1597–1664) is ranked among the leading exponents of Dutch Classicism, a school of art whose form and content were based on examples from classical antiquity. Besides working as a painter, De Bray was also active as a poet and architect. In 1616 he is first mentioned in Haarlem, where he trained under two famous painters: Cornelis Cornelisz van Haarlem (1562–1638) and Hendrick Goltzius (1558–1617). Like his teachers, De Bray devoted himself mainly to history paintings, although he occasionally produced portraits as well. De Bray seems to have run a joint studio with his three sons, Jan (1626/27–1697), Joseph (c.1628/34–1664) and Dirck (c.1635–1694), who were also painters. In this 'family business', drawings – preliminary studies as well as accurate copies of their own paintings – played a strikingly

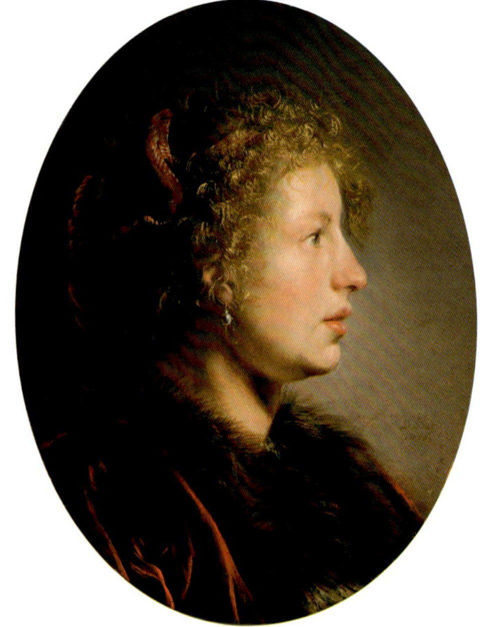

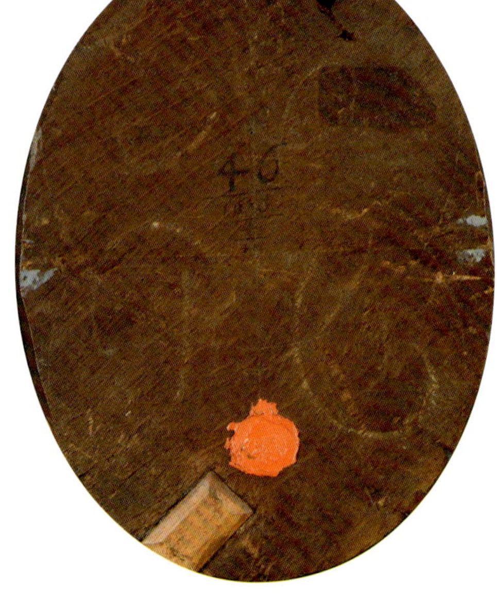

important role as working material. Many of these drawings are precisely dated, to the very day.

The oval panel painting from 1636, from the famous collection of the Spencer family at Althorp House, to which it may have been added as early as the seventeenth century,[93] displays De Bray's great talent. The subtly elaborated illumination focuses all attention on the young woman's face. Her blonde curls are depicted in bold, vigorous strokes. Since the palette is otherwise muted, the red headband and pearl earring are all the more conspicuous. The rapidly painted fur of the woman's coat appears extremely lifelike. This painting is not a portrait but a *tronie*, a bust of an imaginary character. The character recurs in an undated history

painting that De Bray produced – as will become clear – that same year: *Judith with the Head of Holofernes* in the Museo Nacional del Prado, Madrid.[94] In this work the young woman's face is depicted from a three-quarters angle, again with powerful light effects. A drawn copy exists of the painting in Madrid, made by the artist himself in 1636.[95]

The painting, which surfaced only recently, has not only been preserved in fine condition, but sheds new light on the chronology of the painter's oeuvre. For the back of the painting contains some extremely interesting information (see fig.). In the first place, our attention is drawn to two circles and two lines, as well as some points that have been marked with the aid of a pair of compasses.[96] The

panel-maker apparently used compasses
to make a perfectly oval-shaped panel. In
spite of all his efforts, however, the panel
has a rather uneven circumference, and the
wood has an irregular thickness, varying
from 5 to 6 mm. The back of the panel
provides still more information, this time
originating from the artist himself. The
following figures are noted in black ink
in the middle of the panel: '46 / 1636. / 4 /
14'.[97] The artist has numbered his painting
46 and dated it 14 April 1636, just as
precisely as the drawn copies referred to
above. We now know which painting De
Bray made after this: it was the one now in
Madrid! This painting has a similar
numbering on the back: it is numbered 47,
and dated 25 April 1636, 11 days after the
tronie. Similar numbers and dates have
been found on other paintings by De Bray.
They provide a unique source of information when reconstructing the chronology
in De Bray's oeuvre.[98]

Jacob Backer
Young Woman Holding a Fan
c.1644–1645

One could scarcely conceive of a greater
difference than that between Jacob
Backer's smoothly finished portraits
and this *tronie*, which he painted around
1644–1645. In the realm of *tronies*, Jacob
Backer (1608/9–1651) shows himself a
worthy rival of his famous contemporary
Rembrandt, who produced countless
tronies at the beginning of his career. These
fantasy figures, with their diverse apparel,

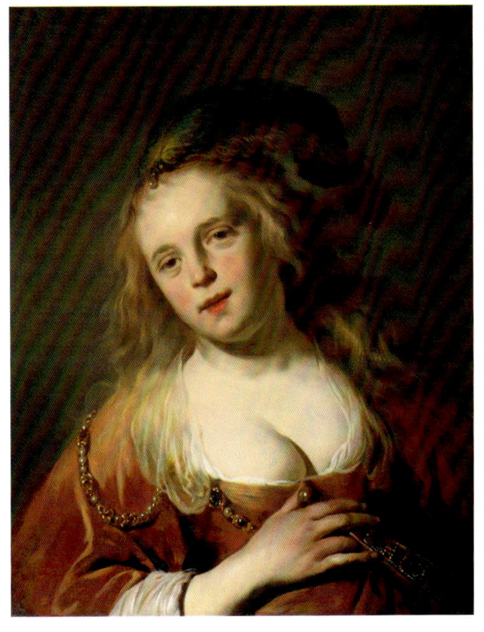

evoked certain associations among
seventeenth-century viewers.[99] *Young
Woman Holding a Fan* has been painted in
extremely loose yet deft brushwork and is
a real feast for the eyes. Backer produced
other paintings in this category, such as
Shepherd with Flute in the Mauritshuis and
Boy with a Beret in Museum Boijmans Van
Beuningen, Rotterdam.[100] These three
remarkably well preserved works were
all painted at great speed and with very
broad brushstrokes. The three were
recently displayed together in an exhibition devoted to Backer in Amsterdam and
Aachen, where the painting discussed here
was one of the highlights. The woman's
voluptuousness is emphasised by her
luxuriant head of hair, decorated with
feathers, and by the gold chain with pearls
on her clothing. Backer has depicted the

details and the reflected light on this
chain, the pearls and the fan extremely
convincingly by adding highlights and
perfectly placed brushstrokes.

This painting may have belonged
to the painter's half-brother Dirck Backer,
since an inventory of the latter's estate
includes 'a female *tronie* with a feather'.[101]

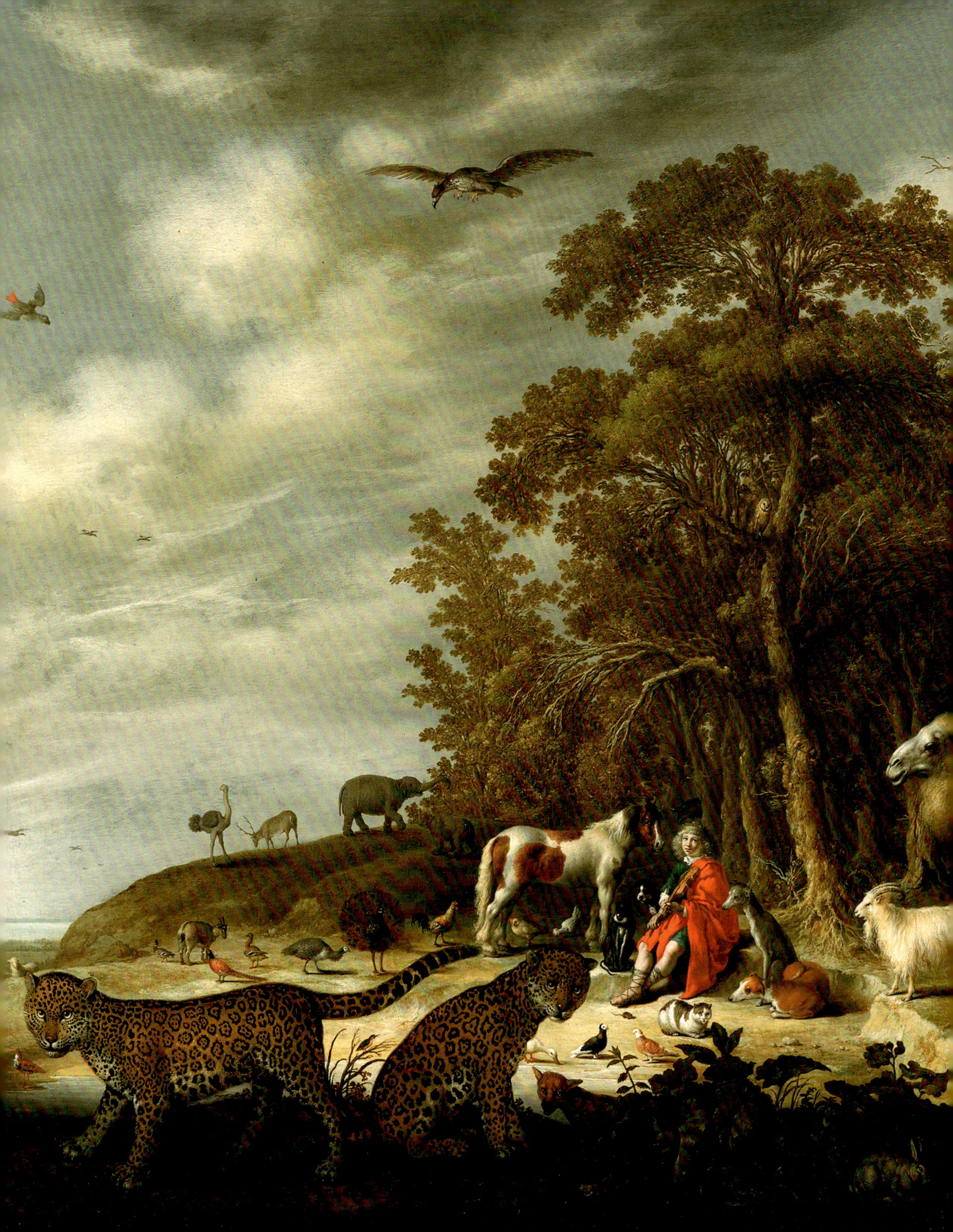

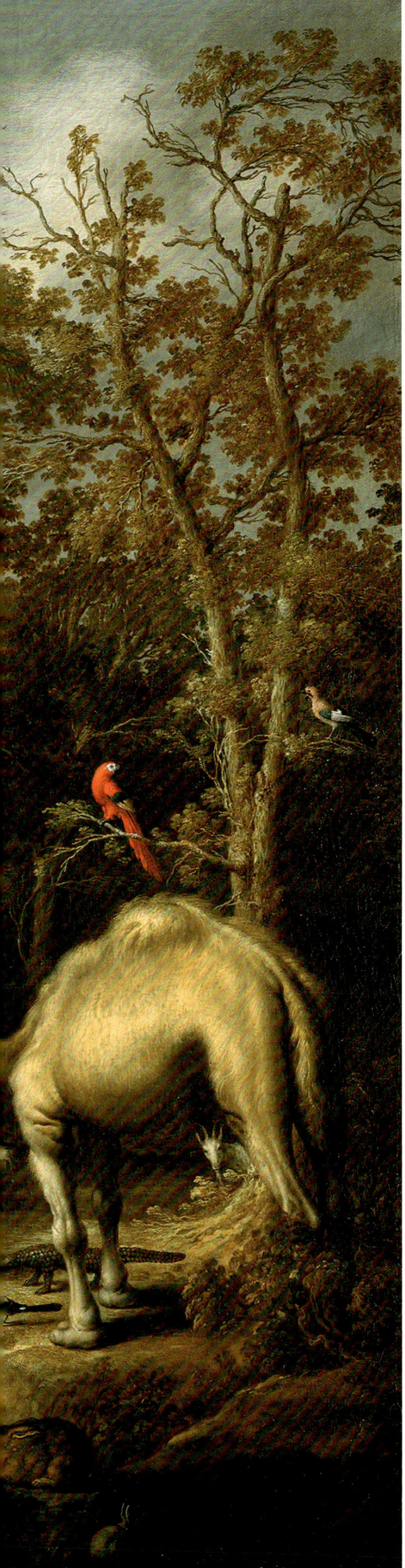

History Paintings

It was long believed that Dutch painters from the Golden Age confined themselves to the everyday, visible reality. Only Rembrandt (1606–1669) was widely known for his impressive scenes from the Bible or classical antiquity. For a long time, history paintings by other artists from the Golden Age were neglected. *Gods, Saints, and Heroes*, a major exhibition in Washington, Detroit and Amsterdam (1980–1981), corrected this misapprehension and revived interest in the subject. It was discovered that numerous artists had painted diverse history paintings of very high quality.

Seventeenth-century handbooks on art reserve their highest terms of appreciation for history painters. After all, to paint a history, one needed first to read a story, to choose a decisive moment from it, to think of a good composition, and then to depict the event with the appropriate decorum. Besides scenes based on biblical accounts and on classical Greek and Roman literature and mythology, allegories and scenes from Dutch history are also included in this category. History painting – along with portraiture – is one of the oldest genres in Dutch painting. With the passage of time, motifs from history paintings developed into independent genres, such as the landscape and still life.

History Paintings

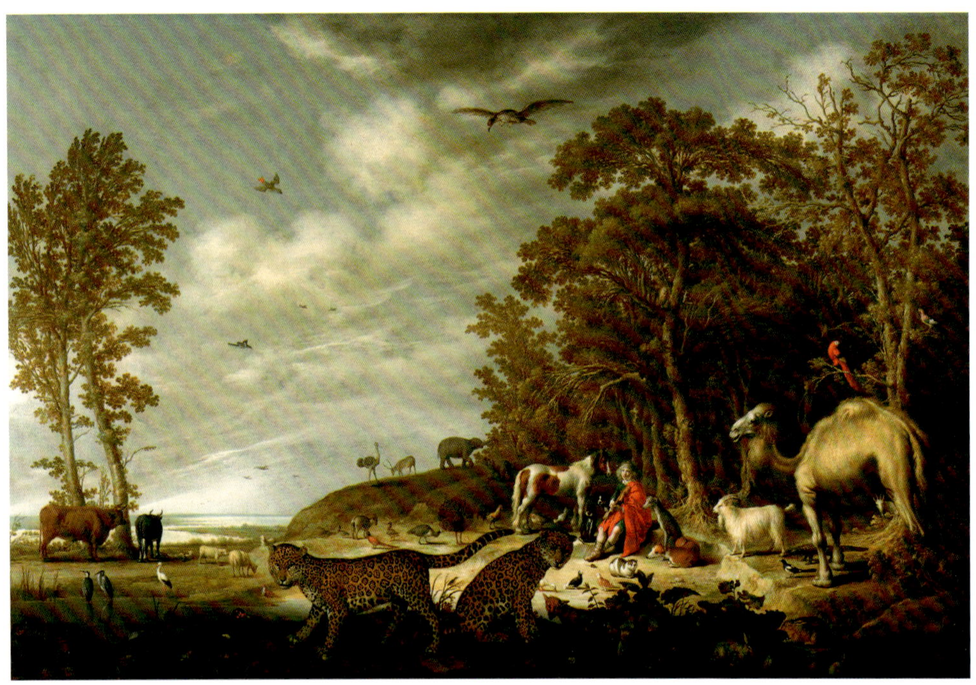

Aelbert Cuyp
Orpheus Charming the Animals
c.1640

Aelbert Cuyp (1620–1691) is the best-known member of a family of painters from Dordrecht. He was probably trained by his father Jacob Cuyp (1594–1651/52), with whom he would frequently collaborate in the 1640s. Although Aelbert worked in other genres, such as portraiture, figurative pieces, cattle pieces and stable interiors, he was first and foremost a landscape painter. At first sight, this large painting indeed appears to be a landscape, but one showing a very unusual scene. It depicts a story from Ovid's *Metamorphoses* about the poet and singer Orpheus. With his music, he was not only able to entice the animals, but he even induced the trees to provide him with shade to protect him from the sun. Rather than the lyre mentioned in Ovid, Cuyp gives Orpheus a violin.

This story was particularly popular among animal painters such as Roelant Savery (1576–1639) and Paulus Potter (p. 33), but it also attracted the attention of the young Cuyp. Besides this painting, which can be dated to around 1640, when the artist was about 20 years of age, he painted a smaller and far less ambitious version of the subject in the same period (Dessau, Anhaltische Gemäldegalerie). Cuyp had already produced a similar scene in 1639, in which Adam gives names to the animals (private collection). The three paintings have several details in common, such as the standing leopard in the foreground. Cuyp probably based himself here on a painting by his father, dating from 1639. Around 1645, Cuyp would tackle Orpheus once again, in a larger painting than the one described here (private collection).[102]

Some might wonder why Cuyp, who today owes his fame primarily to his Italianate landscapes, should have produced history paintings of this kind as a young man. The answer is to be found in seventeenth-century handbooks on art, which systematically praise the merits of history paintings. In order to produce a work of this kind – that is, to depict a story from classical mythology (as here), history, or the Bible – the artist would first have to study the written source, and then use his imagination to translate the text convincingly into an image. According to art theorists, this was a greater challenge than imitating the visible reality, as in paintings such as animal pieces, still lifes, landscapes, interiors and portraits. Sooner or later, however, many Dutch painters gravitated towards these less exalted subjects, because there was more demand for them.

'The jewel in the crown of our collection'.

The Peregrinations of a Painting: Rembrandt's *Portrait of Aeltje Uylenburgh*

Rembrandt's portrait of Aeltje Uylenburgh (1570–1644), the greatest masterpiece in the collection of Eijk and Rose-Marie de Mol van Otterloo, has always been privately owned. Rembrandt painted it in 1632 as the pendant to the portrait – that can now no longer be identified – of Aeltje's husband, the Amsterdam minister Johannes Sylvius (1564–1638). We still know what Sylvius looked like, thanks to the portrait etching Rembrandt made of him in 1633. The artist initially knew Aeltje solely as the niece of his then employer, Hendrick Uylenburgh (1584/89–1661), in whose workshop the two portrait paintings were produced. Following Rembrandt's marriage in 1634 to Saskia Uylenburgh – another, much younger, niece of Uylenburgh's – Sylvius and his wife Aeltje were gradually drawn into the painter's intimate circle of friends.

Partly thanks to a bible that resurfaced only recently, containing a chronicle with details on the Sylvius family, we can reconstruct the places where the couple's portraits were displayed from the time they were painted in 1632. They initially hung in Amsterdam, in the parental home on Leliegracht, and in 1638, the year of Johannes Sylvius's death, they were moved to Aeltje's new house on Herengracht. After her death in 1644, the paintings were inherited by the eldest son, Cornelis Sylvius (1608–1685), who lived with her. In 1647 he moved to Haarlem, where he later became burgomaster. On his death in 1685, the 'portraits of his late father

and mother painted by Rembrandt van Rijn' ('contrefeytselen van sijn . . . vader en moeder sal[iger] door Rembrant van Ryn geschildert') passed to his son Johannes Jr (1652–1710), who also became burgomaster of Haarlem. After his death in 1710 the family portraits came into the possession of his son, Cornelis II Sylvius (1687–1738), who sold the Rembrandts at some unknown point in time. It was around this time that the portrait of Johannes Sylvius vanished from the documented sources.

The next owner of Aeltje's portrait was Jean-Jacques Burlamacchi (1694–1748) of Geneva. This prominent legal scholar and politician had acquired a number of masterpieces during his extended stays in England and Holland in 1720 and 1721. It was probably at this time that he purchased from Cornelis II Sylvius in Haarlem the portrait painted by Rembrandt, which later became known, erroneously, as 'le portrait de la mère de Rembrandt'. Around 1800 Burlamacchi's celebrated collection in Geneva was opened up for foreign visitors. Artists from the surrounding region were also welcomed there, which explains the painted copies that are preserved today in Dessau, Geneva and Lausanne. Around 1825, Burlamacchi's entire collection was sold to a Parisian dealer. The Rembrandt came into the hands of William Coesvelt of London. This internationally active banker and collector saw the painting primarily as an investment, and on 2 May 1828 it was put up for auction by the London art dealer John Smith on his instructions. No purchaser presented

himself, however, and Smith did not sell the painting until 1835, to a friend, the Amsterdam dealer Albertus Brondgeest (1786–1849).

It must have been from Brondgeest that Baron James de Rothschild (1792–1868), the founder of the Parisian branch of the famous firm of bankers, acquired the painting. After his death in 1868, it passed to his widow, Betty de Rothschild (1805–1886). The director of the Berlin museums, Wilhelm (von) Bode (1845–1929), saw the painting displayed in her house around 1880. After the baroness's death in 1886, the Rembrandt passed to her son, Baron Alphonse de Rothschild (1827–1905). A handwritten inventory of his collection, dating from 1903, described the 'Portrait de vieille femme par Rembrandt' as hanging beside the door to the smoking room in the mansion at no. 2 rue Saint-Florentin in Paris, whose interior was arranged in the manner of a museum. In another part of this house hung Vermeer's renowned *Astronomer* (now in Paris, Musée du Louvre). After the banker's death in 1905, the Rembrandt came into the hands of his son, Baron Édouard de Rothschild (1868–1949), who also took charge of the family business. At the beginning of the Second World War his collection was removed to safety on the family's estate in Normandy. In July 1940 the elderly baron fled to America with his youngest daughter, Baroness Bethsabée de Rothschild (1914–1999). The Rembrandt was seized by the Germans, but survived the war unscathed. In 1949, Bethsabée inherited the painting from her deceased

Rembrandt's *Portrait of Aeltje Uylenburgh* (1632) is beyond all doubt the greatest masterpiece in the Van Otterloos' collection. The painting was displayed in the Mauritshuis as part of the exhibition *Dutch Portraits* (2007–2008), a survey of Dutch portrait painting in the Golden Age.

father, after which she settled in Israel in 1962. In 1978 the painting was examined by members of the Rembrandt Research Project in the baroness's house in Tel Aviv. They were the first art historians to have studied the painting for many years. After the baroness's death in 1999, the Rembrandt was put up for auction at Christie's in London, on 13 December 2000. It was then that the sitter's true identity, which is now universally accepted, was first published in the accompanying auction catalogue, by Jaap van der Veen (see p. 79). The Dutch dealer Robert Noortman made the highest bid for the rediscovered Rembrandt, with Eijk and Rose-Marie de Mol van Otterloo acquiring a significant share in it. In the spring of 2005, the couple finally acquired full ownership of the portrait (see pp. 20–21), after which it was displayed on loan in the Mauritshuis, The Hague, in the summer of that year. For the three months of the current exhibition, it can briefly be seen there once again.

This account is based on a detailed reconstruction of the peregrinations of Rembrandt's portrait by Ben Broos (to be published in *Oud Holland*).

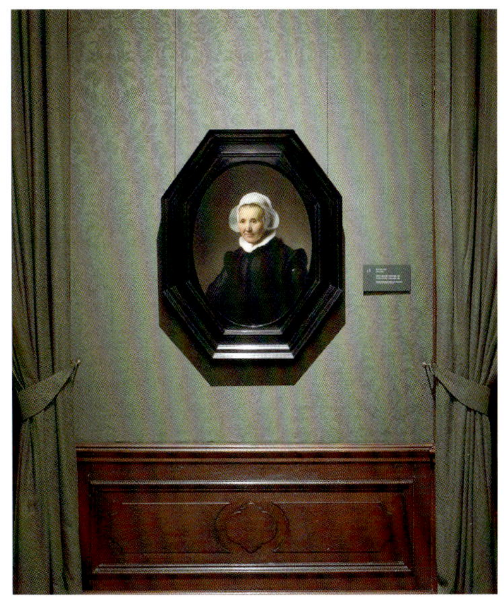

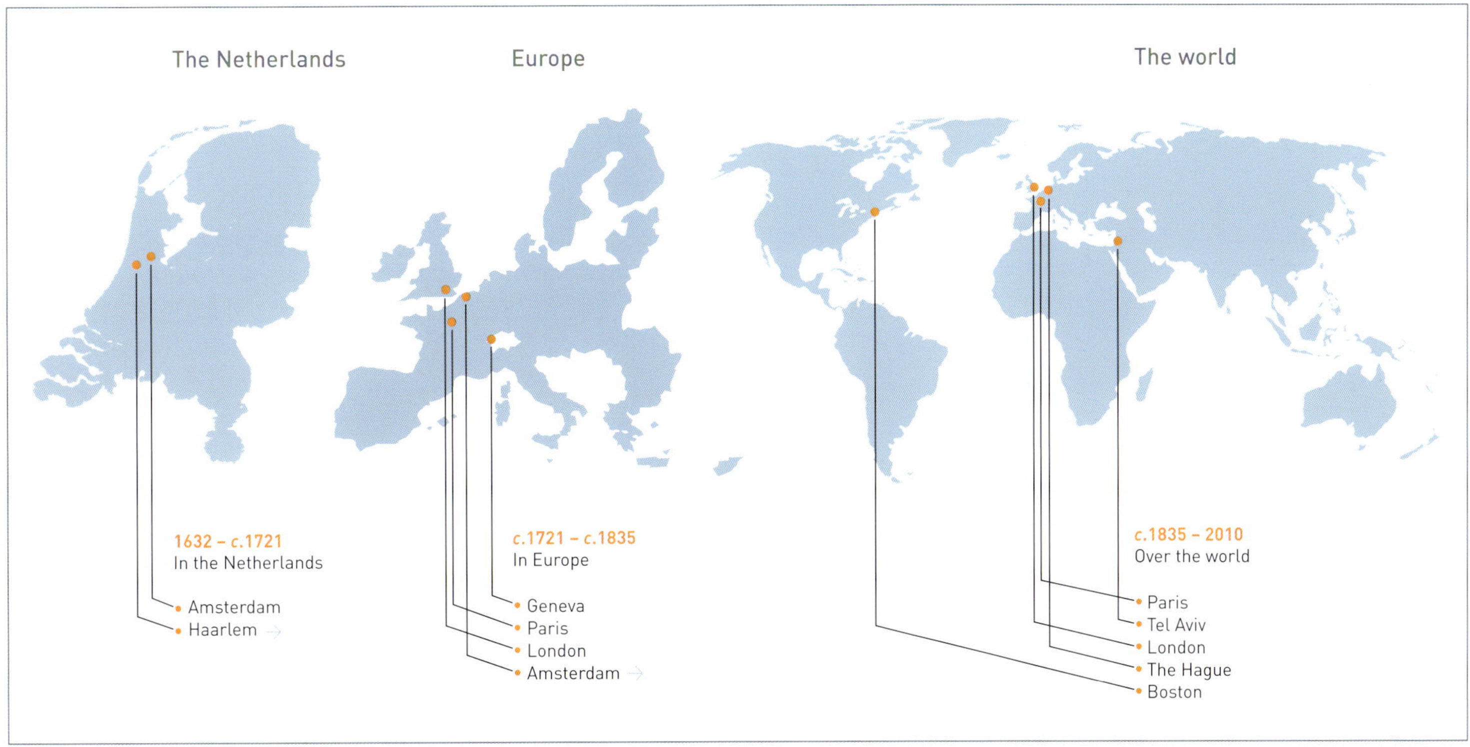

Highlights

The Paintings in Alphabetical Order

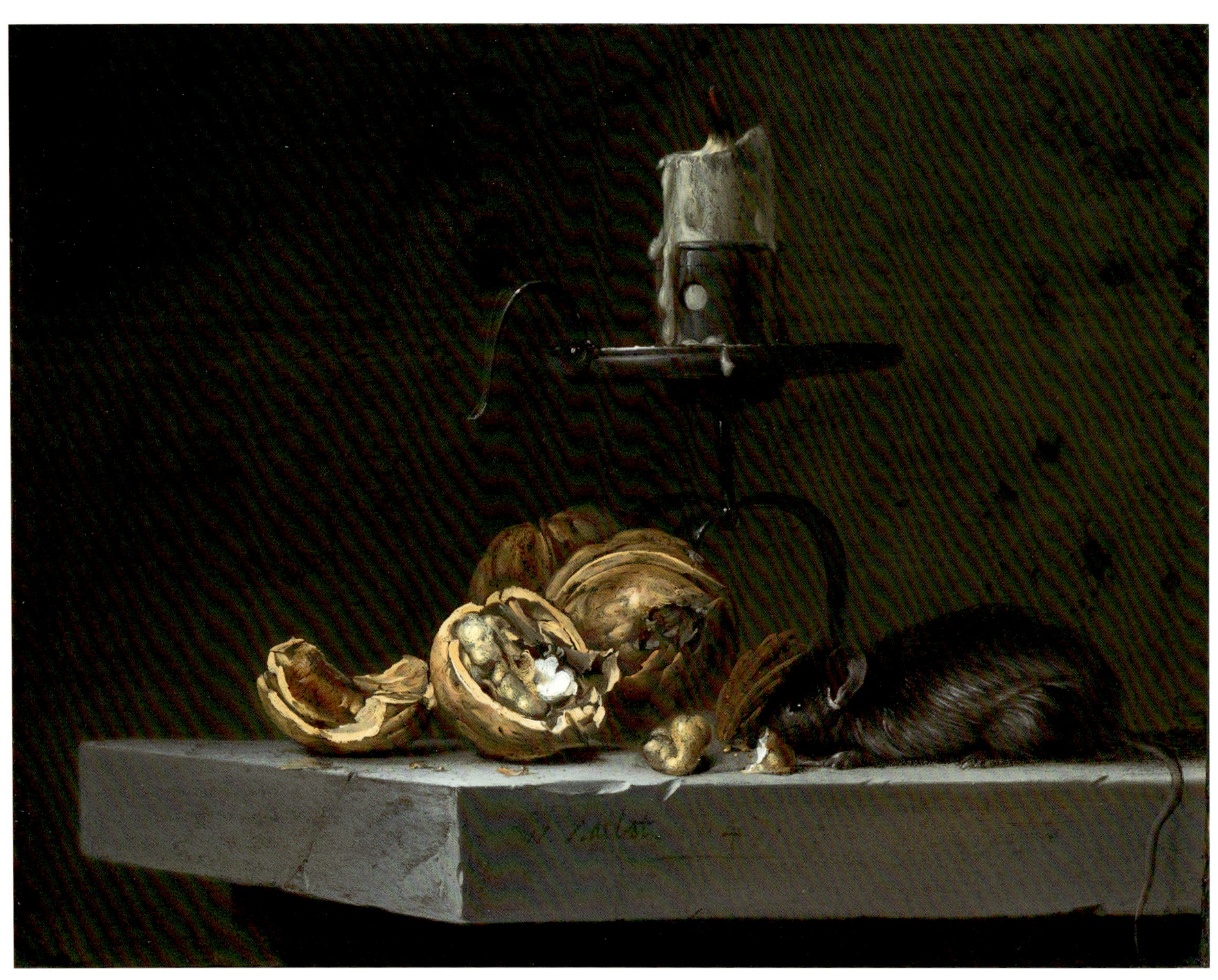

  Balthasar van der Ast
Flower Still Life, c.1630

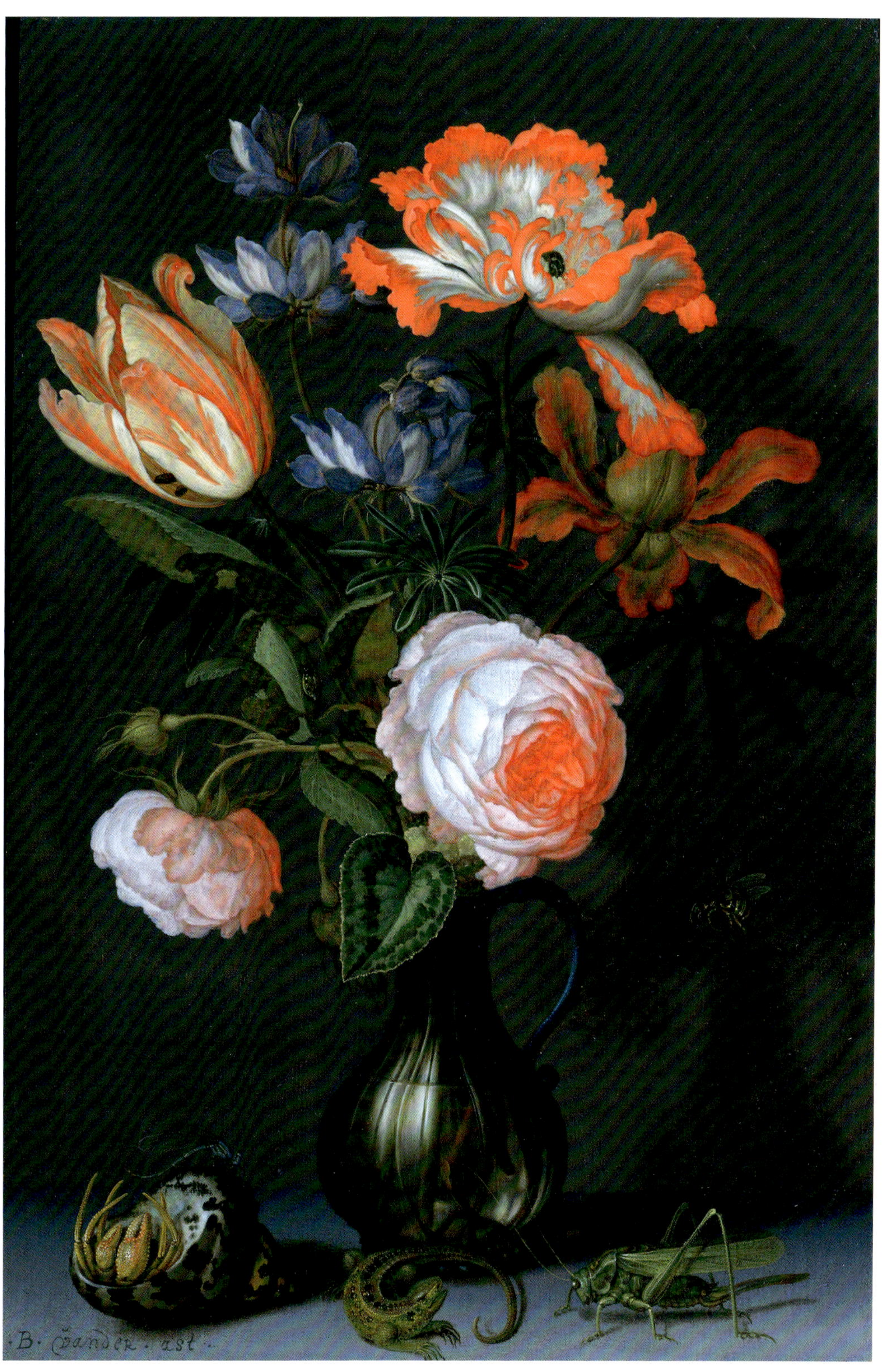

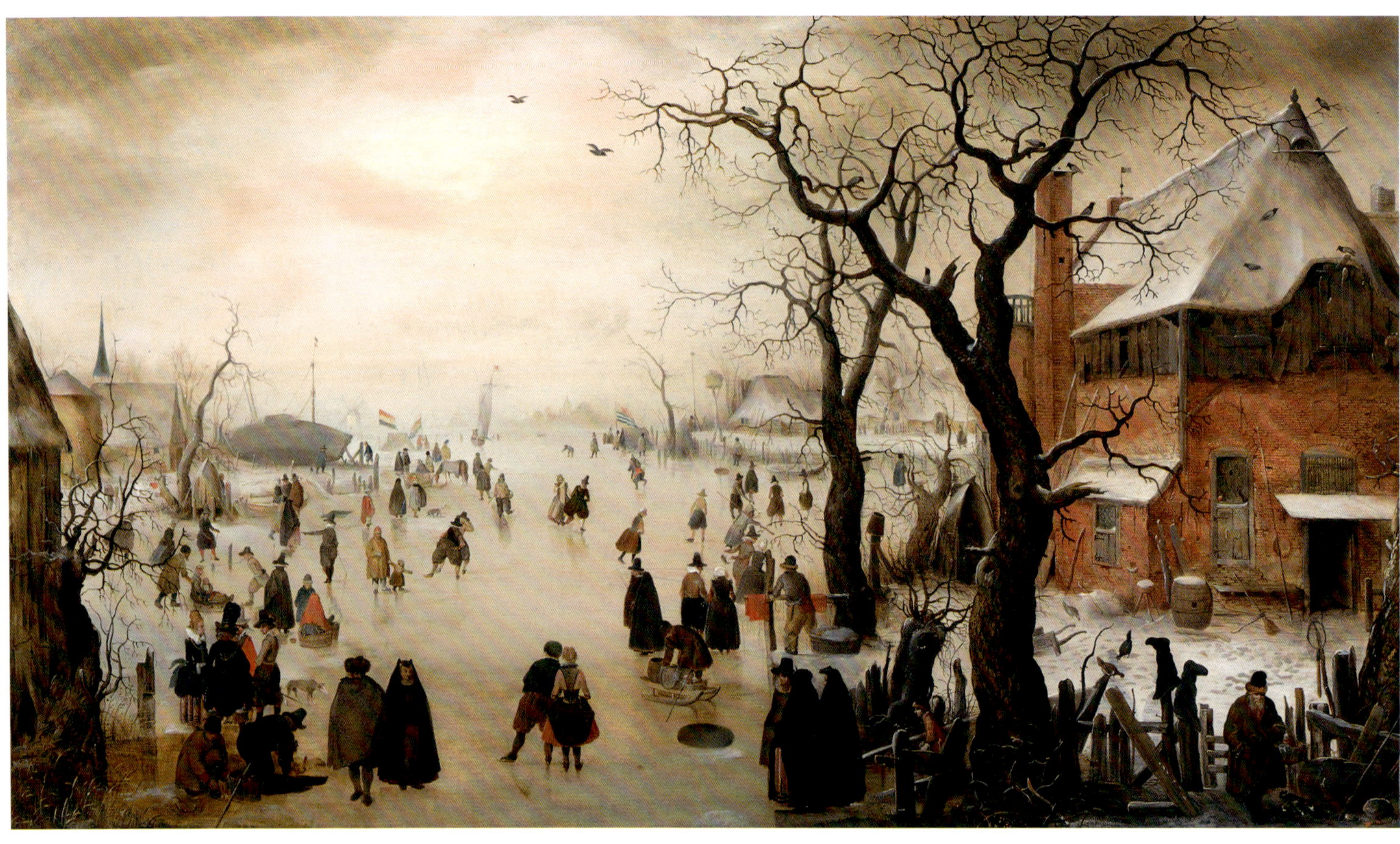

3   Hendrick Avercamp
Winter Landscape with Skaters, c.1610–1615

Young Woman Holding a Fan, c.1644–1645

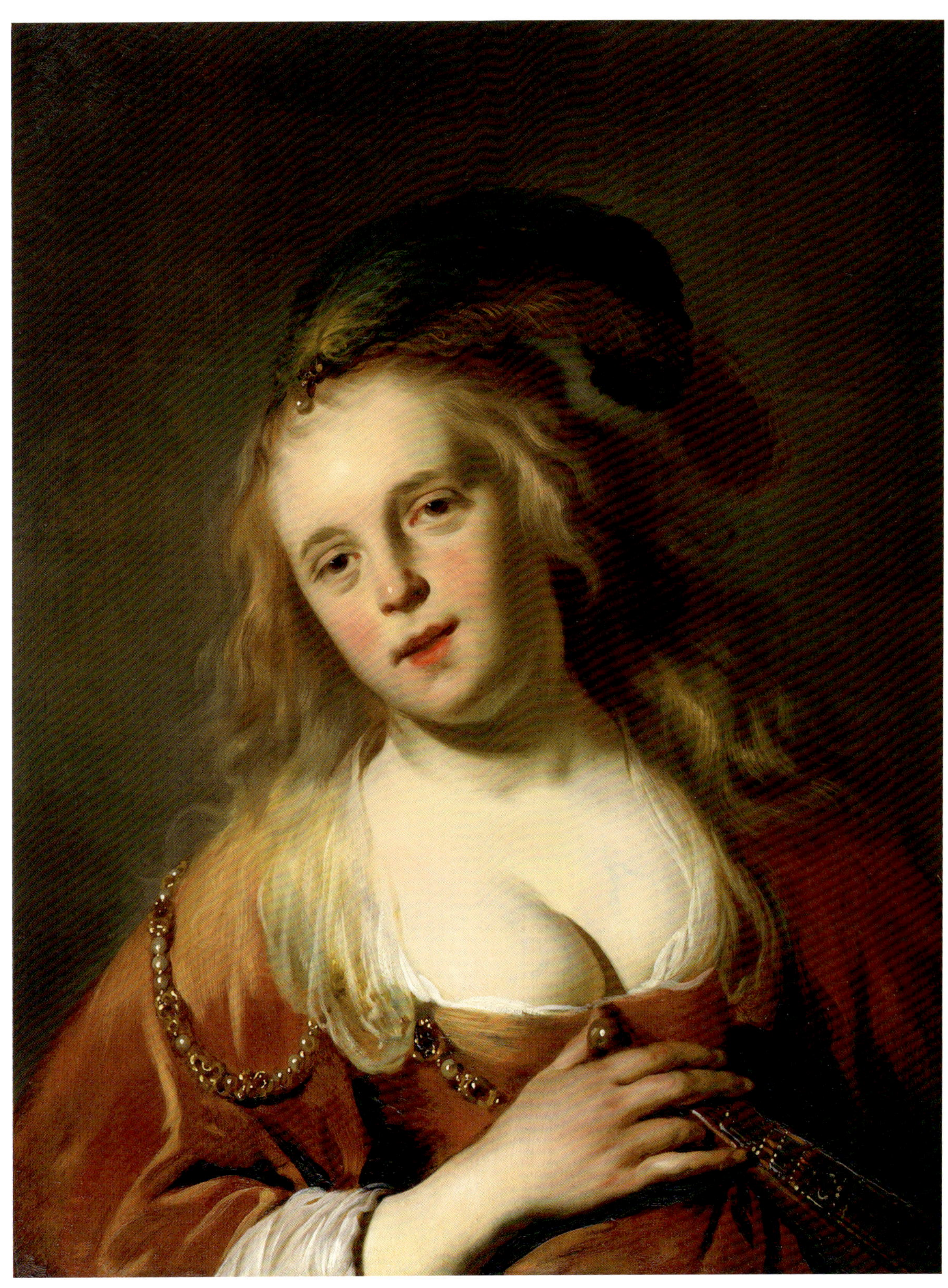

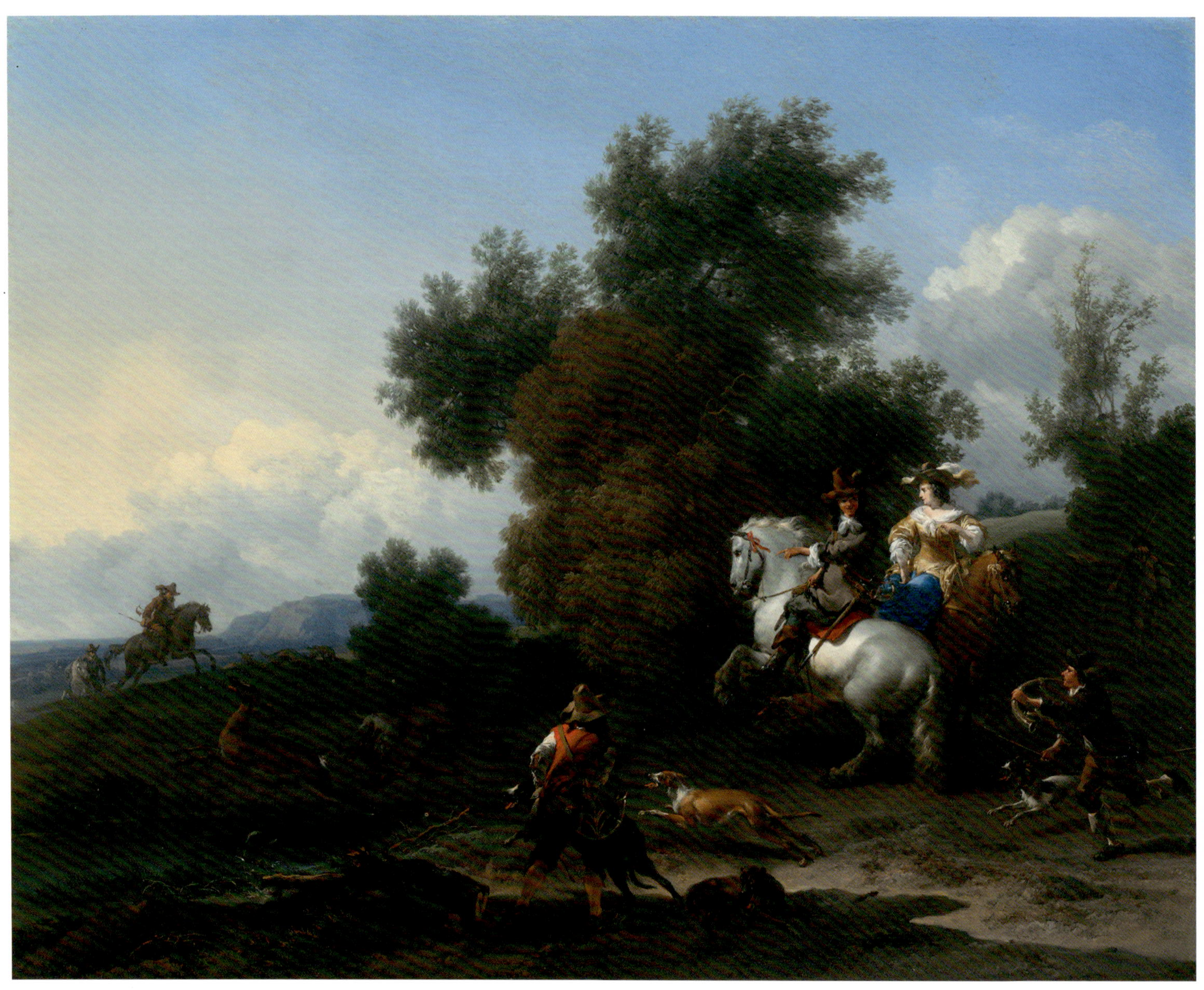

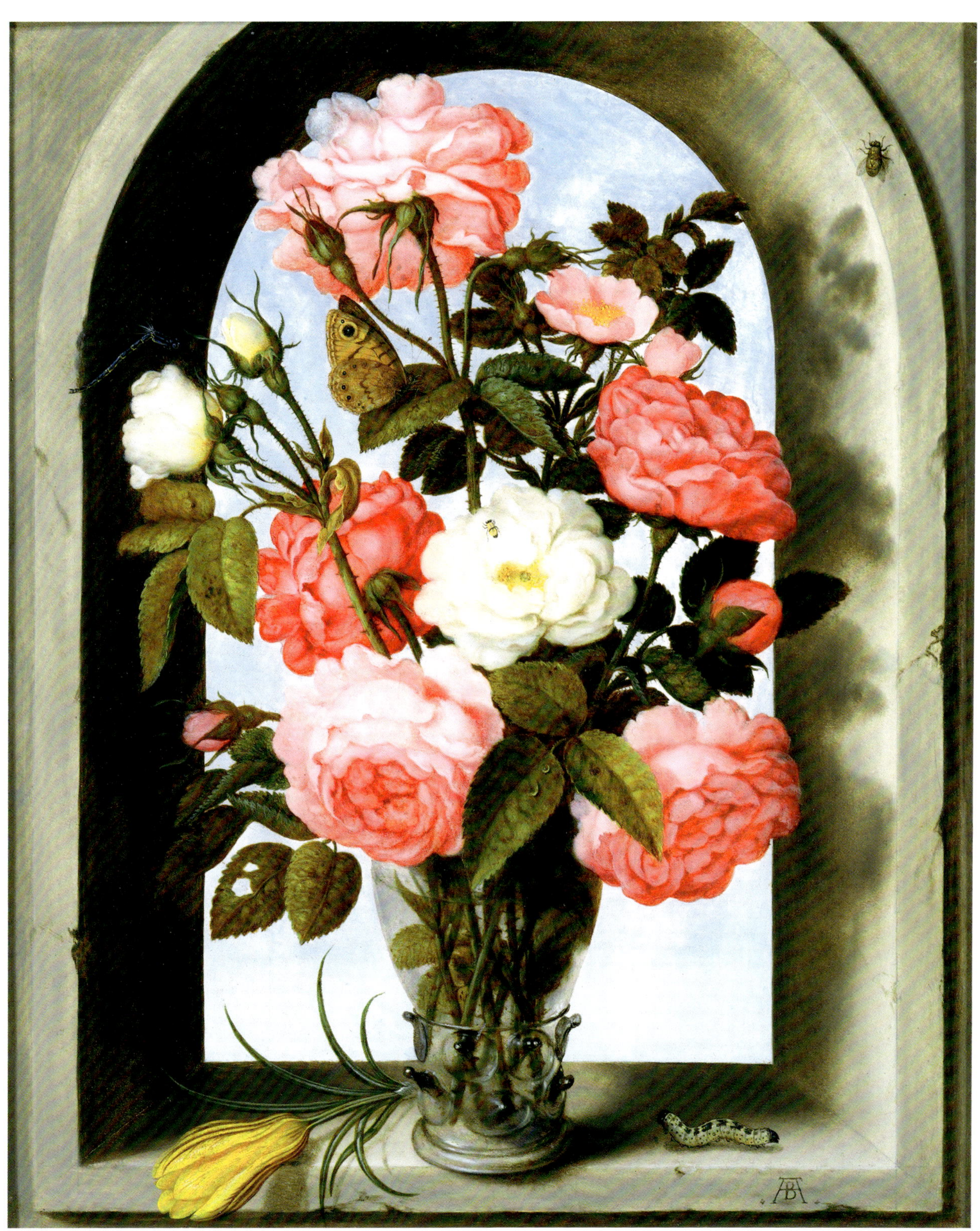

Italianate Landscape with Travellers, c. 1645 – 1650

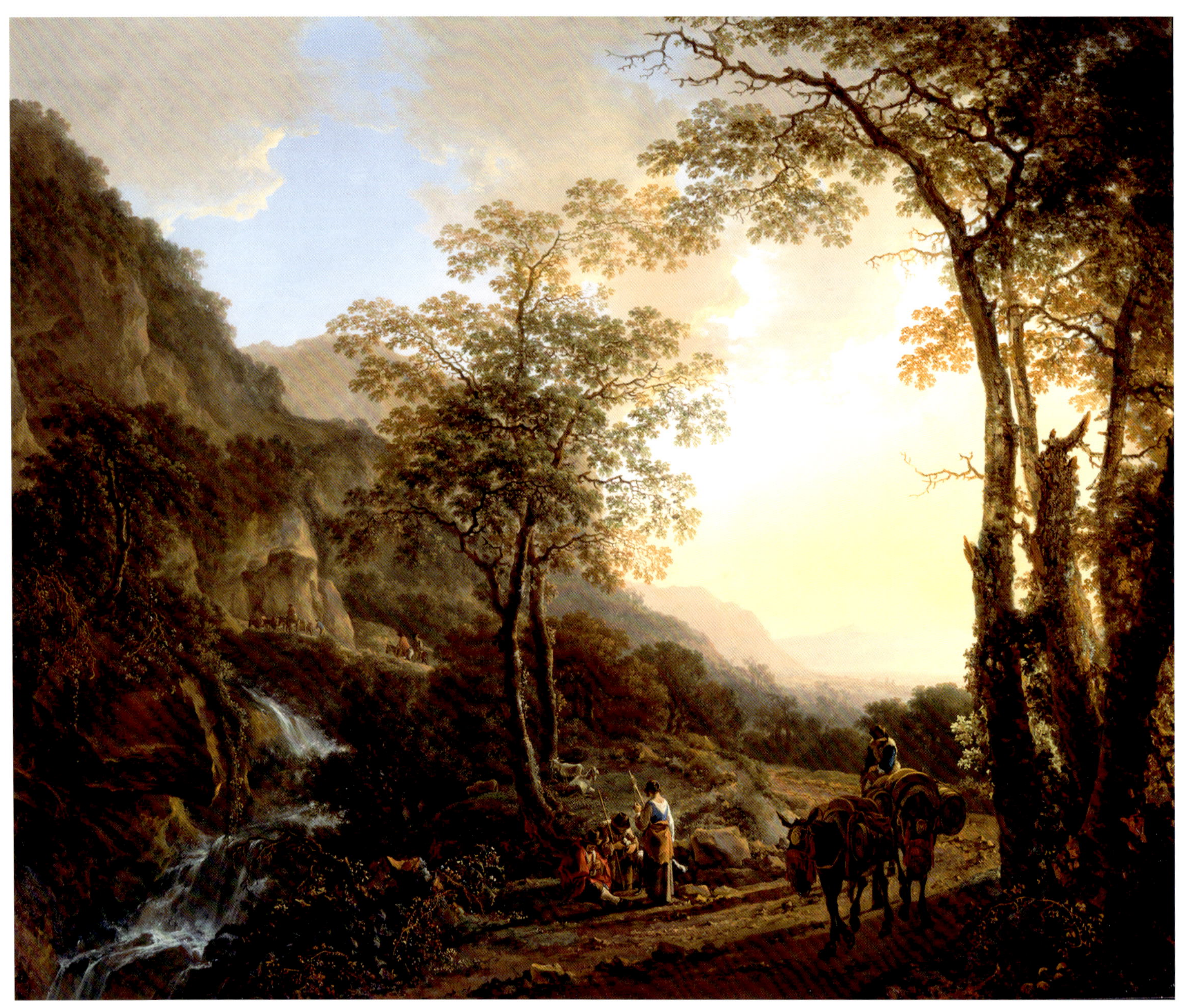

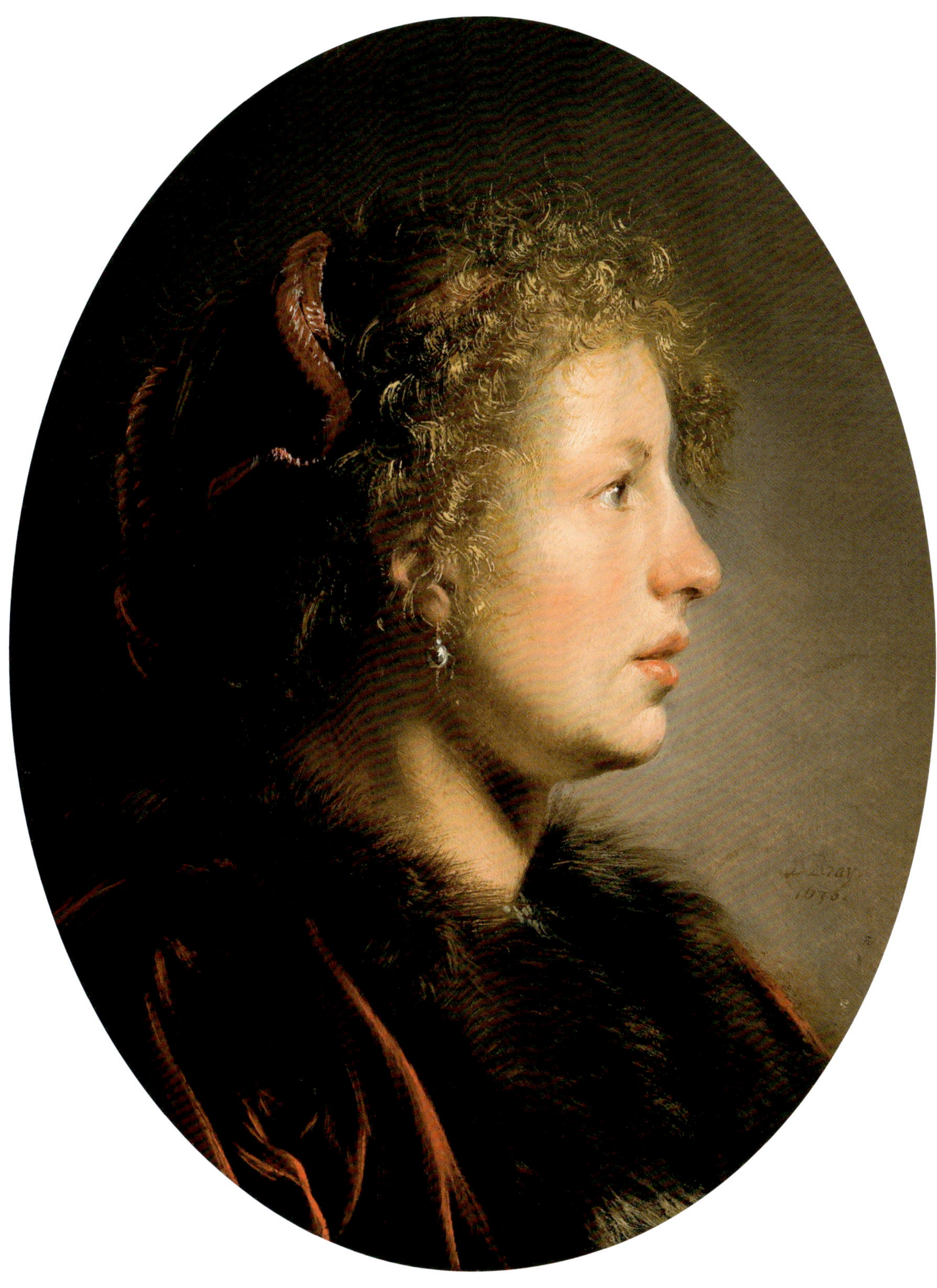

Boats in a Calm, 1651

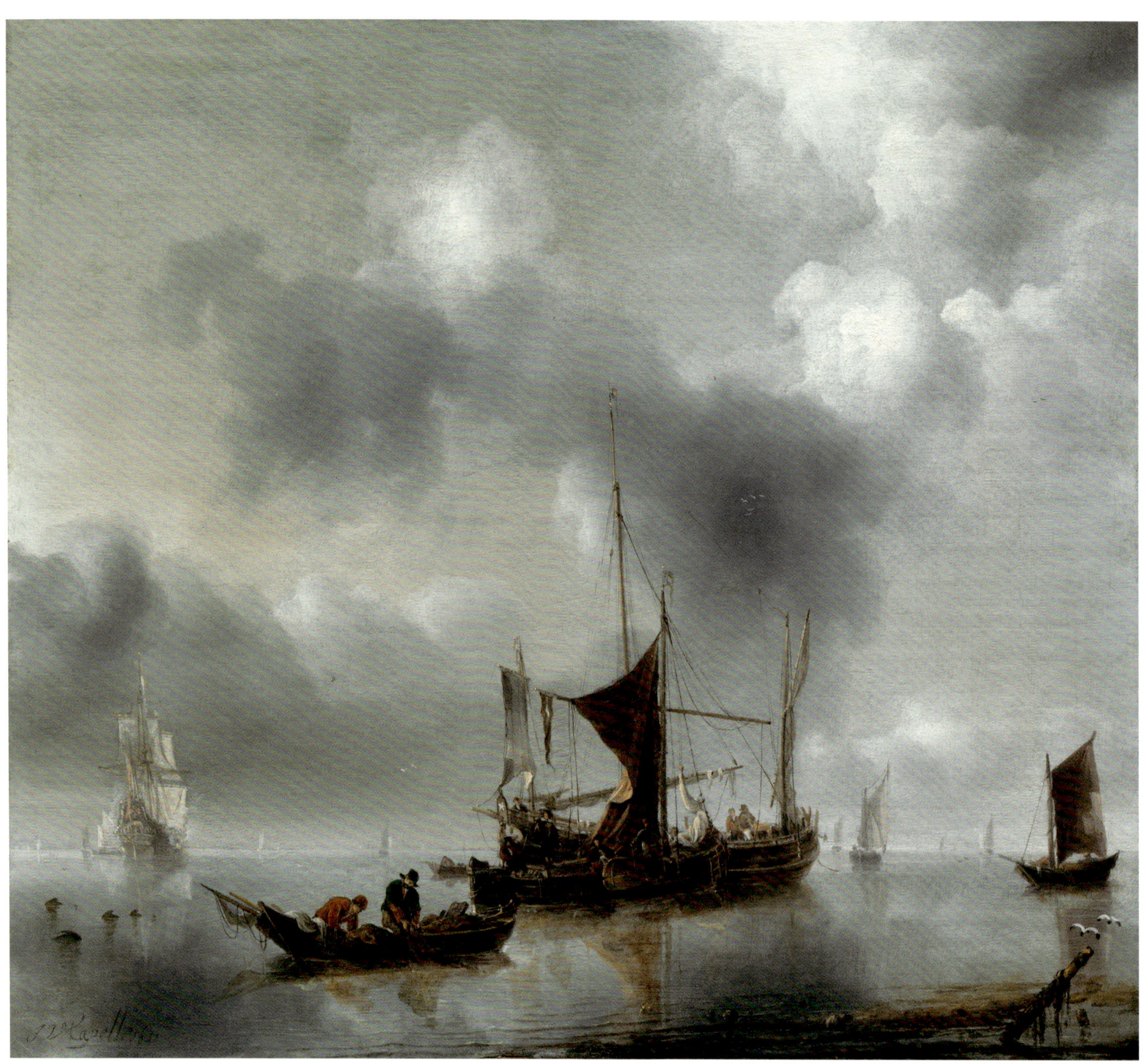

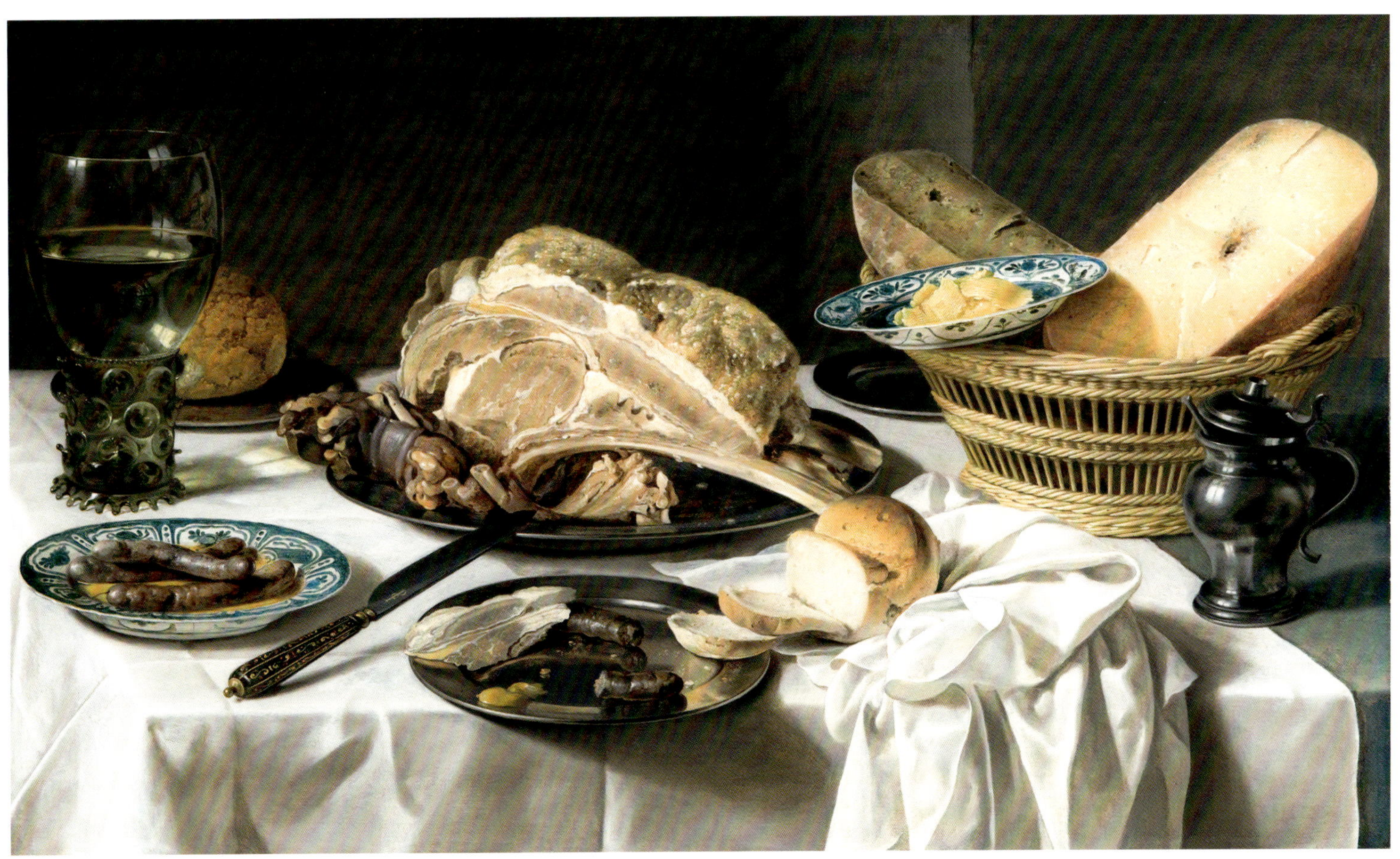

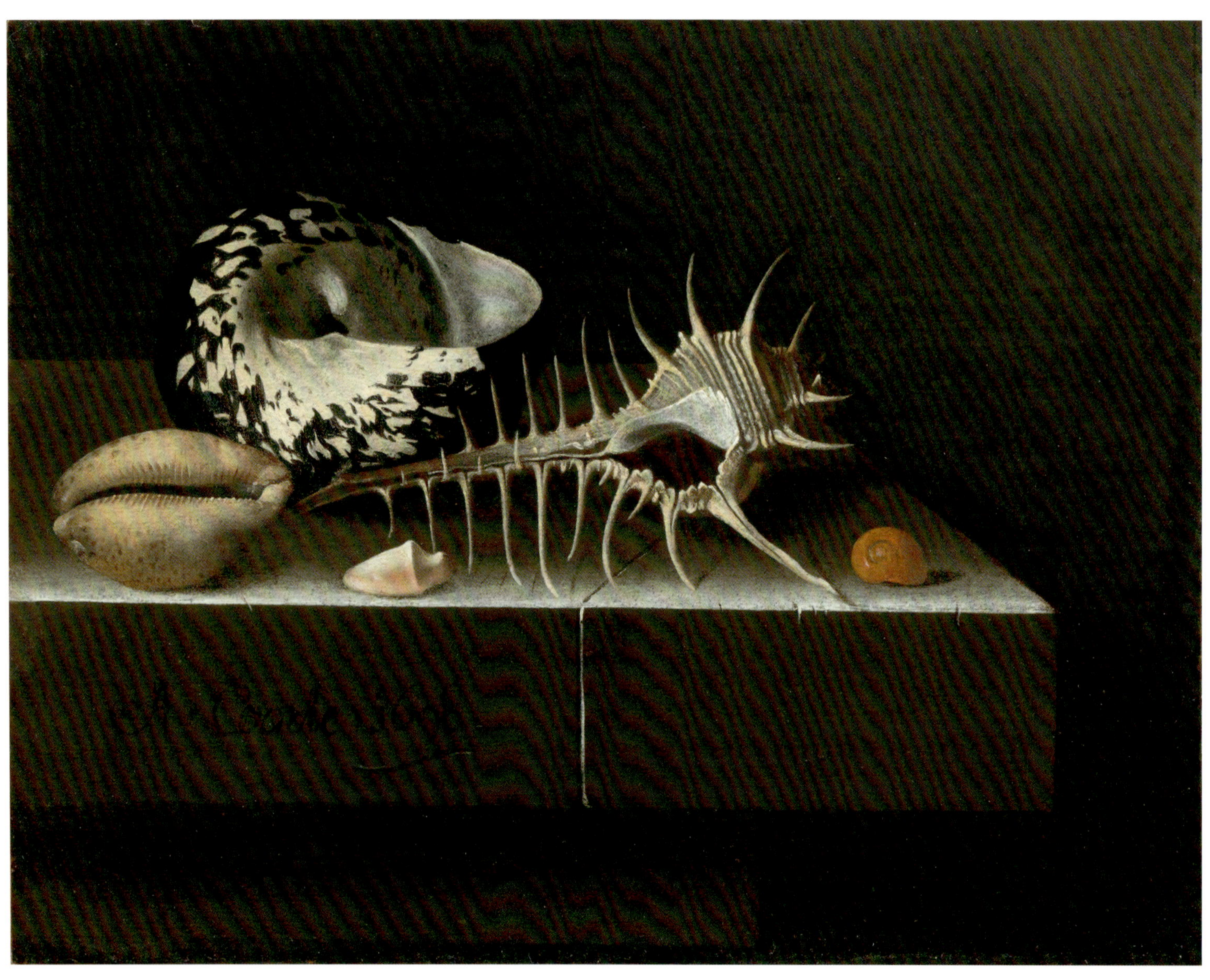

12 Aelbert Cuyp
Orpheus Charming the Animals, c.1640

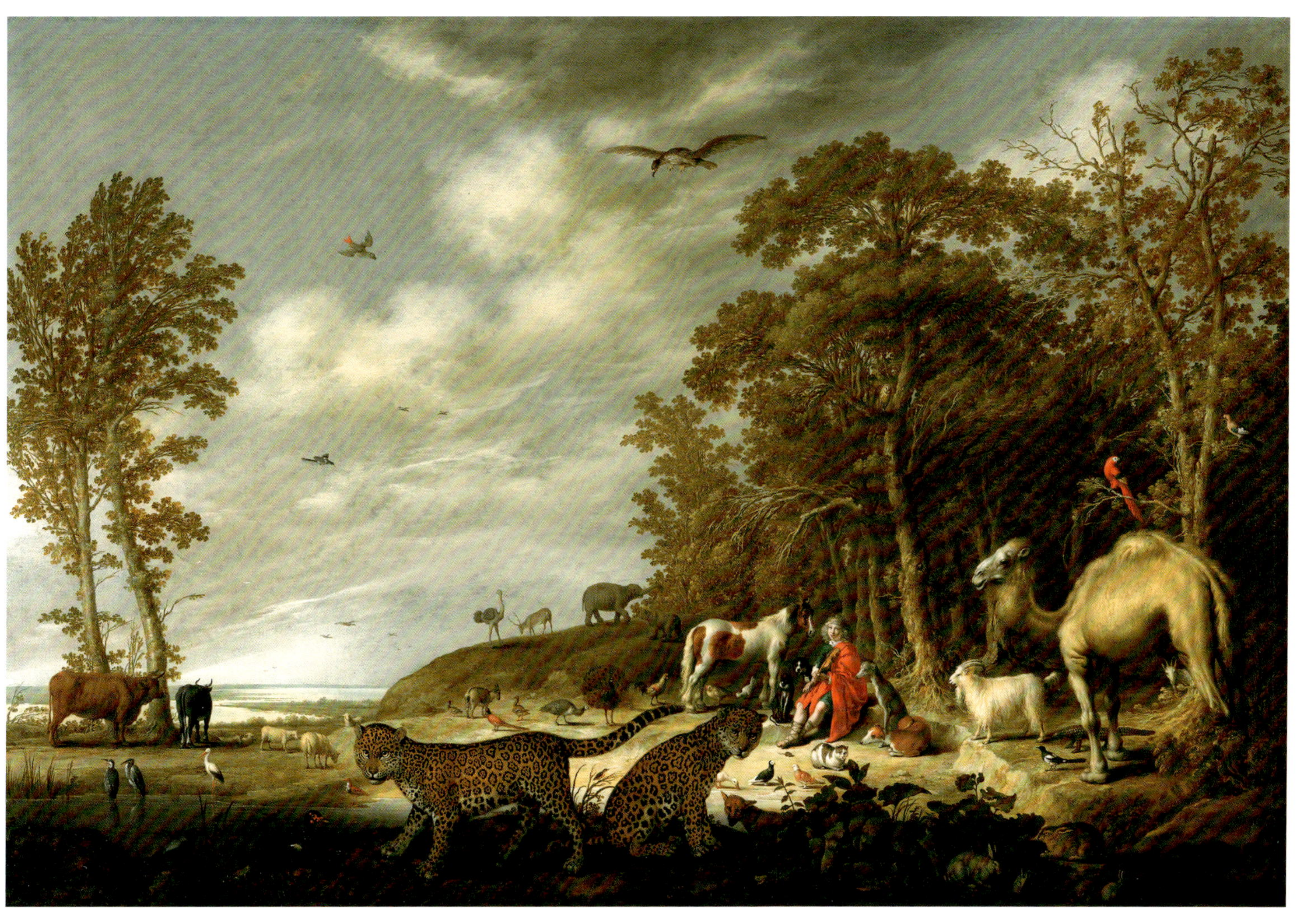

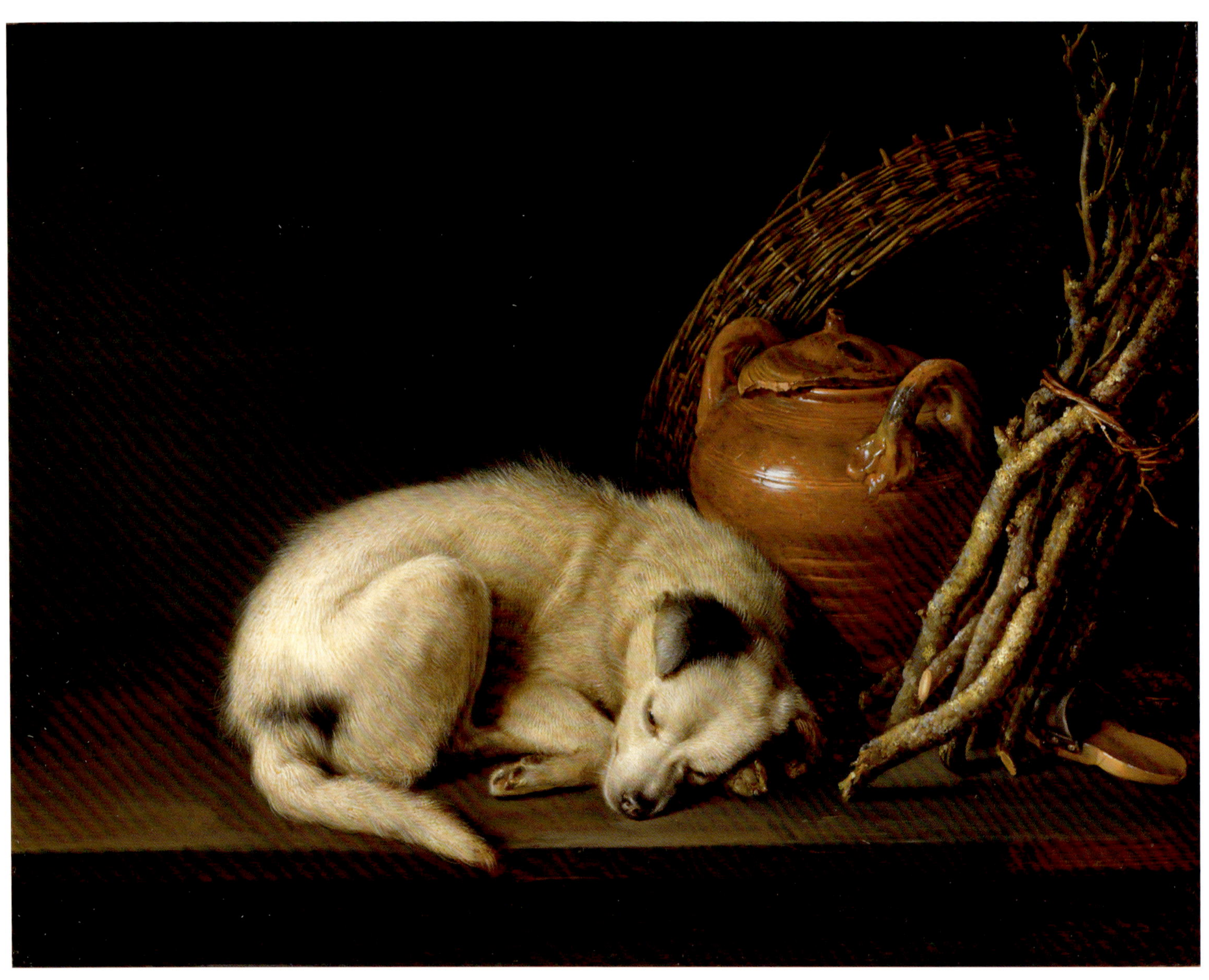

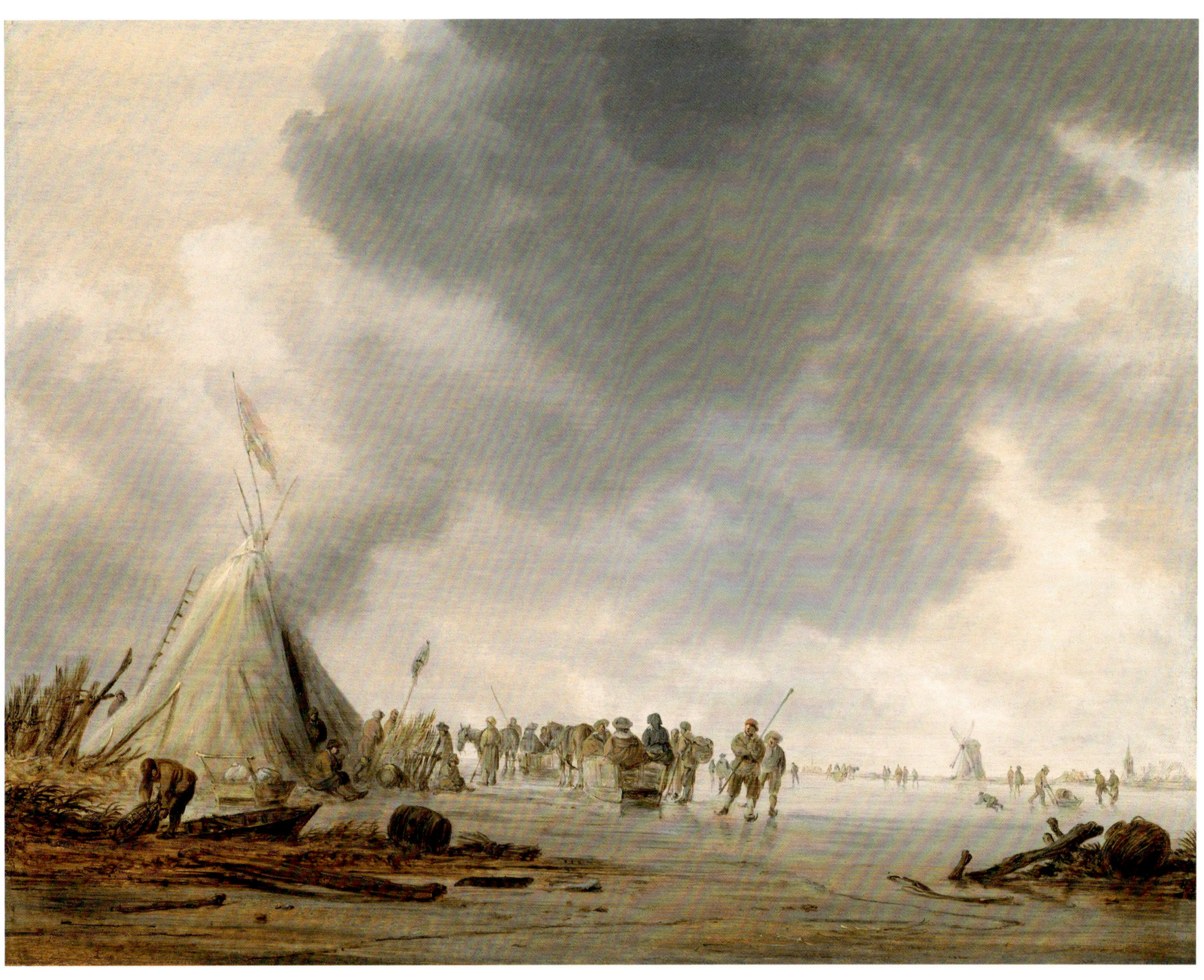

14 Jan van Goyen
Winter Landscape with Skaters, 1637

Still Life with a Tazza, 1633

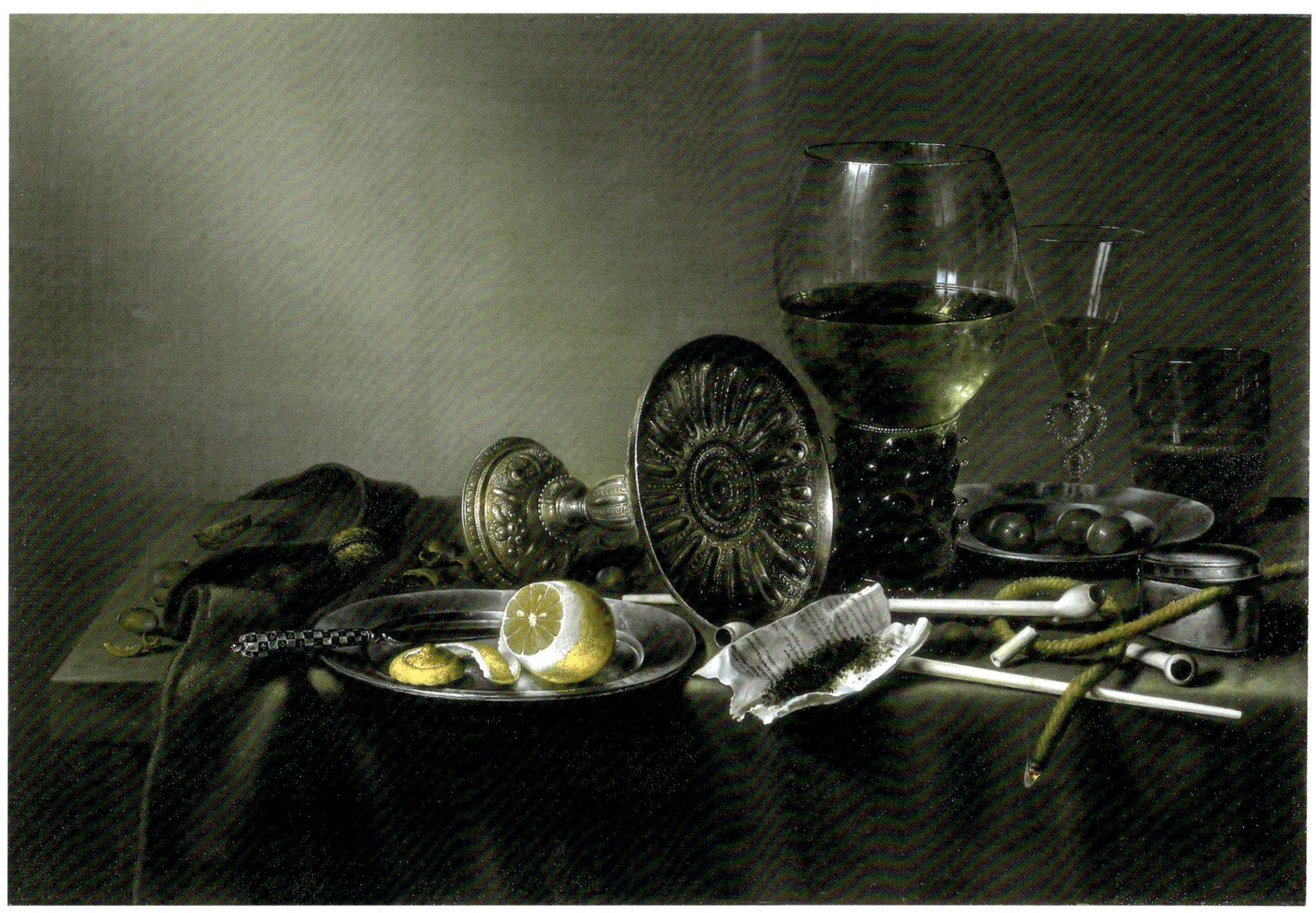

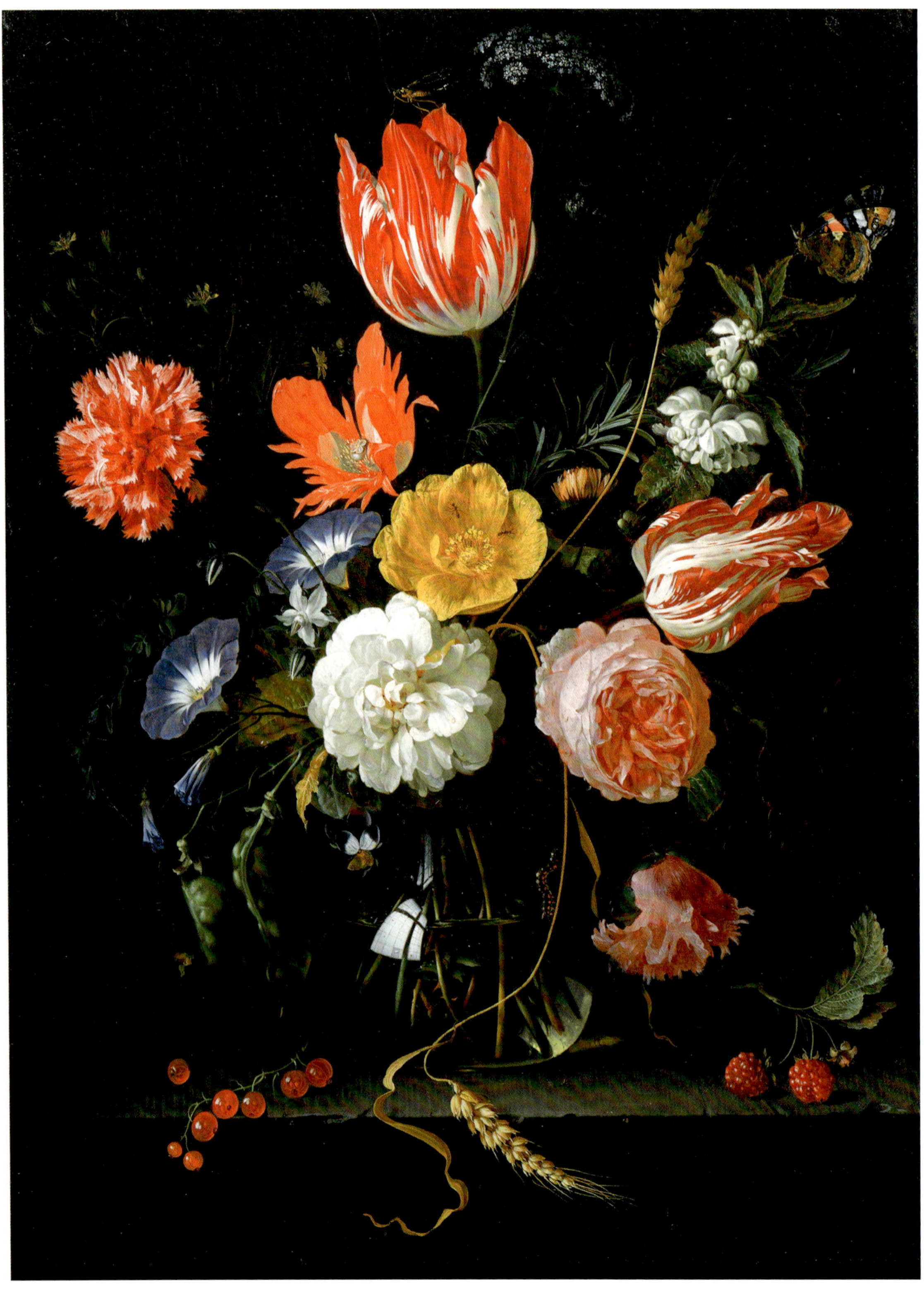

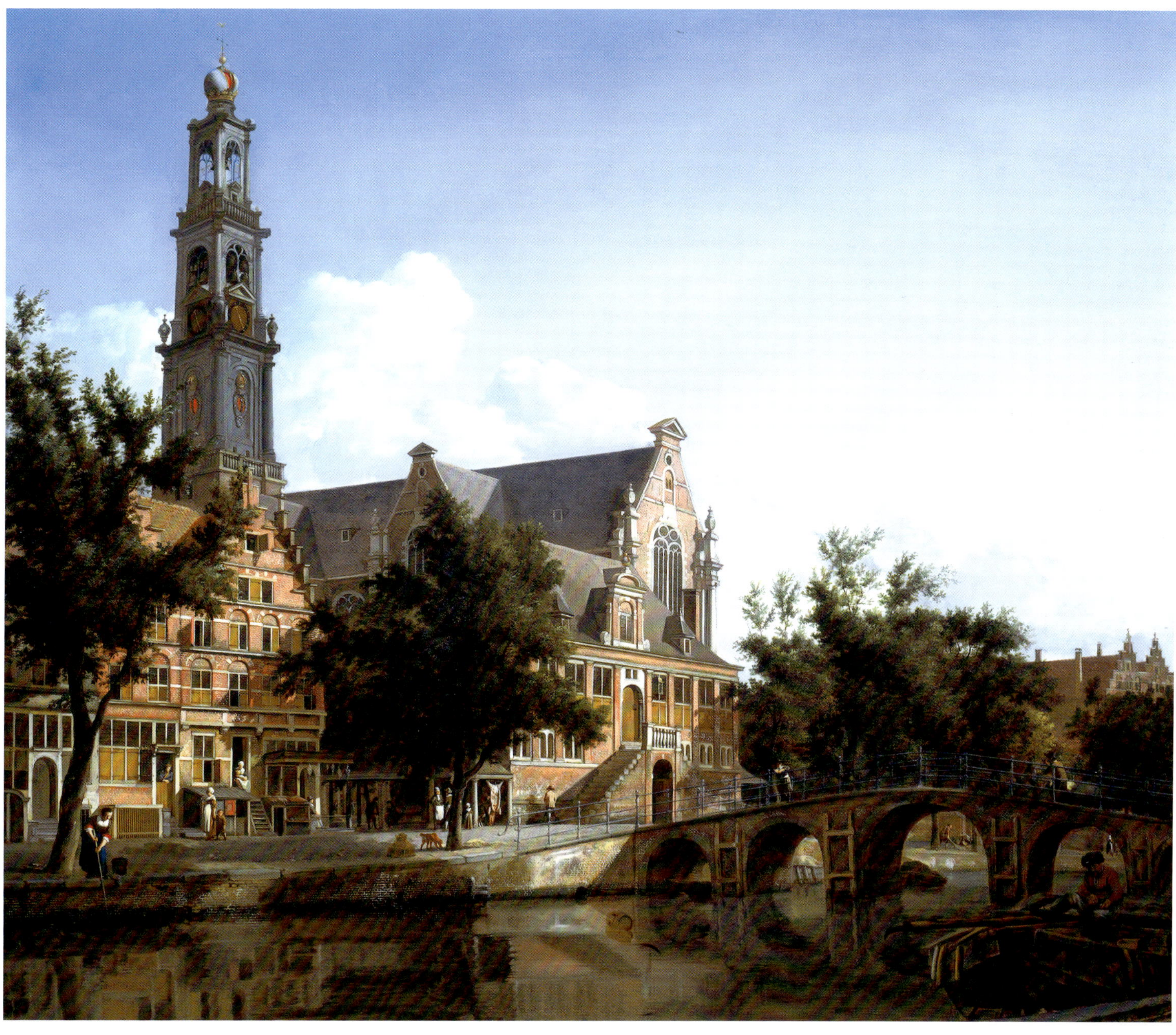

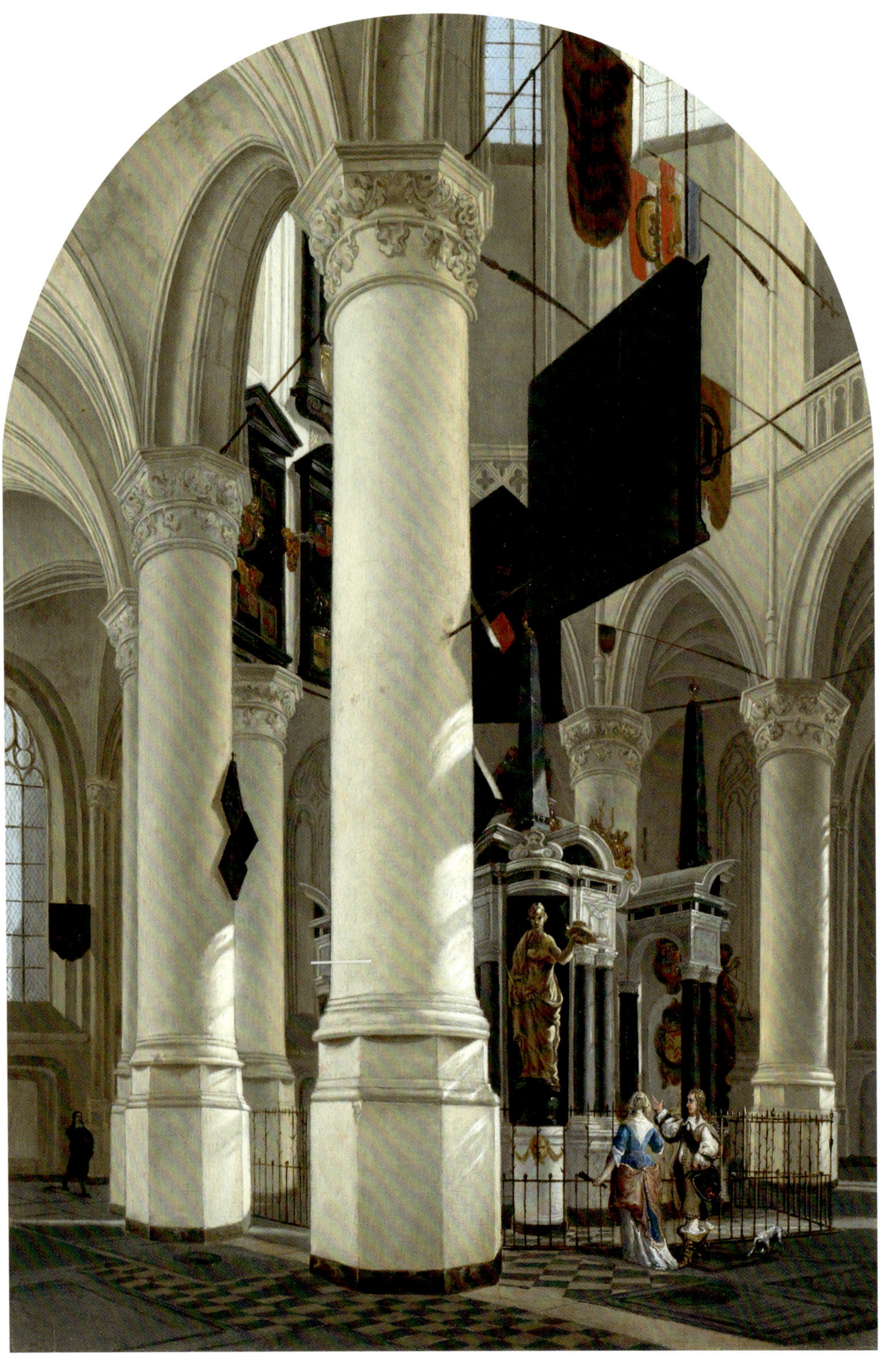

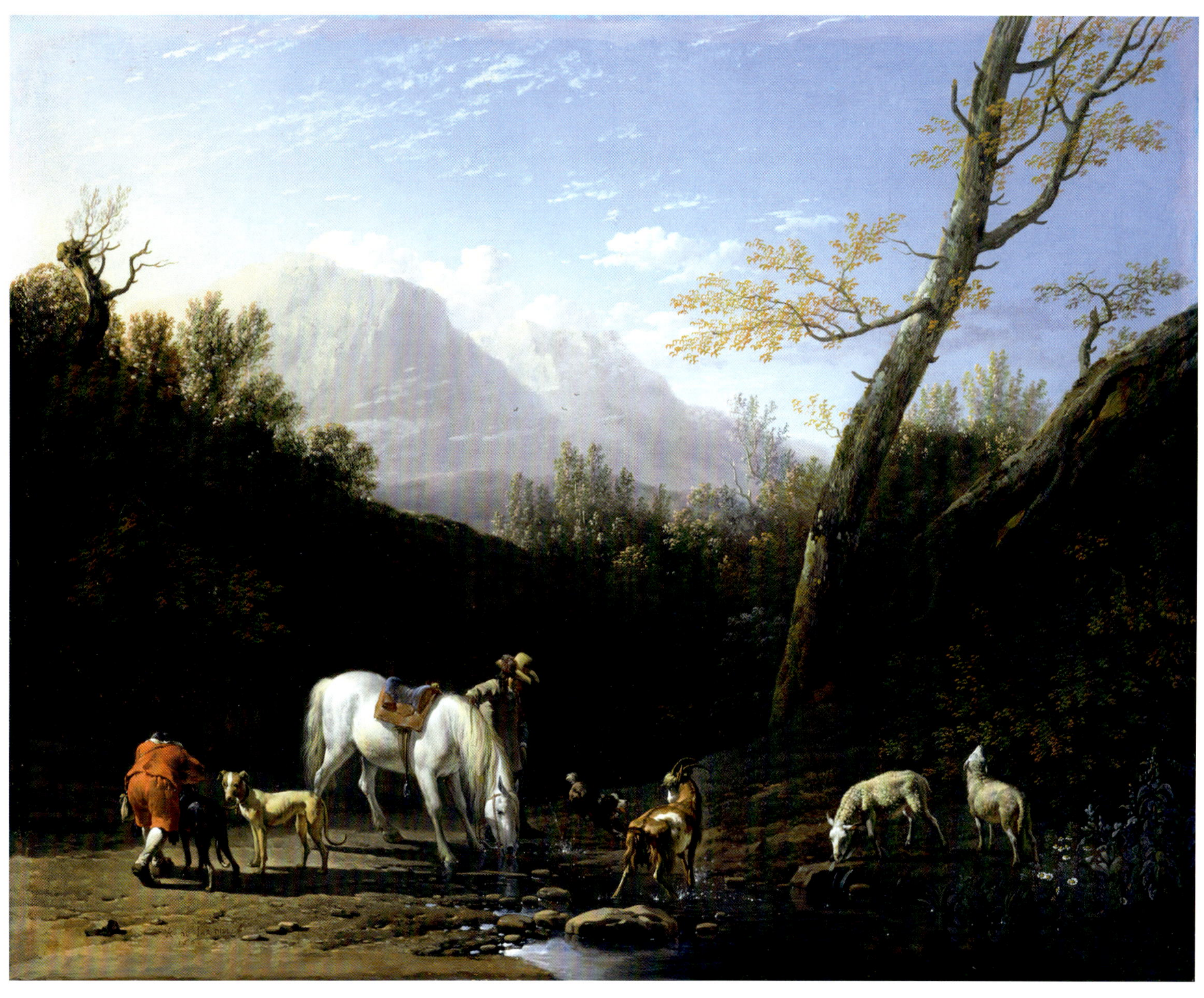

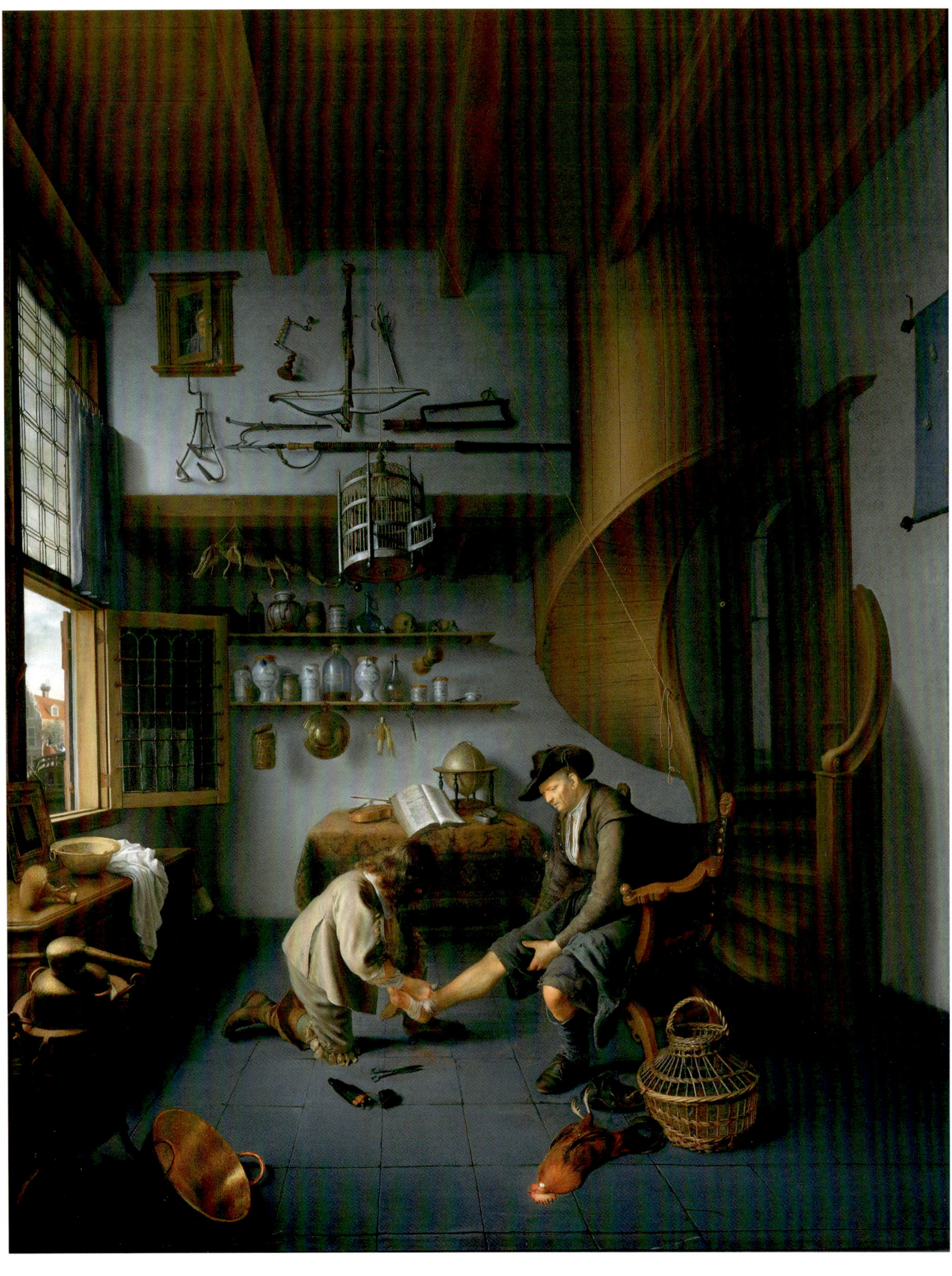

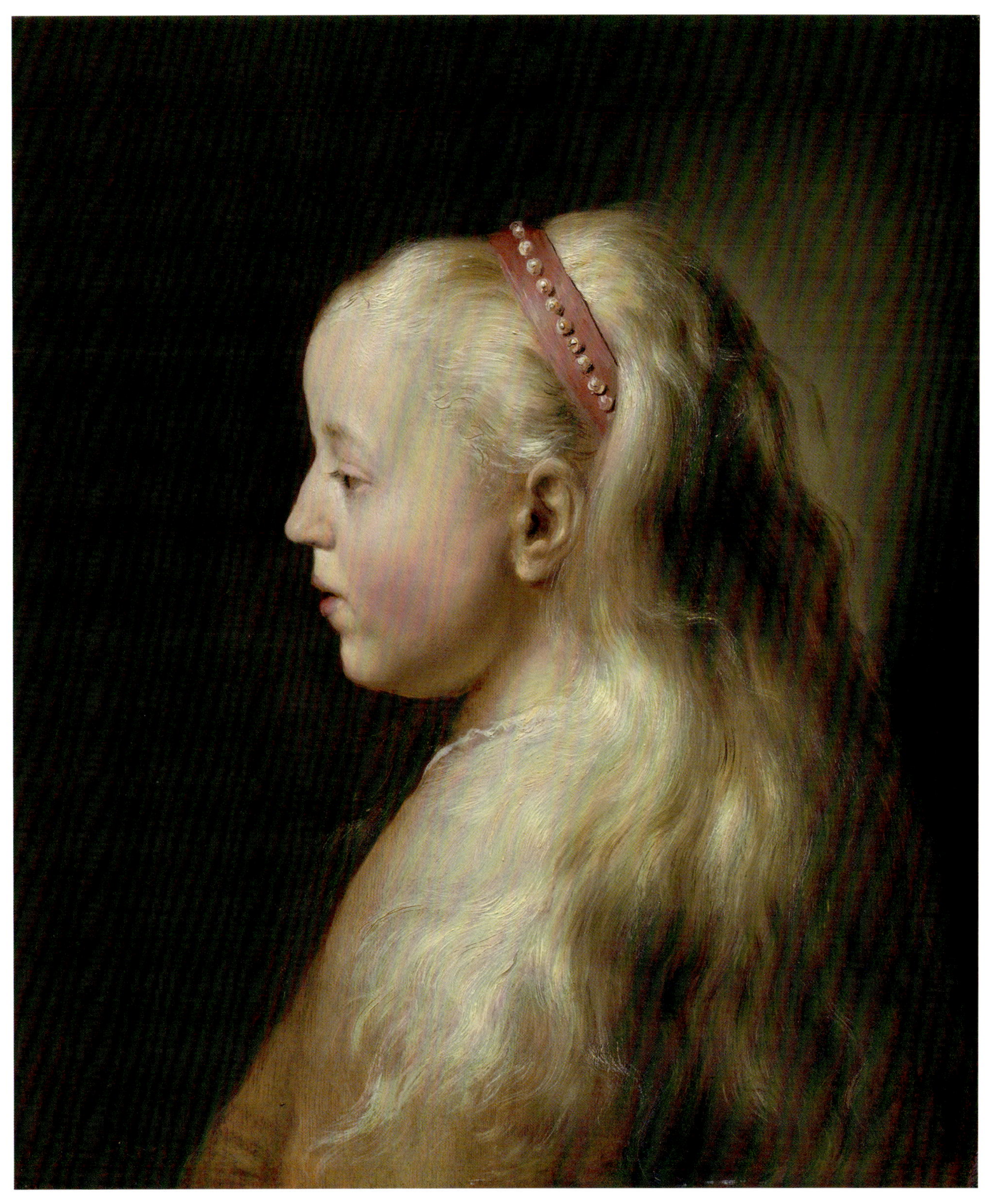

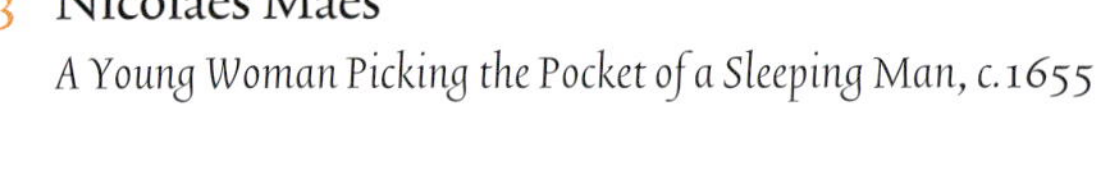

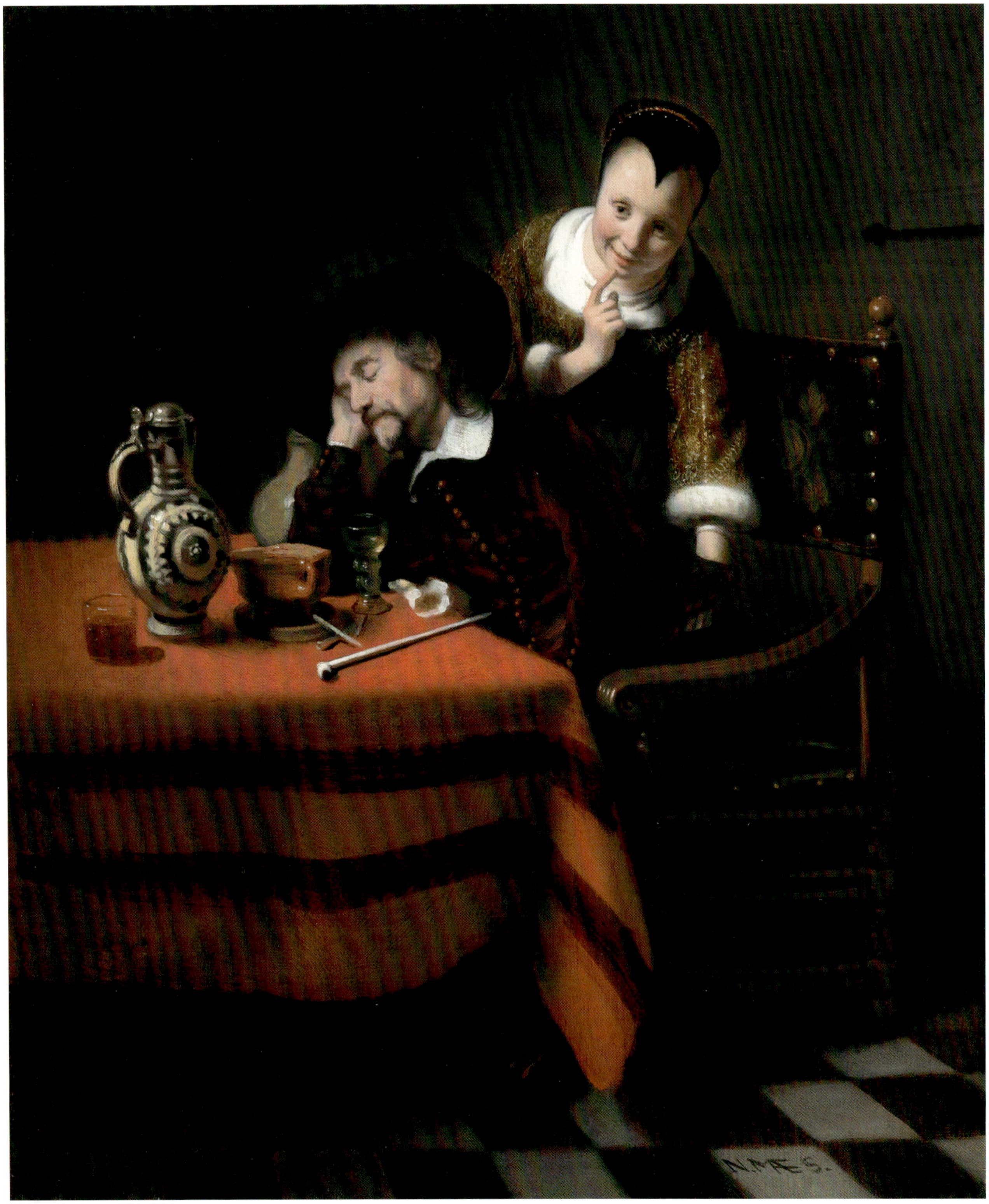

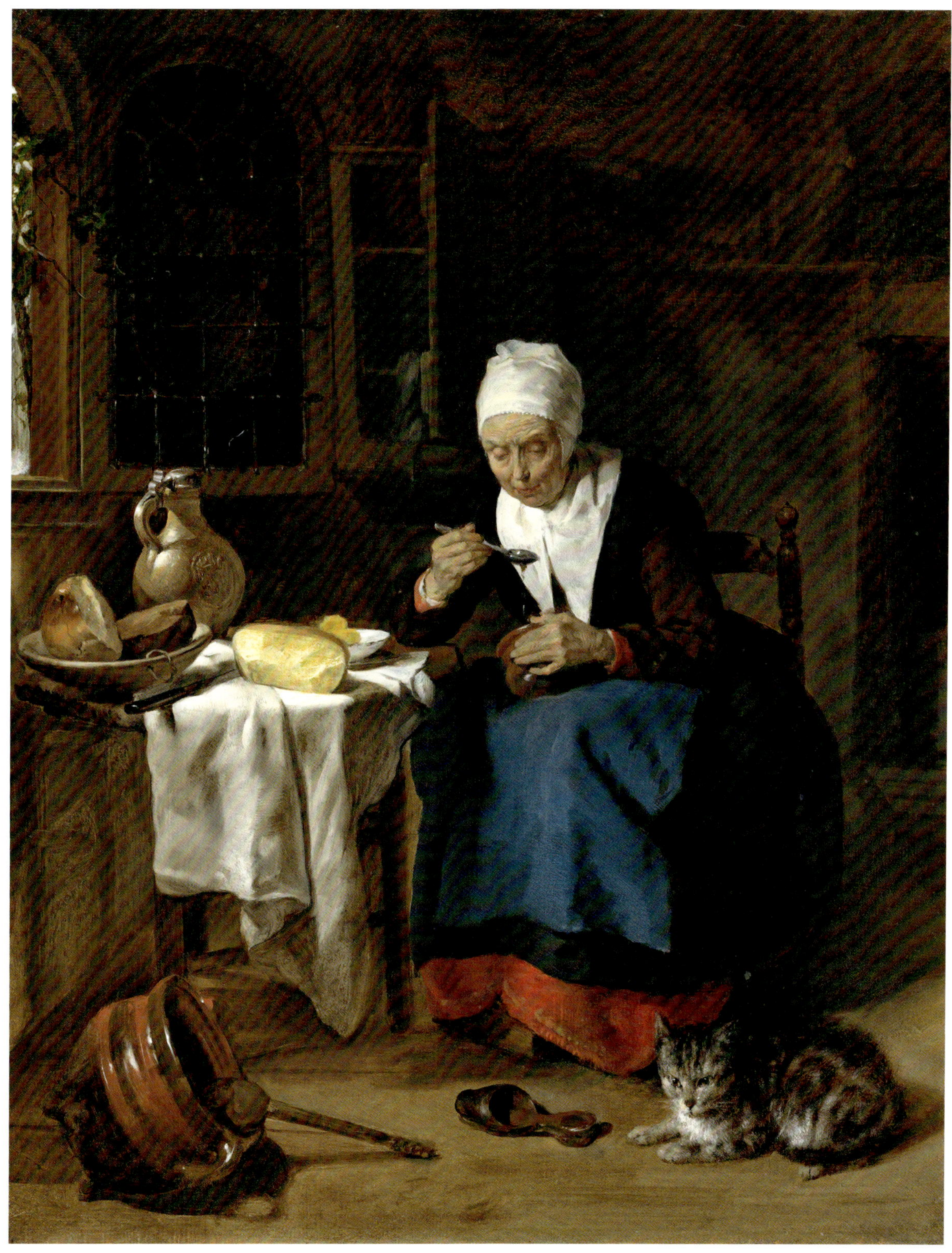

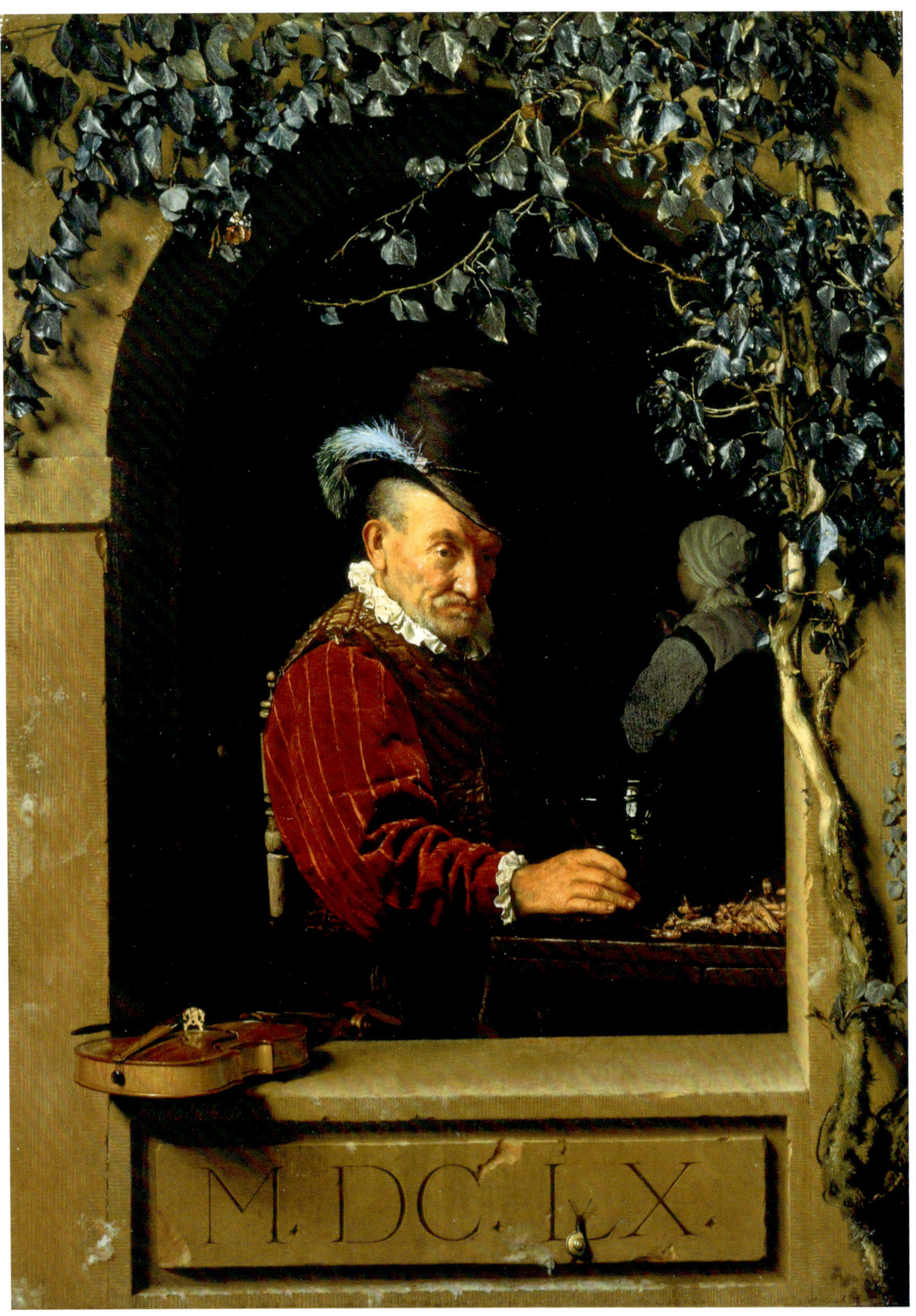

Figures in a Snowstorm, c.1655–1660

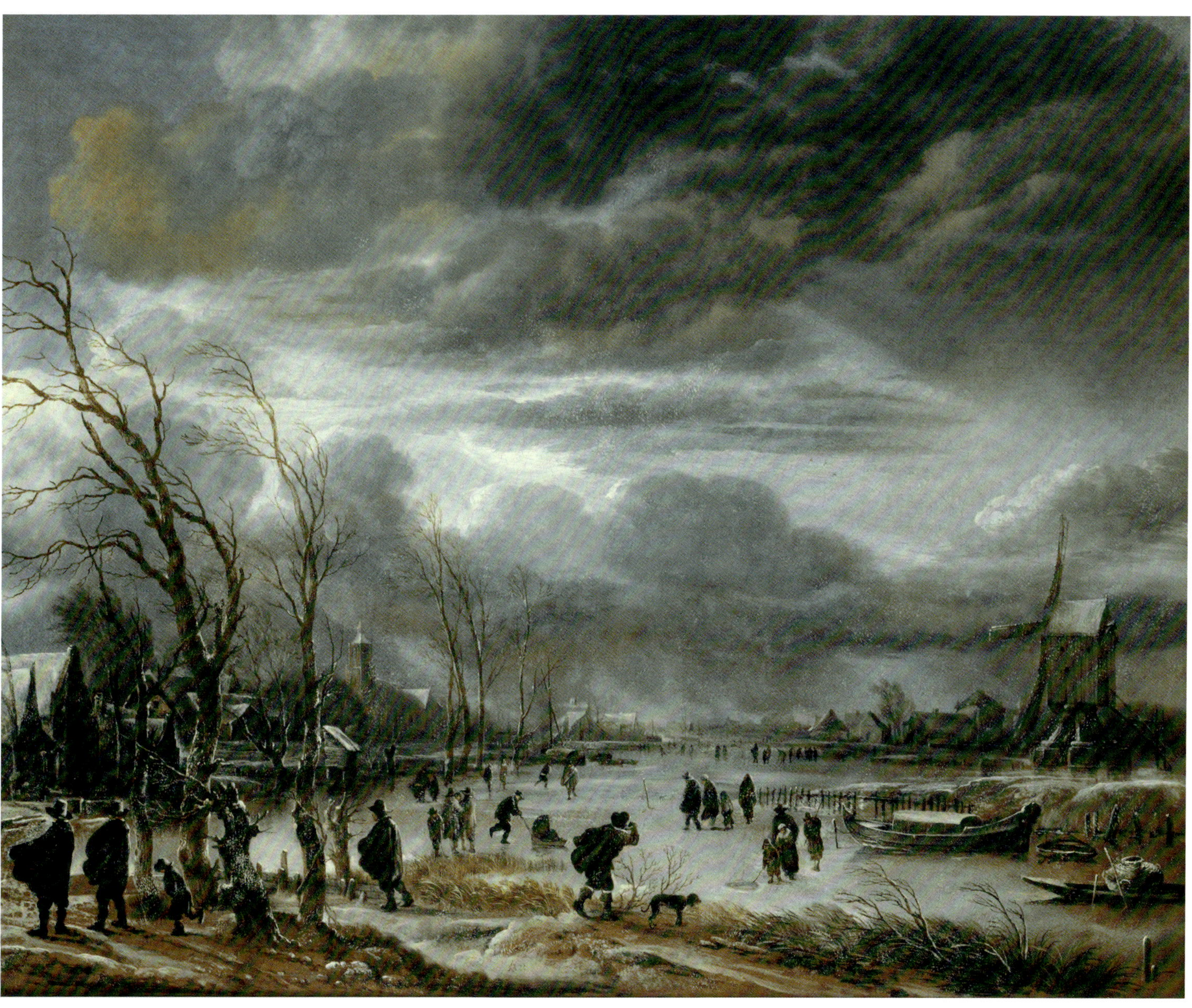

A Peasant Family in a Cottage Interior, 1661

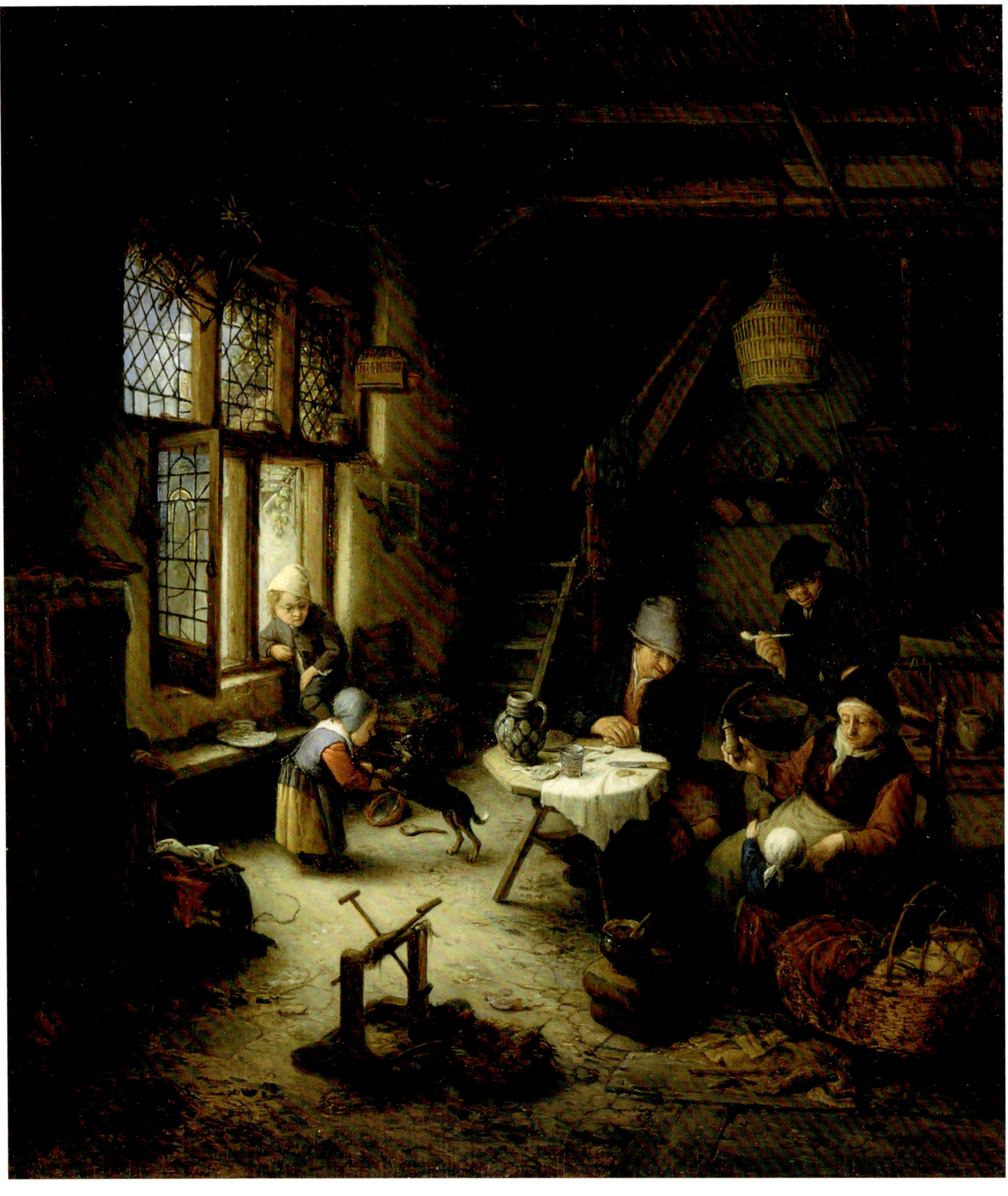

Harbour Scene, c.1650

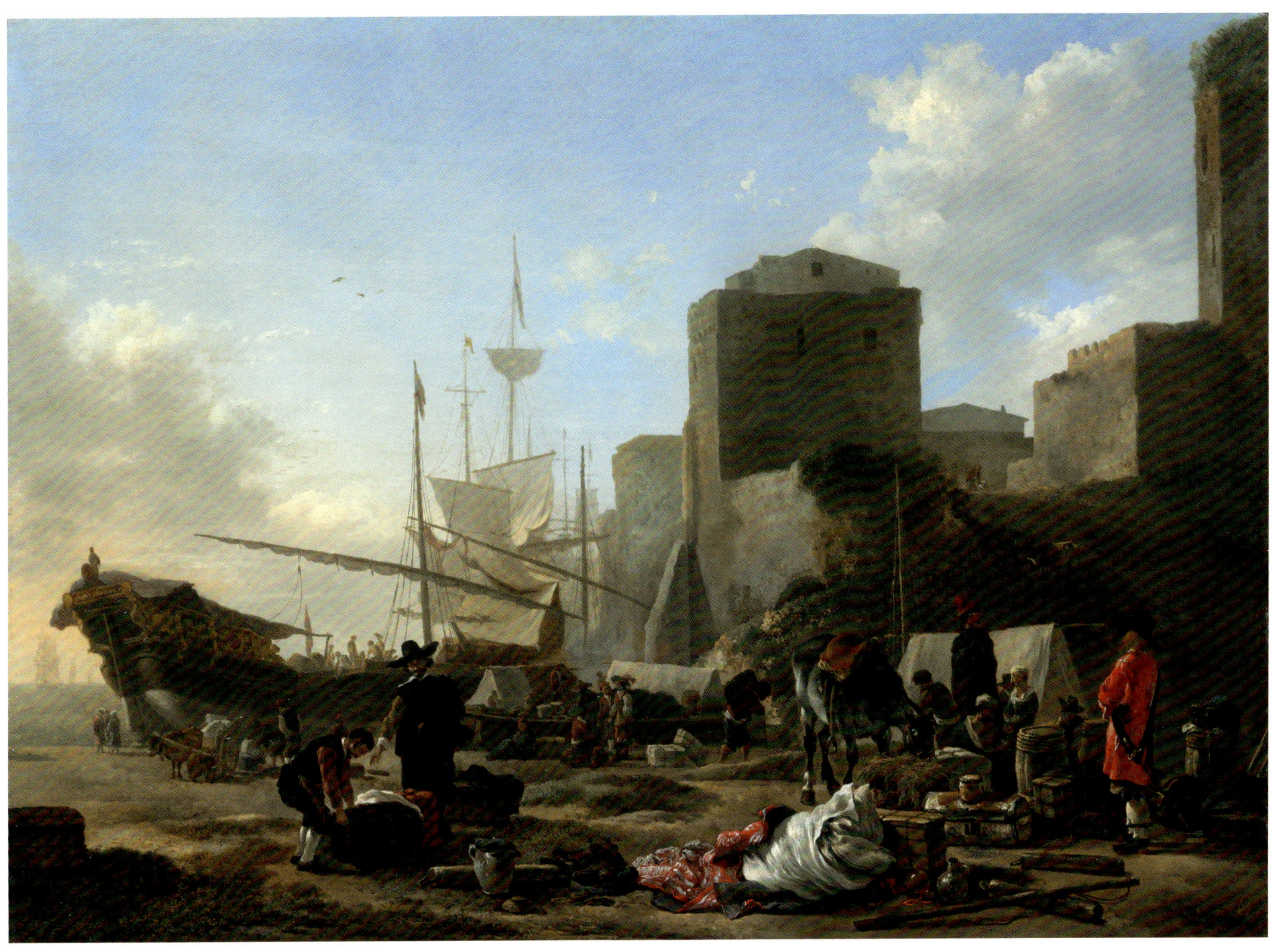

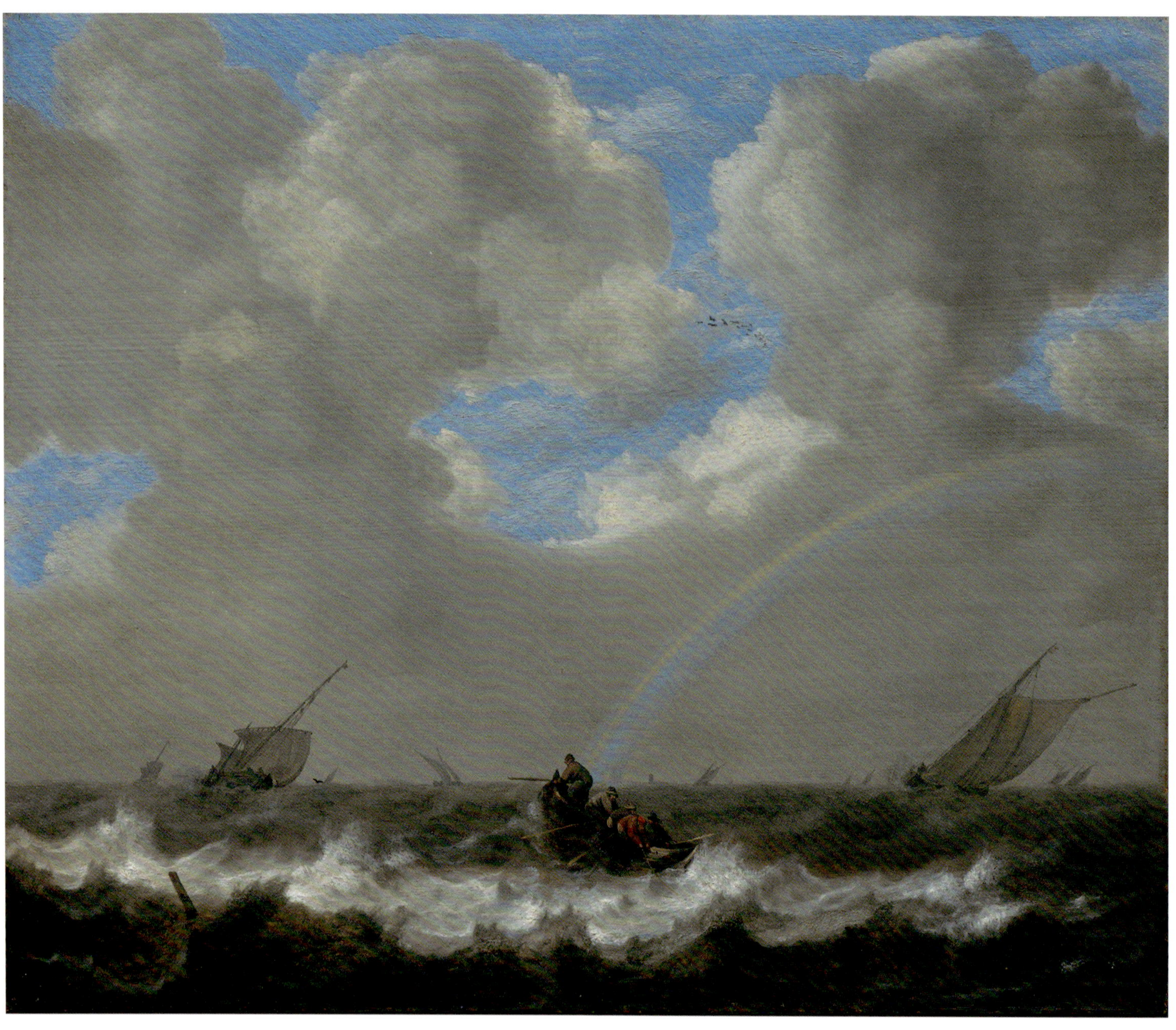

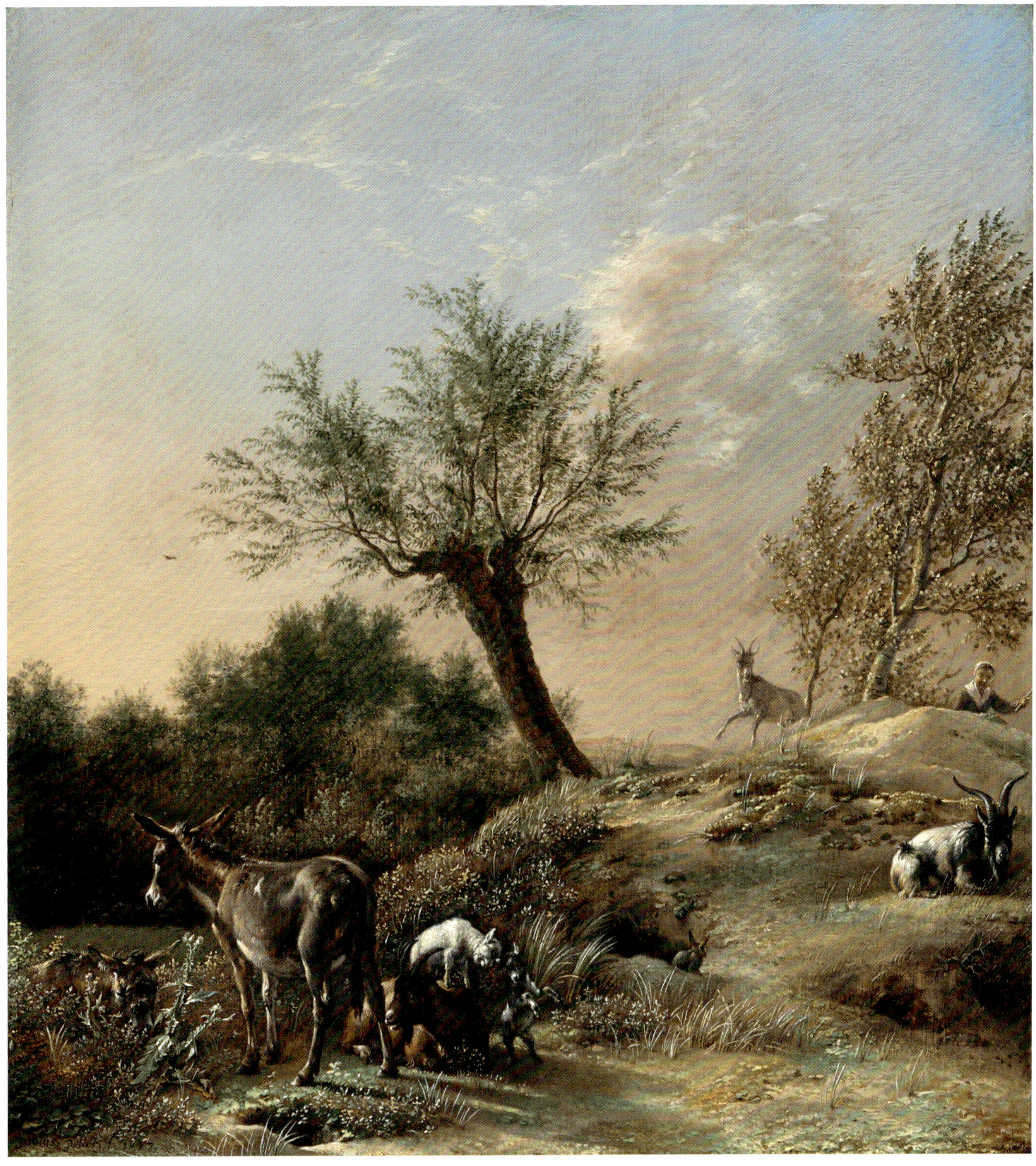

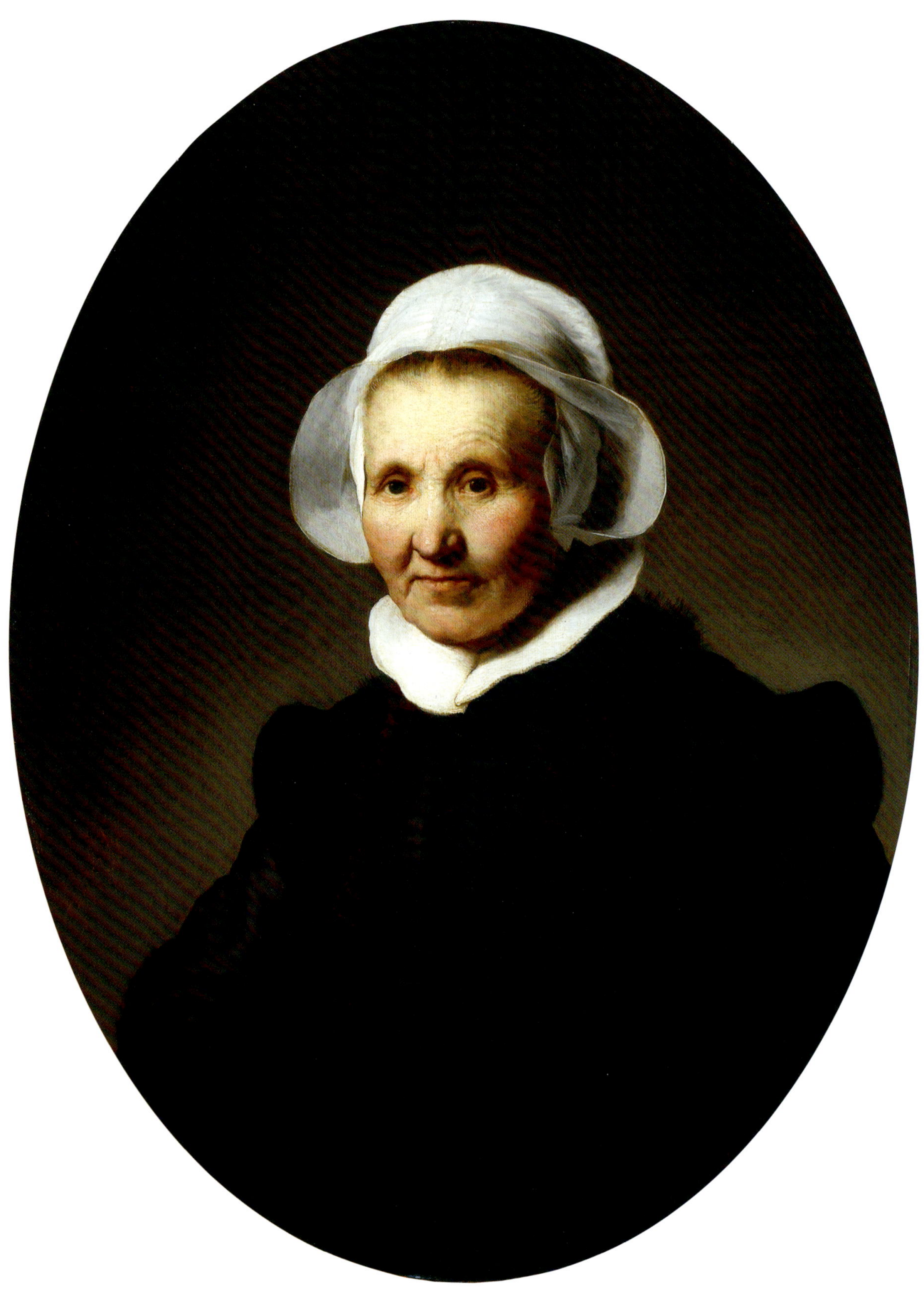

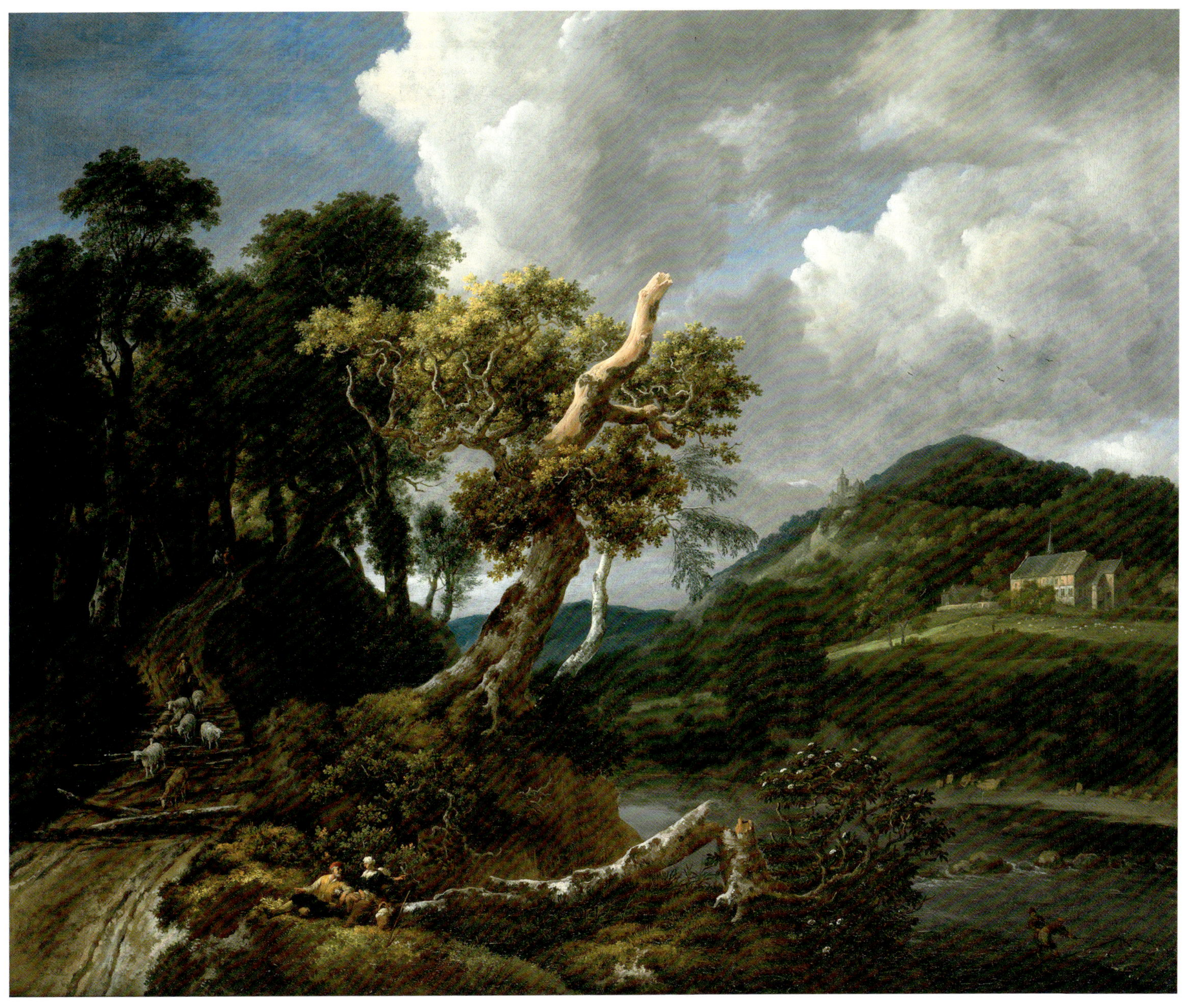

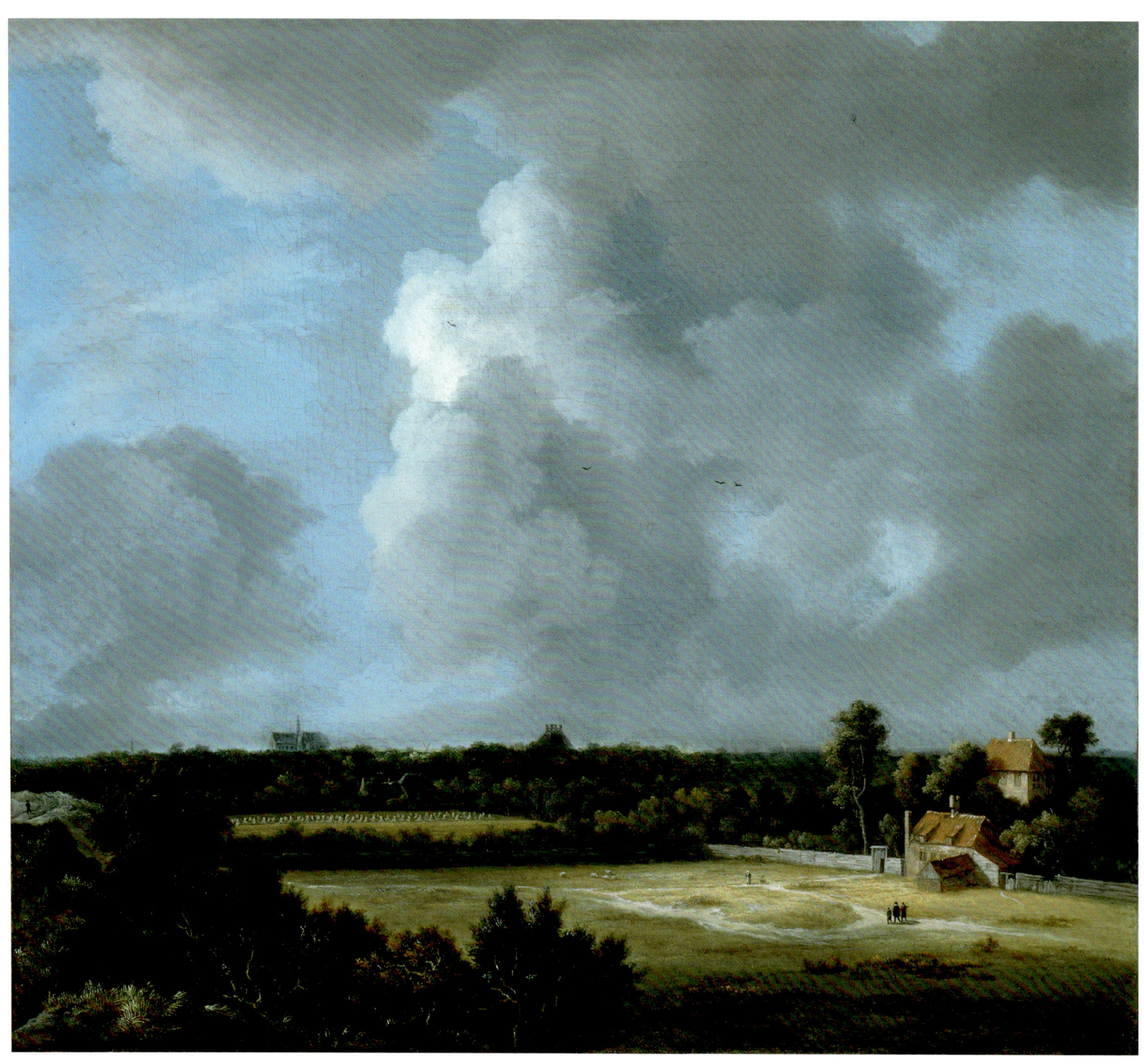

Winter Landscape with Windmills, c.1675

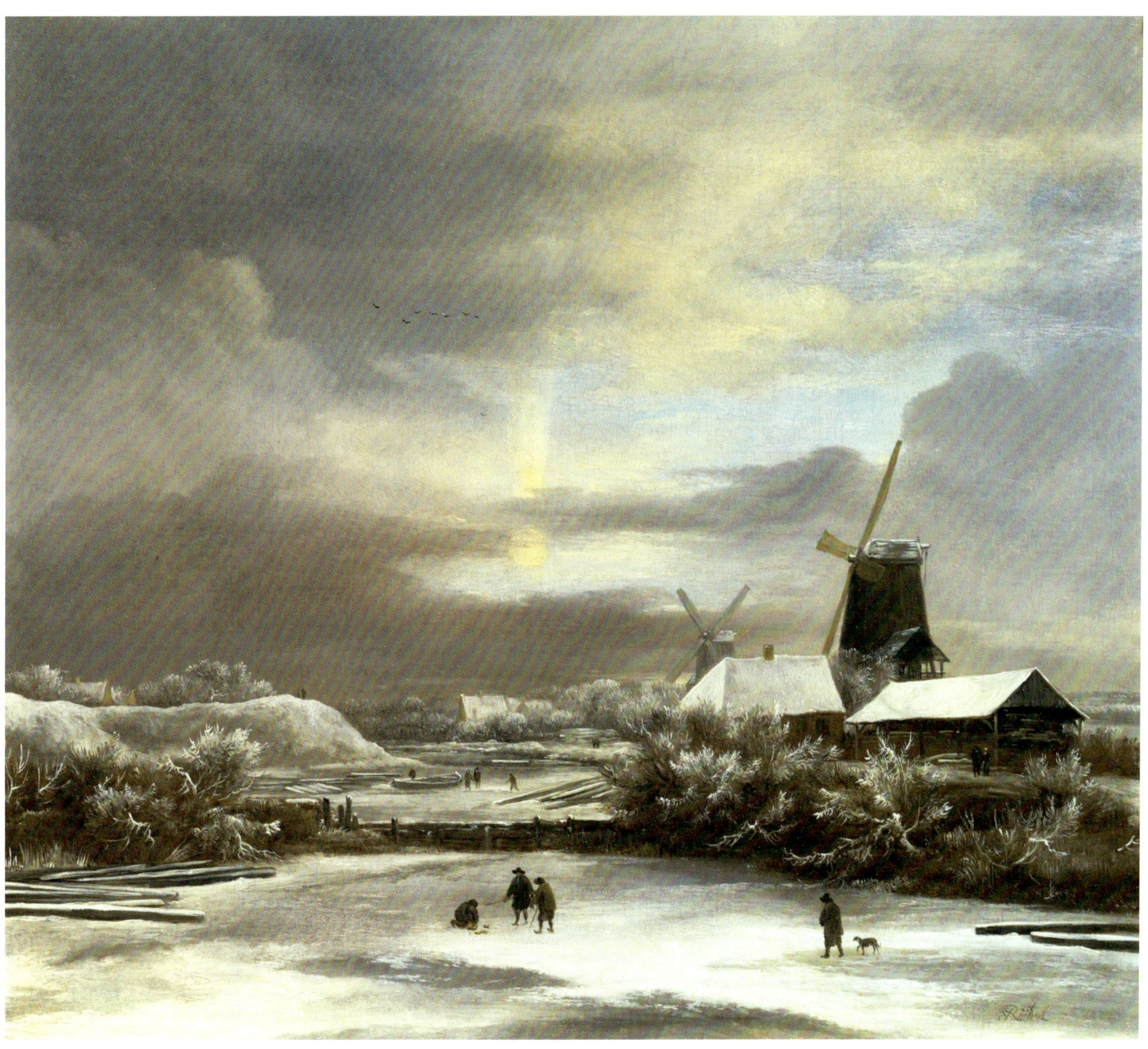

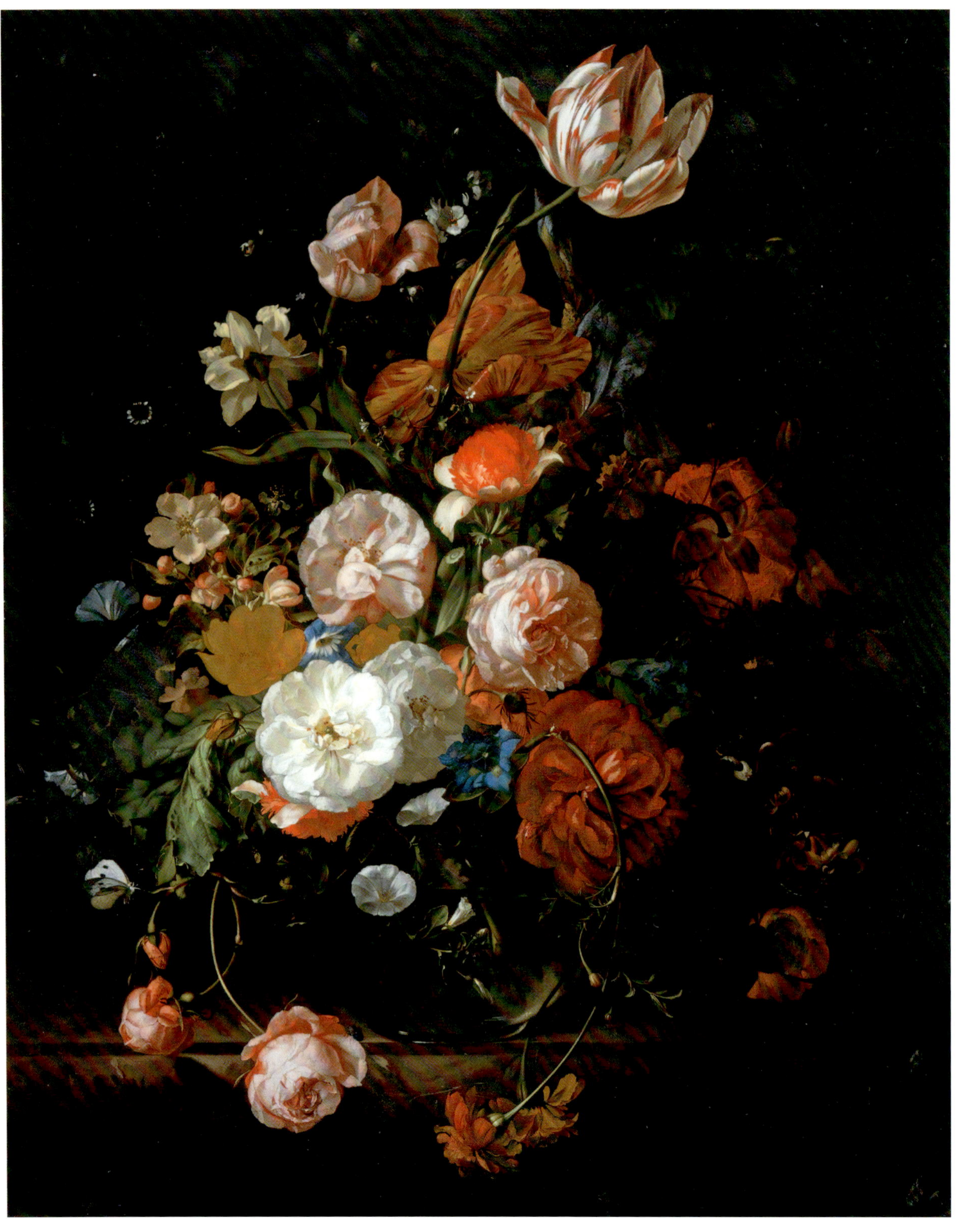

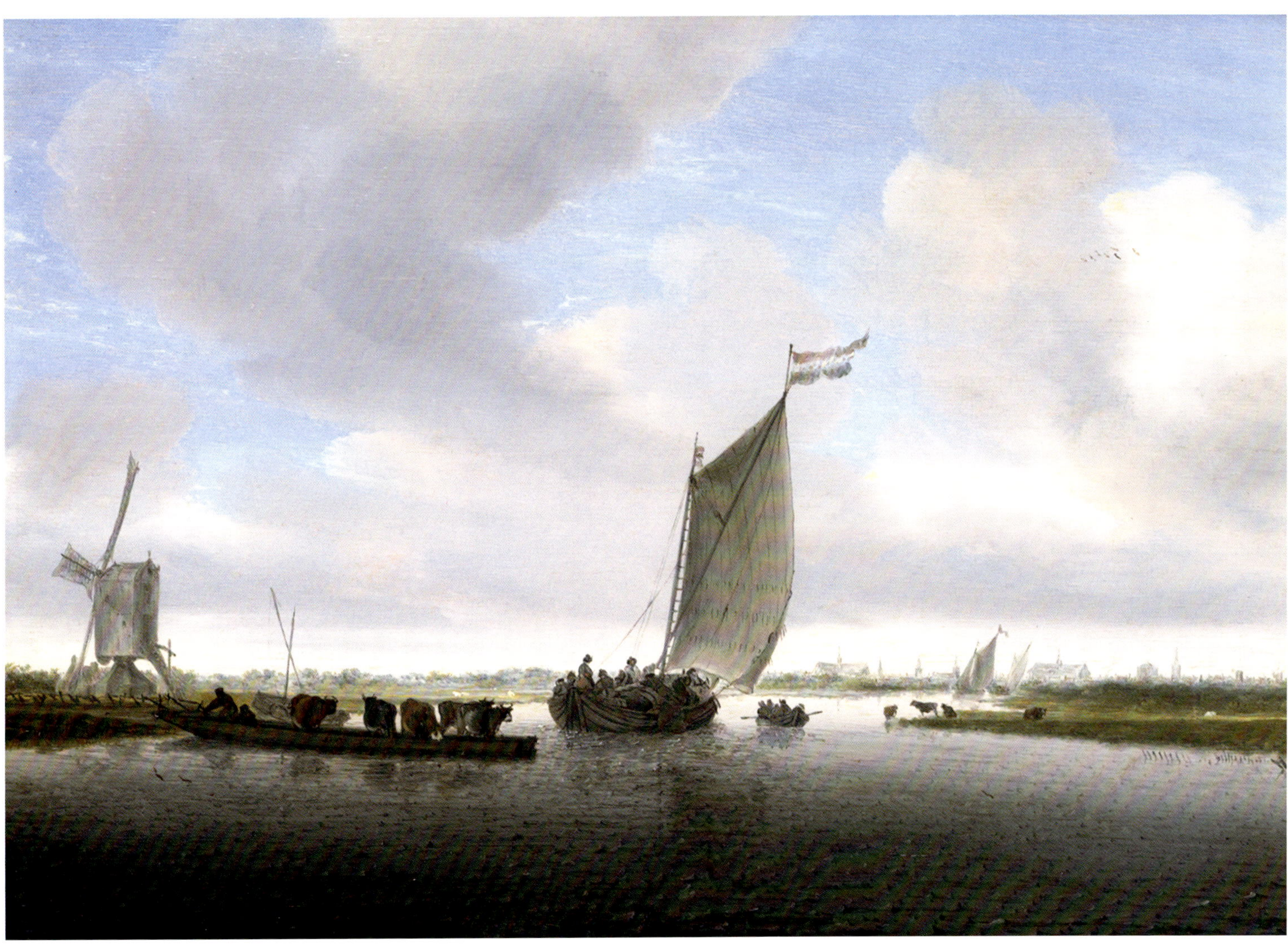

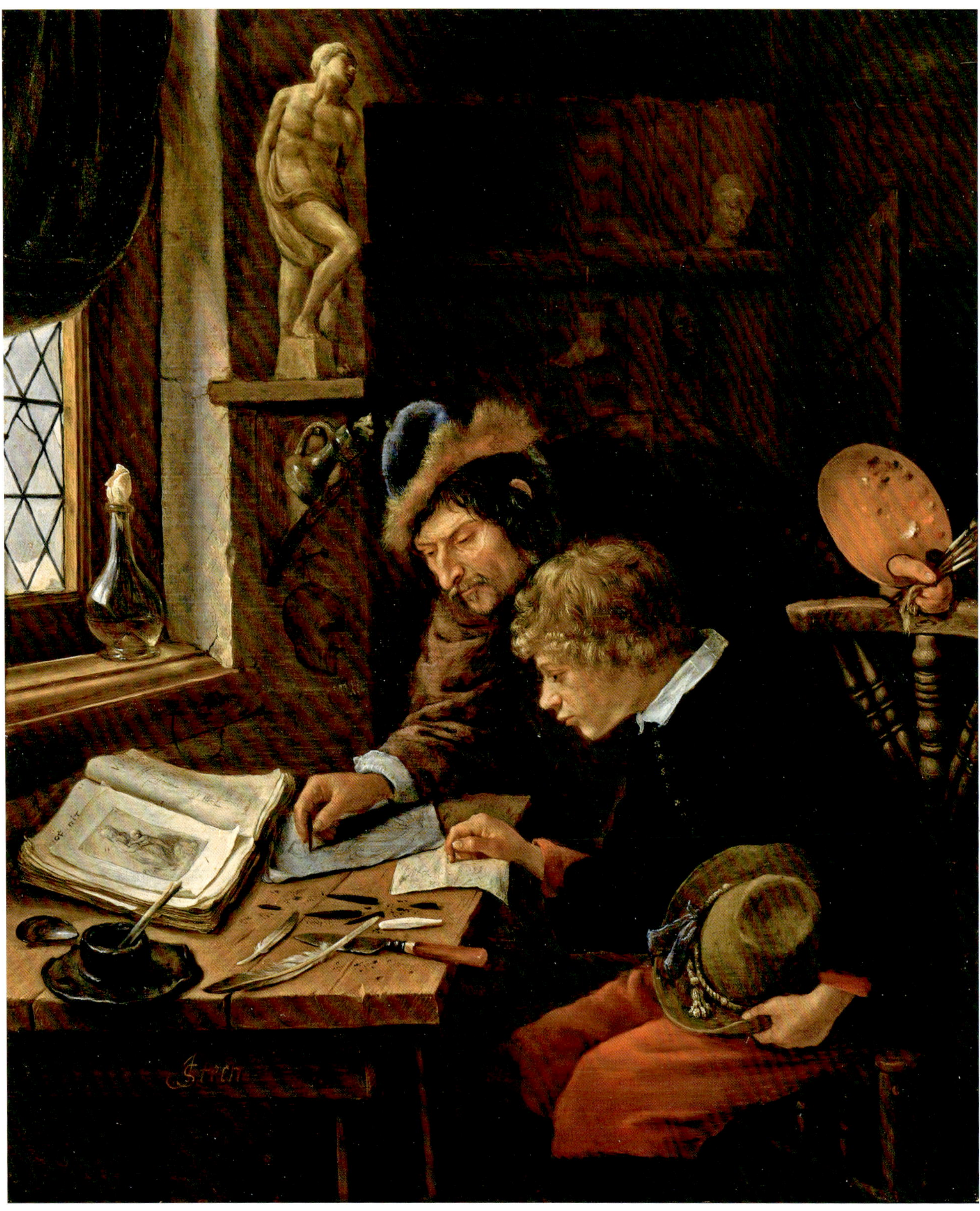

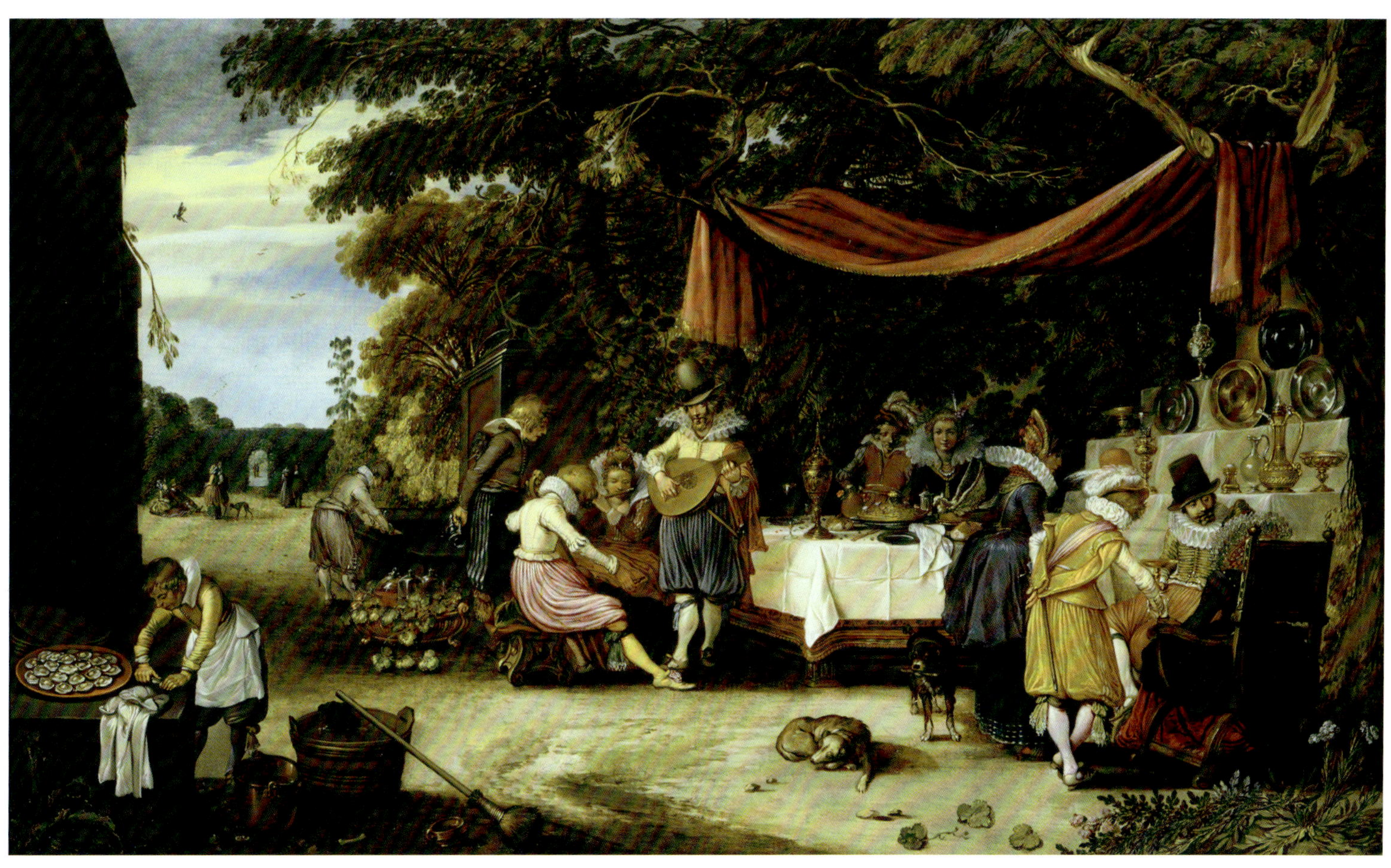

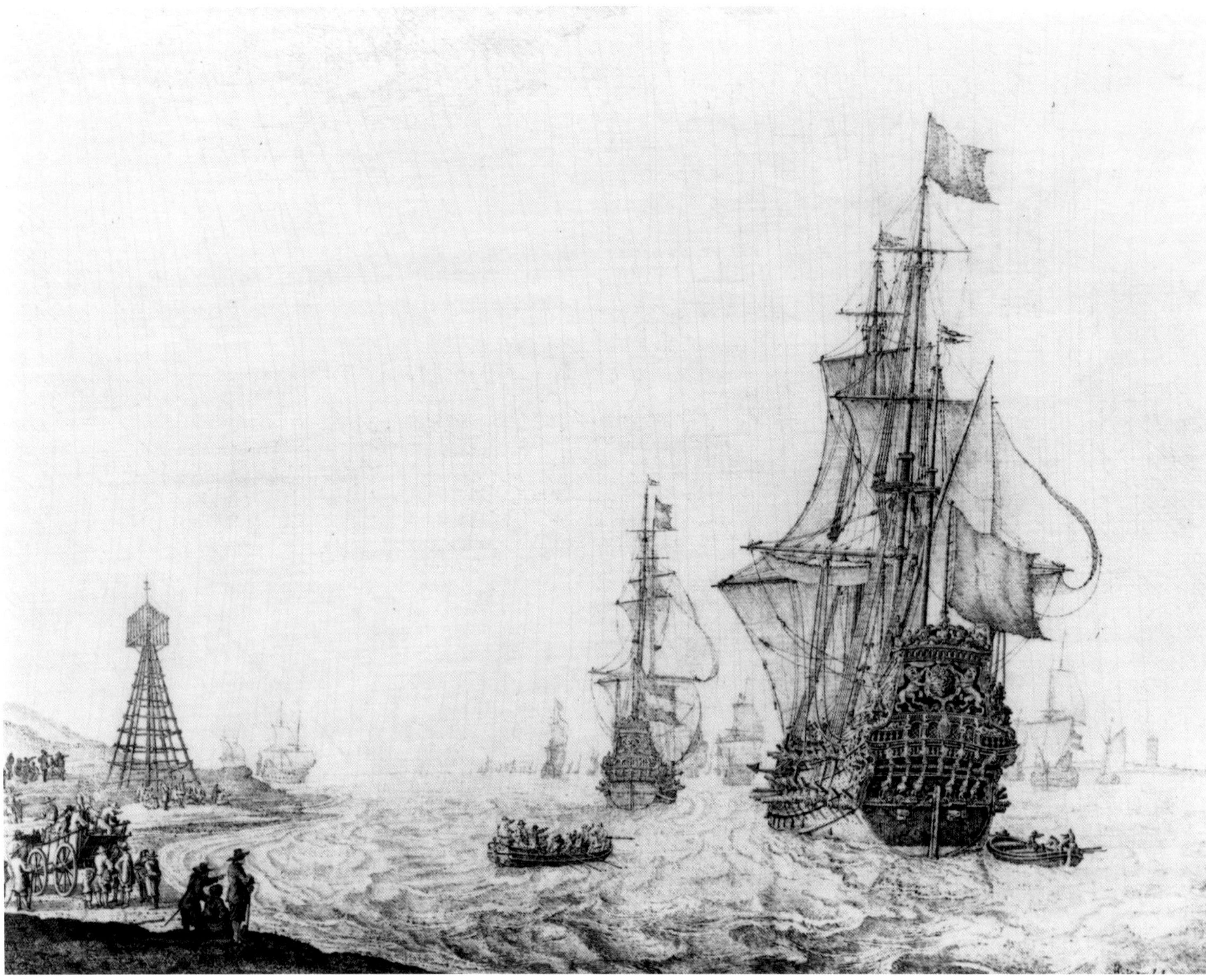

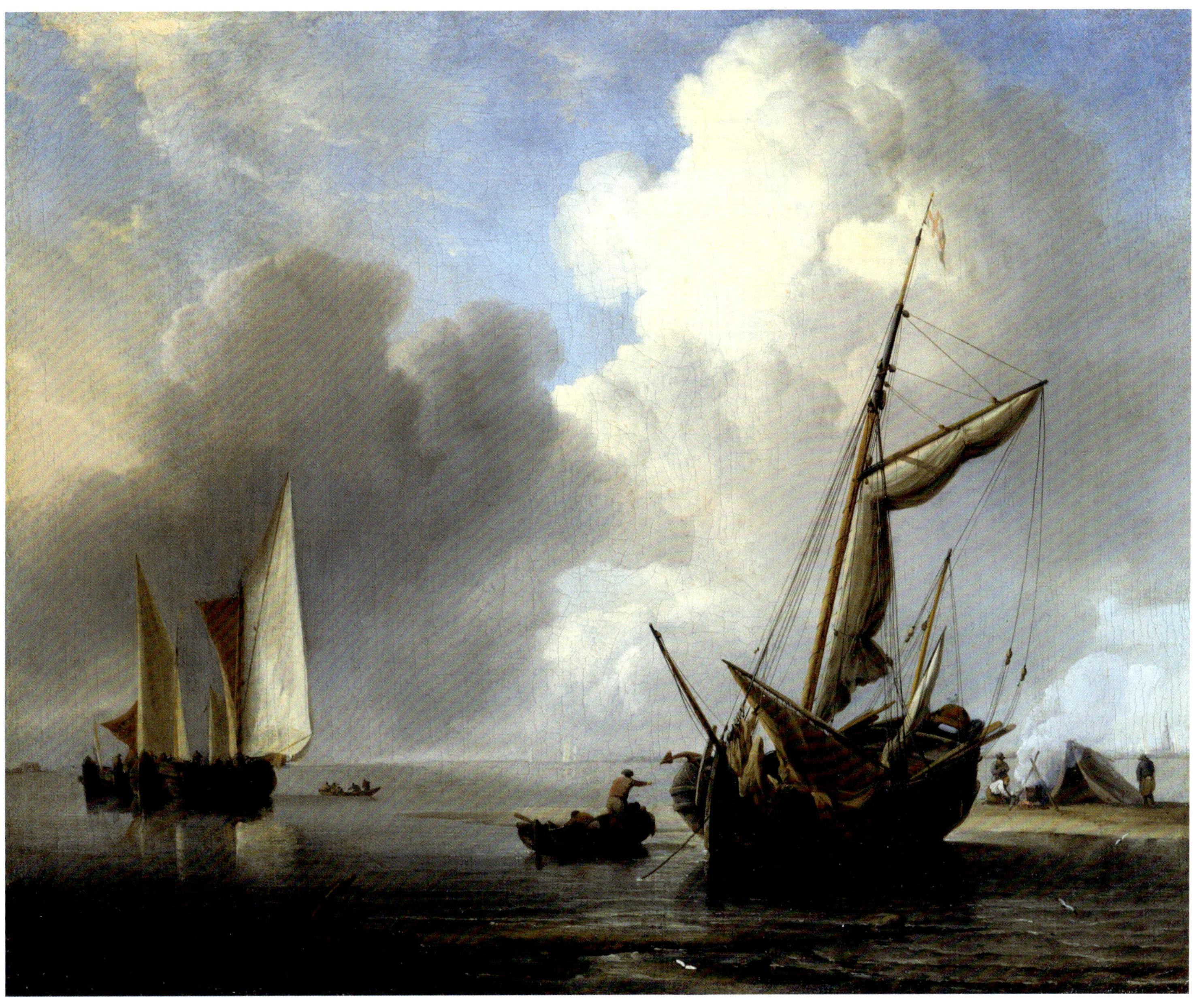

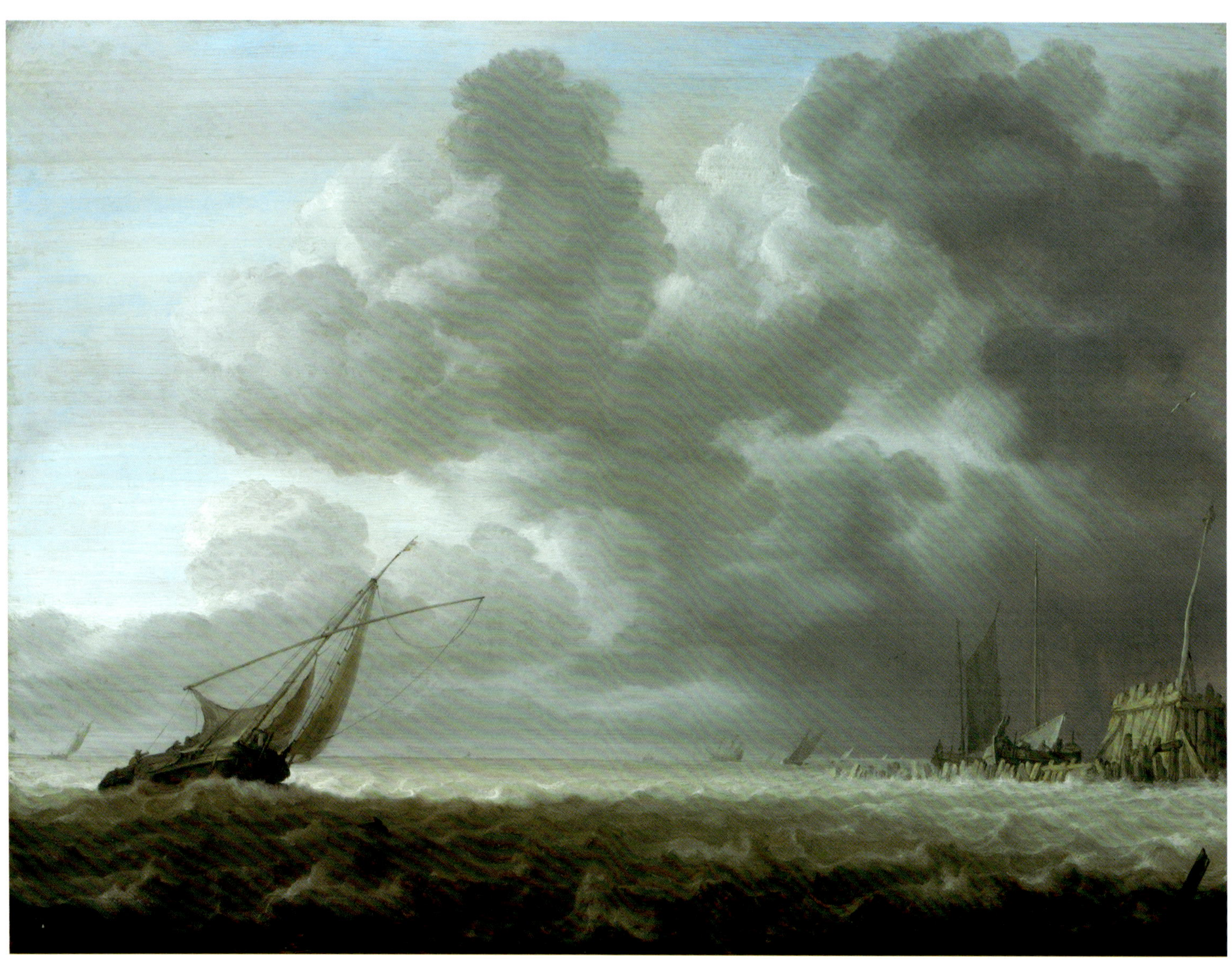

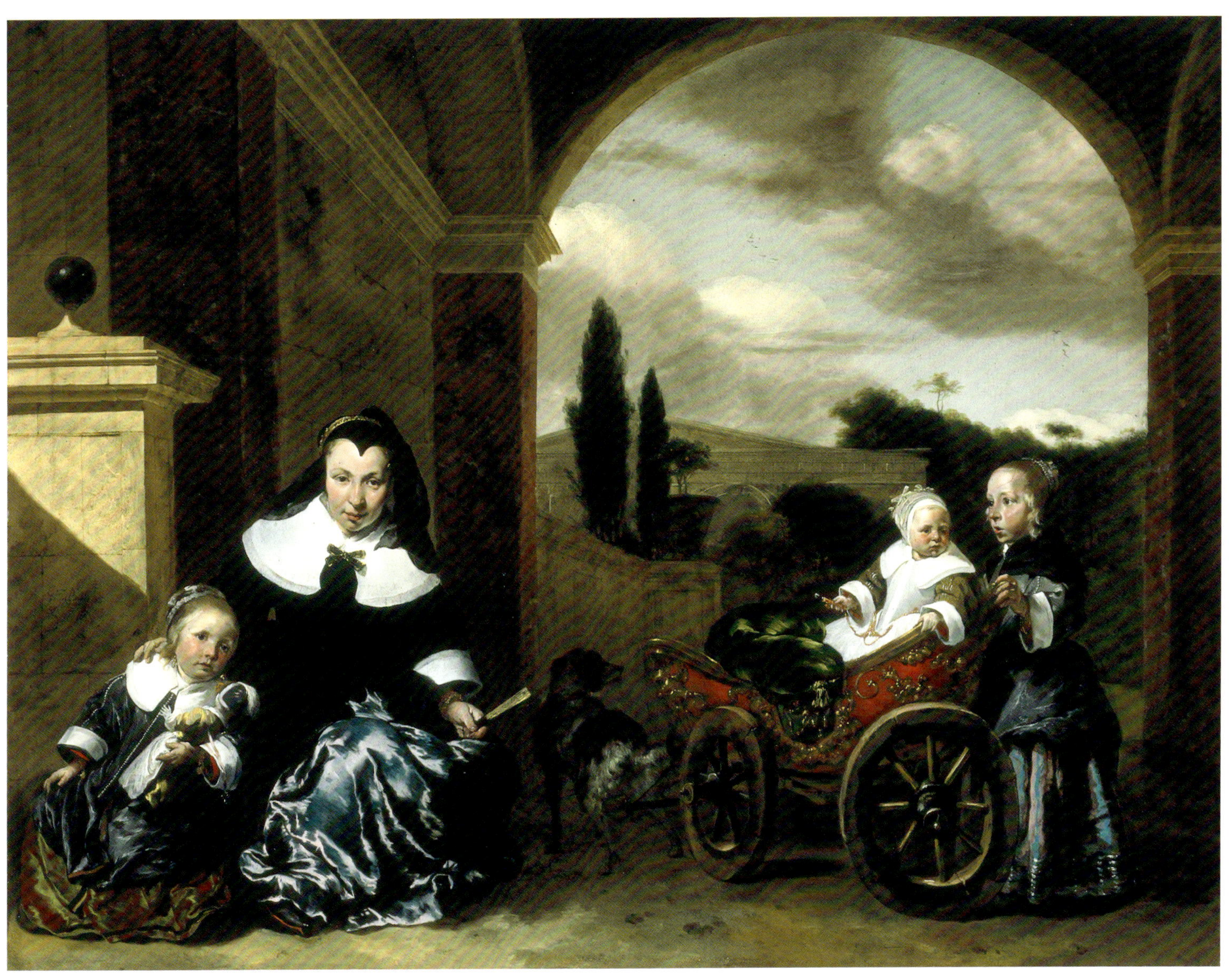

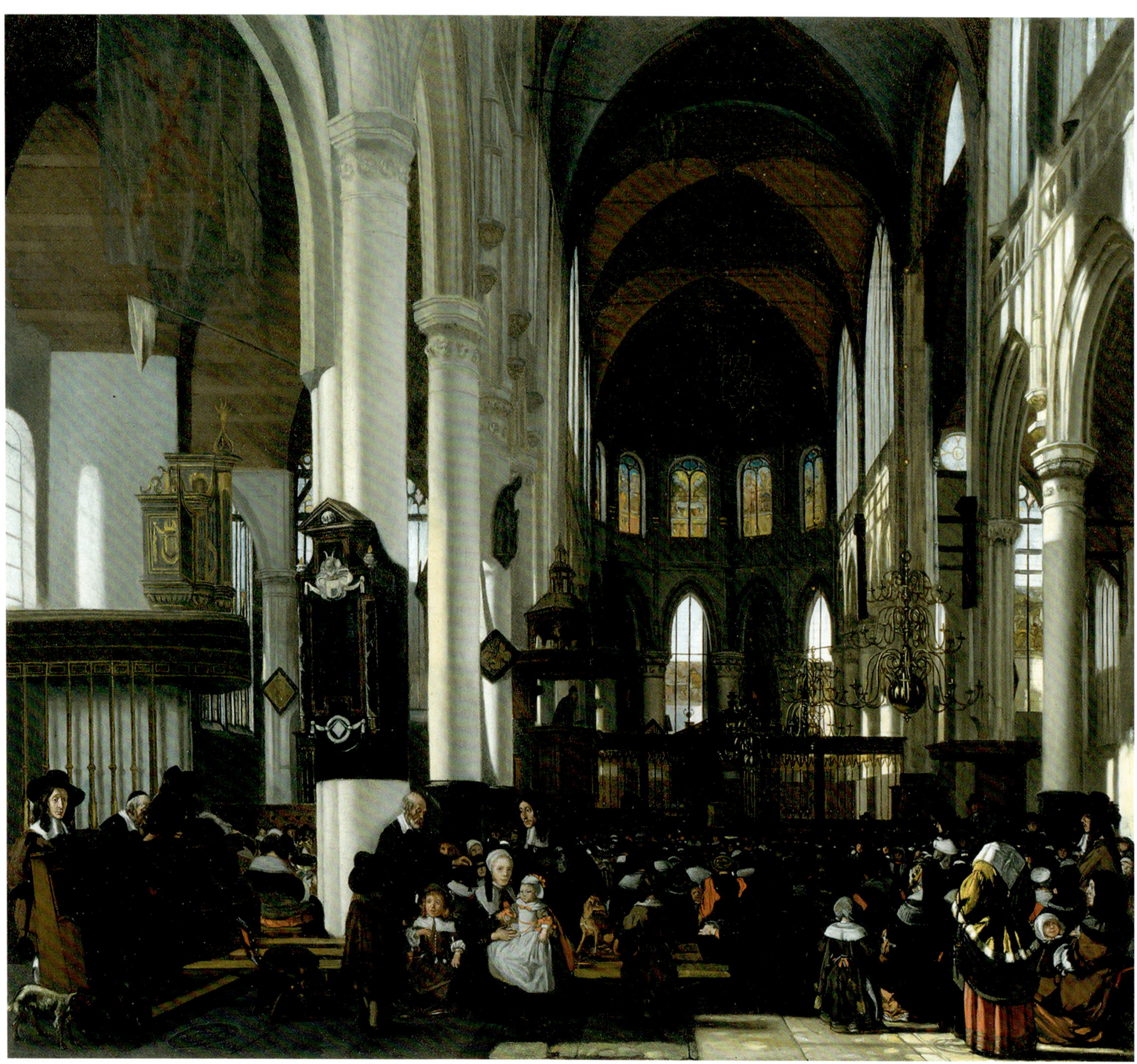

The Stag Hunt, c.1659–1660

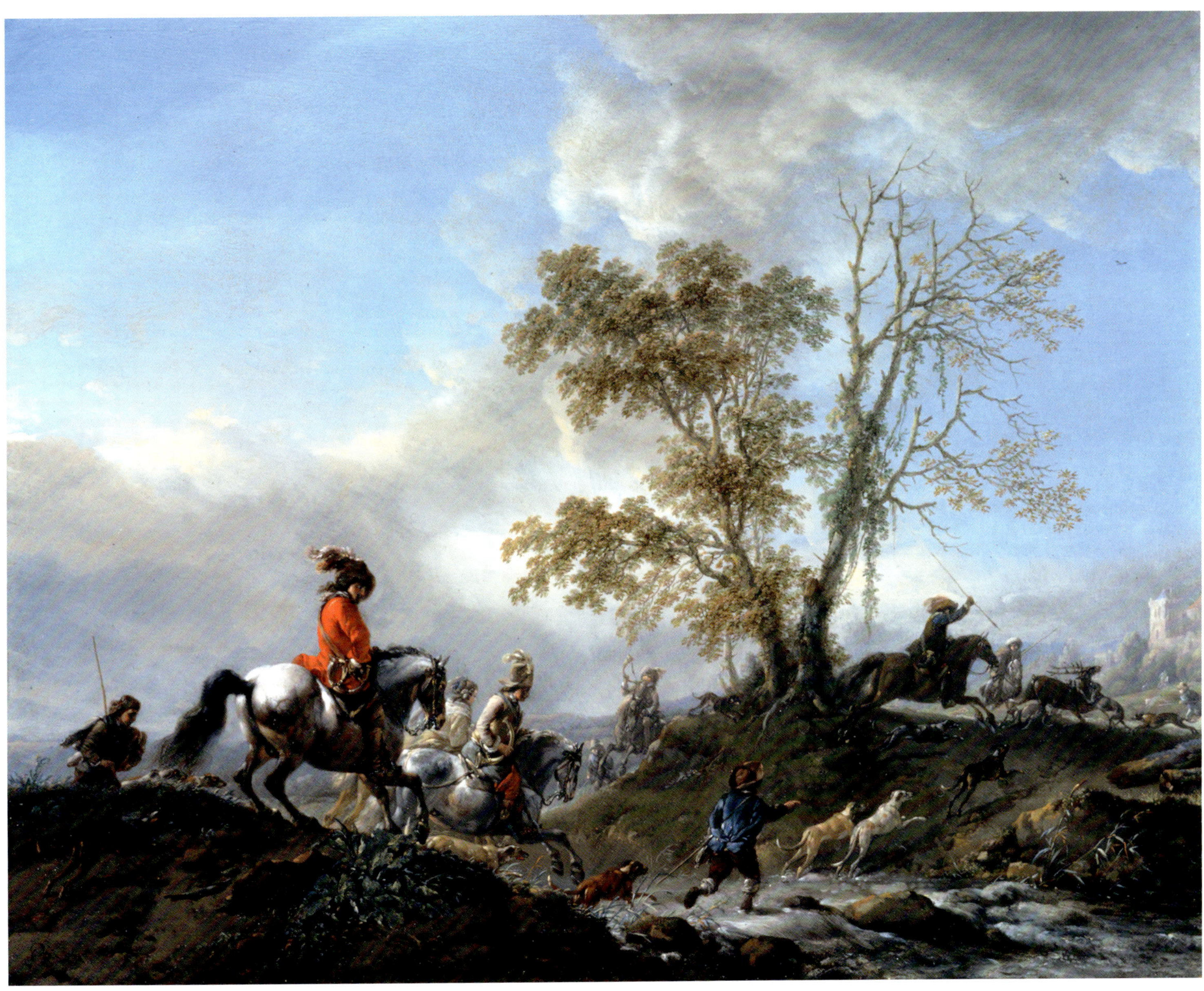

Appendices

List of Works Exhibited

1 Willem van Aelst, 1627– after 1683
Still Life with a Candle, Walnuts and a Mouse,
1647
Copper, 19 × 25 cm
At lower left: *.W.V. aelst. [16]47*
Acquired in 2002

2 Balthasar van der Ast, 1593/94–1657
Flower Still Life, c.1630
Panel, 37 × 25 cm
At lower right: *. B . vander . ast .*
Acquired in 1998

3 Hendrick Avercamp, 1585–1634
Winter Landscape with Skaters, c.1610–1615
Panel, 53 × 95 cm
At lower centre, on the beer barrel:
HA (in ligature)
Acquired in 2005

4 Jacob Backer, 1608/9–1651
Young Woman Holding a Fan, c.1644–1645
Panel, 69 × 57 cm
At upper right: *JAB* (in ligature)
Acquired in 1996

5 Nicolaes Berchem, 1621/22–1683
Landscape with a Stag Hunt, c.1660–1670
Panel, 38 × 49 cm
At lower left: *Berchem*
Acquired in 1993

6 Ambrosius Bosschaert the Elder,
1573–1621
Still Life with Roses in a Glass Vase, c.1619
Copper, 28 × 23 cm
At lower right: *.AB.* (in ligature)
Acquired in 1994

7 Jan Both, c.1615–1652
Italianate Landscape with Travellers,
c.1645–1650
Canvas, 138 × 168 cm
At lower right: *JBoth* (JB in ligature)
Acquired in 2007

8 Salomon de Bray, 1597–1664
Bust of a Young Woman in Profile, 1636
Panel (oval), 27 × 21 cm
At lower right: *SD Bray. / 1636.*
(SD in ligature)
Acquired in 2009

9 Jan van de Cappelle, 1626–1679
Boats in a Calm, 1651
Canvas, 48 × 53 cm
At lower left: *I V Capelle 1651*
(VC in ligature)
Acquired in 2005

10 Pieter Claesz, 1596/97–1660
Still Life with a Ham and Cheeses, c.1627–1628
Panel, 51 × 90 cm
On the knife: *PC* (in ligature)
Acquired in 2009

11 Adriaen Coorte, active c.1683–1707
Still Life with Shells, 1698
Paper on panel, 17 × 22 cm
At lower left: *A. Coorte. i698.*
Acquired in 1995

12 Aelbert Cuyp, 1620–1691
Orpheus Charming the Animals, c.1640
Canvas, 113 × 167 cm
At lower right: *A. cuyp*
Acquired in 1997

13 Gerrit Dou, 1613–1675
A Resting Dog, 1650
Panel, 17 × 22 cm
At lower centre: *GDov. 1650*
(GD in ligature)
Acquired in 2005

14 Jan van Goyen, 1596–1656
Winter Landscape with Skaters, 1637
Panel, 31 × 41 cm
At lower left: *VG 1637*
Acquired in 1997

15 Frans Hals, 1582/83–1666
Portrait of a Preacher, c.1660
Panel, 36 × 30 cm
At lower right: *FH* (in ligature)
Acquired in 2006

16 Willem Heda, 1594–1680
Still Life with a Tazza, 1633
Panel, 51 × 76 cm
At lower left: - HEDA / 1633 -.
Acquired in 1996

17 Jan Davidsz de Heem, 1606–1683/84
A Glass Vase with Flowers, c.1655–1660
Panel, 47 × 36 cm
At lower centre: J D De Heem
Acquired in 1997

18 Jan van der Heyden, 1637–1712
View of the Westerkerk in Amsterdam,
c.1667–1670
Panel, 54 × 64 cm
At lower right: *VHeyd* (VH in ligature)
Acquired in 2000

19 Gerard Houckgeest, 1600–1661
The Nieuwe Kerk in Delft, with the Tomb of
William the Silent, c.1651–1652
Panel (upper corners rounded),
60 × 41 cm
Acquired in 2002

20 Karel du Jardin, 1626–1678
A Horseman at a River, 1660
Canvas, 36 × 46 cm
At lower left: K. DV. IARDIN. *f.* / 1660.
Acquired in 2006

21 Isaack Koedijck, 1617/18–1668
A Barber Surgeon Tending a Man's Foot,
c.1649–1650
Panel, 91 × 72 cm
On the table: I Koedijk
Acquired in 1994

22 Jan Lievens, 1607–1674
Bust of a Young Girl, c.1631–1632
Panel, 45 × 38 cm
At lower left: L
Acquired in 2007

23 Nicolaes Maes, 1634–1693
A Young Woman Picking the Pocket of a Sleeping
Man, c.1655
Panel, 36 × 30 cm
At lower right: N. *MAES.* (MAE in
ligature)
Acquired in 2002

24 Gabriel Metsu, 1629–1667
An Old Woman Eating Porridge, c.1657
Panel, 36 × 28 cm
On the cupboard: *Gmetsú* (Gm in ligature)
Acquired in 2009

25 Frans van Mieris the Elder, 1635–1681
The Old Fiddler, 1660
Panel, 28 × 21 cm
Under the fiddle: *F. van Mieris. fe. A°* /
M. DC. LX.
Acquired in 2000

26 Aert van der Neer, 1603/4–1677
Figures in a Snowstorm, c.1655–1660
Canvas, 61 × 76 cm
At lower left: *AV DN*
(AV and DN in ligature)
Acquired in 2008

27 Adriaen van Ostade, 1610–1685
A Peasant Family in a Cottage Interior, 1661
Panel, 35 × 31 cm
At lower right: *Av Ostade* / 1661
(Av in ligature)
Acquired in 2006

28 Adam Pijnacker, 1620/21–1673
Harbour Scene, c.1650
Panel, 33 × 47 cm
At lower right: *APÿnacker* (AP in ligature)
Acquired in 2001

29 Jan Porcellis, 1583/84–1632
Boats on a Choppy Sea, c.1631
Panel, 32 × 39 cm
At lower left, on the driftwood: IP
Acquired in 2003

30 Paulus Potter, 1625–1654
'The Rabbit Warren', 1647
Panel, 40 × 36 cm
At lower left: *Paulus. Potter. f. 1647.*
Acquired in 1996

31 Rembrandt, 1606–1669
Portrait of Aeltje Uylenburgh, 1632
Panel (oval), 74 × 56 cm
At upper right: *RHL van Ryn / 1632*
(RHL in ligature); at upper left: *Æ 62*
Acquired in 2005

32 Jacob van Ruisdael, 1628–1682
Wooded Landscape, c.1655–1660
Canvas, 109 × 142 cm
At lower centre: *vRuisdael* (vR in ligature)
Acquired in 1998

33 Jacob van Ruisdael, 1628–1682
Landscape with a View of Haarlem,
c.1670–1675
Canvas, 36 × 40 cm
Acquired in 1997

34 Jacob van Ruisdael, 1628–1682
Winter Landscape with Windmills, c.1675
Canvas, 39 × 43 cm
At lower right: *JvRuisdael* (JvR in ligature)
Acquired in 2004

35 Rachel Ruysch, 1664–1750
Flower Still Life, 1709
Canvas, 78 × 64 cm
At lower right: *Rachel Ruysch 1709*
Acquired in 2007

36 Salomon van Ruysdael, 1600/3–1670
River Landscape with a Sailing-Boat, 1655?
Panel, 31 × 44 cm
On the boat on the left: *SvR / 1655*
(SvR in ligature; indistinctly dated)
Acquired in 2006

37 Jan Steen, 1626–1679
The Drawing Lesson, c.1660–1665
Panel, 24 × 21 cm
At lower left: *JSteen* (JS in ligature)
Acquired in 1998

38 Esaias van de Velde, 1587–1630
An Elegant Company in a Garden, 1614
Canvas, 52 × 86 cm
At lower left: *E. VANDEN. VELDE. / 1614*
Acquired in 2008

39 Willem van de Velde the Elder, 1611–1693
The Brederode Setting Sail from Vlieland, 9 June
1645, c.1645
Panel, 25 × 33 cm
At lower right: *w.v.velde*
On the ship on the right: BRE DE RO DE
Acquired in 2007

40 Willem van de Velde the Younger,
1633–1707
Fishing Boats by the Shore, c.1660–1665
Canvas, 30 × 37 cm
Acquired in 2004

41 Simon de Vlieger, 1600/1–1653
Sailing Ships in a Breeze, c.1648–1649
Panel, 46 × 62 cm
At lower right, on the driftwood: *S. Vlieger*
Acquired in 1999

42 Jan Baptist Weenix, 1621–1659
Portrait of the De Kempenaer Family, c.1653
Canvas, 93 × 121 cm
On the balustrade: *Gio: Batta. / Weenix fe.*
Acquired in 1996

43 Emanuel de Witte, 1616/18–1691/92
Interior of the Oude Kerk in Amsterdam,
c.1660–1665
Canvas, 66 × 73 cm
Acquired in 1998

44 Philips Wouwerman, 1619–1668
The Stag Hunt, c.1659–1660
Copper, 27 × 35 cm
At lower left: PHILS. W (PHILS in ligature)
Acquired in 2002

List by Year of Acquisition

Notes

* In the preparations for the exhibition and for this publication, help was received from numerous institutions and individuals. The documentation of the Netherlands Institute for Art History (RKD) in The Hague was an invaluable research aid. The author wishes to take this opportunity to thank all those who helped to make the exhibition and the book possible. A special word of thanks is due to Rose-Marie and Eijk de Mol van Otterloo, for their extraordinary hospitality in the United States. Frits Duparc, the former director of the Mauritshuis, was also extremely helpful. His manuscript texts on the Van Otterloos' paintings in many cases provided a point of departure for the catalogue texts published here. Ben Broos, former chief curator of the Mauritshuis, kindly made available his manuscript on the fascinating provenance of Rembrandt's *Portrait of Aeltje Uylenburgh*. In addition, the author wishes to thank all fellow staff members of the Mauritshuis who were involved in this project for the fruitful and pleasant spirit of cooperation of our working relationship.

1 This text is based on discussions with Eijk and Rose-Marie de Mol van Otterloo, as well as on an interview that they gave to *The Art Newspaper* in September 2009 (Dobrzynski 2009), and on publications by Suzanna de Sitter (2010) and Femke Diercks (in De Mol van Otterloo 2010).

2 Cf. e.g. Boston 2002.

3 For the concept 'the visible world', see also Dordrecht 1992–1993, p. 10.

4 Besides the Cuyp (see p. 88), based on Ovid's *Metamorphoses*, and a Moeyaert based on a biblical tale (p. 20, fig. 2), these are David Teniers the Younger's *Temptation of St Anthony*, dating from around 1650 (see note 6), and Berchem's representation of the apostle Peter (De Mol van Otterloo 2010, no. 8).

5 See pp. 38–39 and ibid., no. 25.

6 Besides the Brueghel there is an early still life from about 1610 by Osias Beert, as well as a sixteenth-century winter landscape by Jacob Grimmer and a history painting made around 1650 by David Teniers the Younger (see De Mol van Otterloo 2010, nos. 7, 14, 26, 59).

7 See Carter 1981–1982; see also Carter 1992–1993.

8 See the comprehensive discussion by Femke Diercks in De Mol van Otterloo 2010.

9 See ibid., no. 39. The painting was purchased from relatives of Eijk de Mol van Otterloo.

10 When the painting was purchased by Robert Noortman at a public auction in London (Christie's, 13 December 2000, no. 52), the Van Otterloos acquired a share in it, partly in the hope of being able to purchase it for their collection at some point in the future. They fulfilled this ambition three years after the auction.

11 See Buvelot 2005 and Van der Ploeg/ Buvelot 2008, p. 19 and fig. 16 (on loan to The Hague); [anon.], 'Superb Rembrandt Painting Makes Its U.S. Debut at The Museum of Fine Arts, Boston', www.artdaily.com, 21 February 2008 (on loan to Boston). In Boston the Rembrandt was shown from 2008 onwards along with eight other paintings from the Van Otterloos' collection.

12 See Greenwich-New York 2008–2009, no. 22 (ill.).

13 For recent developments on the art market, see Buvelot 2010.

14 De Mol van Otterloo 2010. Over the past few years, other private collections have also been published in collection catalogues; see e.g. Van Dedem 2002; Kremer 2008–2009 and Vienna 2010.

15 See Van Suchtelen in The Hague 2001–2002, pp. 12–15 and De Kraker in Amsterdam-Washington 2009–2010, pp. 23–29.

16 See Verslype and Wallert in Amsterdam-Washington 2009–2010, pp. 138–139.

17 Beck 1972–1973, nos. 1–98; Beck 1987, pp. 138–149.

18 Buijsen in The Hague 1994–1995, no. 8.

19 Paris, Frits Lugt Collection; see Buvelot in The Hague 2002, p. 145.

20 Manchester, City Art Gallery; see Buijsen in The Hague 1994–1995, p. 86, note 1.

21 Harwood 1988.

22 See The Hague 2009.

23 Slive 2001, p. 353, no. 479.

24 See Verhoef 2010, figs. 9–11. There is a winter landscape by Jacob Grimmer in the Van Otterloos' collection (see note 6).

25 Van Mander/Miedema 1973, pp. 206–209, 545; see Van Suchtelen in The Hague 2001–2002, p. 104.

26 Kassel-The Hague 2009–2010.

27 Schumacher 2006, vol. 1, nos. A 109–226; nos. B 11–23.

28 The same applies to a stag hunt depicted by Wouwerman, now in Paris, Musée du Louvre; see Schumacher 2006, no. A 155 and fig. 146.

29 Duparc 1993, p. 277; for other paintings by Wouwerman on copper, see Schumacher 2006, nos. A 36, 86, 147, 155, 169, 195, 196, 221, 362, 401.

30 For a discussion of painting on copper, see Phoenix-Kansas City-The Hague 1998–1999.

31 Sale London, Sotheby's, 12 December 2002, lot 26.

32 At the publication of Kilian 2005, pp. 166–167, no. 61, the painting's whereabouts were as yet unknown.

33 Smith 1829–1842, vol. 5, p. 240, no. 25.

34 See Sutton in Madrid 1994–1995, pp. 76–77, no. 7.

35 For a detailed description of the painting, see Van Suchtelen in The Hague-Washington 2008–2009, pp. 122–125, no. 23.

36 Ibid., no. 24.

37 Slive 2001, nos. 35–37, 40, 42, 46–48, 52–54, 60, 62, 64, 65, 68, 70; see also Van Suchtelen in The Hague-Washington 2008–2009, no. 35.

38 Slive 2001, pp. 21, 468–489.

39 See Walsh 1971, pp. 119, 246, no. A 50.

40 Amsterdam, Rijksmuseum; see Van Suchtelen in Amsterdam 1993–1994, no. 210.

41 See Kattenburg 1988; Robinson 1990, vol. 1, pp. 44–45, no. 817.

42 Leiden, Stedelijk Museum De Lakenhal and Greenwich, National Maritime Museum. For the technique of pen painting, see Bijl 2010.

43 See Kelch 1971.

44 See the detailed description of the painting in Minneapolis-Toledo-Los Angeles 1990–1991, pp. 189–191, no. 47.

45 See Russell 1975, pp. 21–22, 70, no. 69.

46 Stechow 1975, p. 112, no. 290.

47 Robinson 1990, vol. 2, p. 713, no. 440.

48 See Brunner-Bulst 2004 and Haarlem-Zürich-Washington 2004–2005.

49 Kaufmann 1988, no. 9.6; see Rüger in New York-London 2001, pp. 212, 213, note 4.

50 See www.let.leidenuniv.nl/Dutch/Huygens/HUY82.html; with thanks to my colleague Lea van der Vinde.

51 Sale New York, Christie's, 25 May 2005, lot 12.

52 The shells have been identified, from left to right, as *Trona stercoraria*, *Cittarium pica*, *Murex tribulus* (the skeleton-shaped shell), with in front of it *Cyphoma gibbosum*, and to the right probably *Nerita spec*; see Buvelot 2008, p. 104.

53 Ibid., pp. 50–54 and nos. 21–22, 31–32, 34–35.

54 Sale Gerardus Beljard, Middelburg, 13–18 October 1806, no. 23: '4 Stuks met Steene Tafels, waarop Hoorns en Schulpen [sic], door H. [sic] Coorte op geschildert en gefernist Papier in Olieverw, op Panel en Doek geplakt'; ibid., p. 122.

55 Sale T.A. Samuel, London, Sotheby's, 26 March 1969, lot 35; see ibid., p. 102.

56 See Meijer in Amsterdam 1993–1994, p. 607, no. 279.

57 For the collection of Johann Wilhelm von der Pfalz, see Munich 2009.

58 See Kolfin 2005.

59 See Sutton in Philadelphia-Berlin-London 1984, pp. 229–230, no. 59.

60 See Robinson 1987, pp. 291–297.

61 See Krempel 2000, p. 362, no. D 39.

62 See Waiboer in Rotterdam-Frankfurt am Main 2004–2005, pp. 210–212, no. 58.

63 'Hier zit de Wijze-man, hy laat hem niet meer tappen / Tot 't noenmaal, dan alleen drie matelijke nappen'; Braunschweig 1978, pp. 99, 100, note 1; The Hague-Washington 2005–2006, p. 138 and fig. 22b.

64 Buvelot/Naumann 2008, p. 102.

65 Naumann 1981, no. 33a.

66 Ibid., nos. 33d–t.

67 Ibid., no. 21; see Naumann in The Hague-Washington 2005–2006, p. 33, fig. 1; Buvelot/Naumann 2008, p. 102.

68 See Chapman in Washington-Amsterdam 1996–1997, no. 27.

69 Scholten 2003, p. 74.

70 See Liedtke in New York-London 2001, pp. 299–301, no. 38.

71 Scholten 2003, pp. 84–85, figs. 79–82.

72 A painting by Saenredam dating from 1660 is included in the Van Otterloos' collection (see De Mol van Otterloo 2010, no. 55).

73 Hamburg, Hamburger Kunsthalle; New York-London 2001, no. 37.

74 Manke 1963, nos. 65, 72.

75 See the detailed account of the painting by J. Roding in The Hague-San Francisco 1990–1991, esp. p. 480 and fig. 3.

76 For the painting, see Bredius/Gerson 1969, no. 333; *Corpus*, vol. 2, no. A 63; Buvelot 2005; Buvelot in London-The

Hague 2007–2008, no. 52. This is a revised version of the latter text, dating from 2007.

77 Sale catalogue London, Christie's, 13 December 2000, pp. 132–137, no. 52.

78 Bredius/Gerson 1969, no. 160; *Corpus*, vol. 2, no. A 59. For the putative pendant of this painting, see ibid., no. A 62.

79 See note 77.

80 See *Corpus*, vol. 2, no. A 55.

81 See Bedaux in Haarlem-Antwerp 2000–2001, p. 224 and note 2; see also Moes 1897–1905, vol. 1, p. 507, nos. 4108–4110.

82 See Kuus in Haarlem-Antwerp 2000–2001, p. 226.

83 See Bedaux in ibid., p. 226 and note 5.

84 This is a revised version of my text in London-The Hague 2007–2008, no. 26.

85 Amiens, Musée de Picardie; Slive 1970–1974, no. 215; Slive in Washington-London-Haarlem 1989–1990, pp. 352–353, no. 81.

86 Broos in Mauritshuis 2004, no. 25; Slive 1970–1974, no. 210. See also ibid., no. 208.

87 Hofstede de Groot 1907–1928, vol. 3, p. 79; see also Slive 1970–1974, vol. 3, p. 107.

88 Slive 1970–1974, vol. 3, pp. 107, 108; Broos in Mauritshuis 2004, p. 118, note 25.

89 Slive in Washington-London-Haarlem 1989–1990, nos. 85–86; Slive 1970–1974, vol. 3, nos. 221–222.

90 Hollstein 43; see Dickey in Washington-Milwaukee-Amsterdam 2008–2009, p. 191, no. 59.

91 Wheelock in ibid., p. 136, fig. 1.

92 Dickey in ibid., pp. 195–196, nos. 63–66.

93 See Von Moltke 1938–1939, pp. 357, 386, no. 82.

94 Wuestman in Haarlem-London 2008, pp. 42–43, no. 4.

95 Konstanz, Städtische Wessenberg-Galerie; Von Moltke 1938–1939, p. 398, no. Z. 23 and fig. 83; Giltaij/Lammertse 2001, p. 368.

96 This was seen by the author in 2009; see Buvelot/Lammertse 2010. Petria Noble and Carol Pottasch, chief conservator and senior conservator, respectively, of the Mauritshuis, were closely involved in the examination of the painting.

97 The figures '9 9/10', '92' and '10' can also be made out (at upper right), as well as 'Painted D BRA 1[6]36' (at upper left); the latter inscription was probably added when the painting was at Althorp House.

98 See Buvelot/Lammertse 2010.

99 On *tronies*, see Van de Wetering in London-The Hague 1999–2000, p. 21; Hirschfelder 2008.

100 Amsterdam-Aachen 2008–2009, nos. 22, 24.

101 Franken in ibid., p. 144: 'een vrouwe tronie met een pluijm op'.

102 See Chong in Washington-London-Amsterdam 2001–2002, pp. 88–90, no. 1 and figs. 1–2.

Bibliography

Amsterdam 1993–1994
G. Luijten, A. van Suchtelen et al.,
*Dawn of the Golden Age: Northern Netherlandish
Art 1580–1620*, Amsterdam (Rijksmuseum)
1993–1994

Amsterdam-Aachen 2008–2009
P. van den Brink, J. van der Veen et al.,
Jacob Backer (1608/9–1651), Amsterdam
(Museum Het Rembrandthuis),
Aachen (Suermondt-Ludwig-Museum)
2008–2009

Amsterdam-Washington 2009–2010
P. Roelofs et al., *Hendrick Avercamp: Master
of the Ice Scene*, Amsterdam (Rijksmuseum),
Washington (National Gallery of Art)
2009–2010

Beck 1972–1973
H.U. Beck, *Jan van Goyen 1596–1656:
Ein Oeuvreverzeichnis*, 2 vols., Amsterdam
1972–1973

Beck 1987
H.U. Beck, *Jan van Goyen 1596–1656:
Ergänzungsband*, Doornspijk 1987

Bijl 2010
M. Bijl, 'Willem van de Velde: Marine
Draughtsman', *The Rijksmuseum
Bulletin* 58 (2010), pp. 190–197

Boston 2002
R. Baer, *The Poetry of Everyday Life: Dutch
Painting in Boston*, Boston (Museum of
Fine Arts) 2002

Braunschweig 1978
E. de Jongh et al., *Die Sprache der Bilder:
Realität und Bedeutung in der niederländischen
Malerei des 17. Jahrhunderts*, Braunschweig
(Herzog Anton Ulrich-Museum) 1978

Bredius/Gerson 1969
A. Bredius, revised by H. Gerson,
*Rembrandt: The Complete Edition of the
Paintings*, London 1969

Brunner-Bulst 2004
M. Brunner-Bulst, *Pieter Claesz. der
Hauptmeister des Haarlemer Stillebens im
17. Jahrhundert: Kritischer Œuvrekatalog*,
Lingen 2004

Buvelot 2005
Q. Buvelot, 'On Rembrandt's "Portrait
of Aeltje Uylenburgh"', *Mauritshuis in
focus* 18 (2005), no. 3, pp. 22–26

Buvelot 2008
Q. Buvelot, *The still lifes of Adriaen Coorte
(active c.1683–1707): With oeuvre catalogue*,
The Hague-Zwolle 2008

Buvelot 2010
Q. Buvelot, 'Has the Great Age of
Collecting Dutch Old Master Paintings
Come to an End?', in E. Quodbach (ed.),
*Holland's Golden Age in America: Collecting
the Art of Rembrandt, Vermeer and Hals*,
forthcoming

Buvelot/Lammertse 2010
Q. Buvelot & F. Lammertse, 'Numbered
paintings by Salomon de Bray', *The
Burlington Magazine* 152 (2010), pp. 390–392

Buvelot/Naumann 2008
Q. Buvelot & O. Naumann, 'Format
changes in paintings by Frans van Mieris
the Elder', *The Burlington Magazine* 150
(2008), pp. 102–104

Carter 1981–1982
J. Walsh & C.P. Schneider, *A Mirror of Nature:
Dutch Paintings from the Collection of Mr. and
Mrs. Edward William Carter*, Los Angeles (Los
Angeles County Museum of Art), Boston
(Museum of Fine Arts), New York (The
Metropolitan Museum of Art) 1981–1982

Carter 1992–1993
J. Walsh & C.P. Schneider, *A Mirror of
Nature: Dutch Paintings from the Collection of
Mr. and Mrs. Edward William Carter*, Los
Angeles (Los Angeles County Museum
of Art) 1992–1993

Corpus
J. Bruyn, B. Haak, S.H. Levie, P.J.J. van
Thiel, E. van de Wetering, *A Corpus of
Rembrandt Paintings*, 4 vols., Amsterdam,
Rembrandt Research Project Foundation
1982–

Van Dedem 2002
P.C. Sutton, *Dutch & Flemish Paintings:
The Collection of Willem Baron van Dedem*,
London 2002

Dobrzynski 2009
J.H. Dobrzynski, 'Profile: The most
important collectors you've never heard
of', *The Art Newspaper* (September 2009),
no. 205, pp. 34–35

Dordrecht 1992–1993
P. Marijnissen et al. (eds.), *De Zichtbaere
Werelt: Schilderkunst uit de Gouden Eeuw in
Hollands oudste stad*, Dordrecht (Dordrechts
Museum) 1992–1993

Duparc 1993
F.J. Duparc, 'Philips Wouwerman, 1619–
1668', *Oud Holland* 107 (1993), pp. 257–286

Giltaij/Lammertse 2001
J. Giltaij & F. Lammertse, 'Maintaining
a studio archive: Drawn copies by the
De Braij Family', *Master Drawings* 39 (2001),
pp. 367–394

Greenwich-New York 2008–2009
P.C. Sutton et al., *Reclaimed: Paintings from the
Collection of Jacques Goudstikker*, Greenwich

(Bruce Museum), New York (Jewish Museum) 2008–2009

Haarlem-Antwerp 2000–2001
J.B. Bedaux & R. Ekkart (ed.), *Pride and Joy: Children's Portraits in the Netherlands, 1500–1700*, Haarlem (Frans Hals Museum), Antwerp (Koninklijk Museum voor Schone Kunsten) 2000–2001

Haarlem-London 2008
P. Biesboer et al., *Painting Family: The De Brays, Master Painters of 17th century Holland*, Haarlem (Frans Hals Museum), London (Dulwich Picture Gallery) 2008

Haarlem-Zürich-Washington 2004–2005
P. Biesboer et al., *Pieter Claesz: Master of Haarlem Still Life*, Haarlem (Frans Hals Museum), Zürich (Kunsthaus), Washington (National Gallery of Art) 2004–2005

The Hague 1994–1995
A. Walsh, E. Buijsen, B. Broos, ed. Q. Buvelot, *Paulus Potter: Paintings, drawings and etchings*, The Hague (Mauritshuis) 1994–1995

The Hague 2001–2002
A. van Suchtelen et al., *Holland Frozen in Time: The Dutch Winter Landscape in the Golden Age*, The Hague (Mauritshuis) 2001–2002

The Hague 2002
Q. Buvelot, H. Buijs, *A Choice Collection: Seventeenth-Century Dutch Paintings from the Frits Lugt Collection*, The Hague (Mauritshuis) 2002

The Hague 2009
Q. Buvelot, *Jacob van Ruisdael Paints Bentheim*, The Hague (Mauritshuis) 2009

The Hague-San Francisco 1990–1991
B. Broos et al., *Great Dutch Paintings from America*, The Hague (Mauritshuis), San Francisco (The Fine Arts Museums of San Francisco) 1990–1991

The Hague-Washington 2005–2006
Q. Buvelot et al., *Frans van Mieris 1635–1681*, The Hague (Mauritshuis), Washington (National Gallery of Art) 2005–2006

The Hague-Washington 2008–2009
A. van Suchtelen, A. Wheelock et al., *Dutch Cityscapes of the Golden Age*, The Hague (Mauritshuis), Washington (National Gallery of Art) 2008–2009

Harwood 1988
L. Harwood, *Adam Pynacker*, Doornspijk 1988

Hirschfelder 2008
D. Hirschfelder, *Tronie und Porträt in der niederländischen Malerei des 17. Jahrhunderts*, Berlin 2008

Hofstede de Groot 1907–1928
C. Hofstede de Groot, *Beschreibendes und kritisches Verzeichnis der Werke der hervorragendsten holländischen Maler des XVII. Jahrhunderts*, 10 vols., Esslingen-Paris 1907–1928

Hollstein
F.W.H. Hollstein, *Dutch and Flemish Etchings, Engravings and Woodcuts, c. 1450–1700*, Amsterdam 1949–

Kassel-The Hague 2009–2010
F. Duparc & Q. Buvelot, *Philips Wouwerman 1619–1668*, Kassel (Gemäldegalerie Alte Meister), The Hague (Mauritshuis) 2009–2010

Kattenburg 1988
R. Kattenburg, *The Brederode off Vlieland*, Amsterdam 1988

Kaufmann 1988
T. DaCosta Kaufmann, *The School of Prague: Painting at the Court of Rudolf II*, Chicago-London 1988

Kelch 1971
J. Kelch, *Studien zu Simon de Vlieger als Marine-maler*, PhD thesis, Berlin 1971

Kilian 2005
J.M. Kilian, *The Paintings of Karel du Jardin (1626–1678): Catalogue Raisonné*, Amsterdam 2005

Kolfin 2005
E. Kolfin, *The young gentry at play: Northern Netherlandish scenes of merry companies 1610–1645*, Leiden 2005

Kremer 2008–2009
P. van der Ploeg et al., *Niederländische Malerei: Die Sammlung Kremer*, Cologne (Wallraf-Richartz-Museum & Fondation Corboud), Kassel (Gemäldegalerie Alte Meister, Museumslandschaft Hessen Kassel), Haarlem (Frans Hals Museum) 2008–2009

Krempel 2000
L. Krempel, *Studien zu den datierten Gemälden des Nicolaes Maes (1634–1693)*, Petersburg 2000

London-The Hague 1999–2000
C. White & Q. Buvelot (eds.), *Rembrandt by Himself*, London (National Gallery), The Hague (Mauritshuis) 1999–2000

London-The Hague 2007–2008
R. Ekkart, Q. Buvelot et al., *Dutch Portraits: The Age of Rembrandt and Frans Hals*, London (National Gallery), The Hague (Mauritshuis) 2007

Madrid 1994–1995
P.C. Sutton et al., *The Golden Age of Dutch Landscape Painting*, Madrid (Museo Thyssen-Bornemisza) 1994–1995

Van Mander/Miedema 1973
K. van Mander, revised by H. Miedema,

Den grondt der edel vry schilder-const, 2 vols.,
Utrecht 1973

Manke 1963
I. Manke, *Emanuel de Witte*, Amsterdam 1963

Mauritshuis 2004
B. Broos, A. van Suchtelen, ed. Q. Buvelot,
Portraits in the Mauritshuis, 1430–1790, The
Hague-Zwolle 2004

**Minneapolis-Toledo-Los Angeles
1990–1991**
G.S. Keyes, *Mirror of Empire: Dutch Marine
Art of the Seventeenth Century*, Minneapolis
(Minneapolis Institute of Arts), Toledo
(Toledo Museum of Art), Los Angeles
(Los Angeles County Museum of Art)
1990–1991

Moes 1897–1905
E.W. Moes, *Iconographia Batava*, 2 vols.,
Amsterdam 1897–1905

De Mol van Otterloo 2010
F.J. Duparc et al., *The Collection of Eijk
and Rose-Marie de Mol van Otterloo*, New
Haven-London 2010 (forthcoming)

Von Moltke 1938–1939
J.W. von Moltke, 'Salomon de Bray',
Marburger Jahrbuch für Kunstgeschichte 11–12
(1938–1939), pp. 309–420

Munich 2009
R. Baumstark, *Kurfürst Johann Wilhelms Bilder*,
2 vols., Munich (Alte Pinakothek) 2009

Naumann 1981
O. Naumann, *Frans van Mieris the Elder
(1635-1681)*, 2 vols., Doornspijk 1981

New York-London 2001
W.A. Liedtke, M.C. Plomp, A. Rüger et al.,
Vermeer and the Delft School, New York (The
Metropolitan Museum of Art), London
(National Gallery) 2001

Philadelphia-Berlin-London 1984
P.C. Sutton et al., *Masters of Seventeenth-
Century Dutch Genre Painting*, Philadelphia
(Philadelphia Museum of Art), Berlin
(Gemäldegalerie, Staatliche Museen zu
Berlin), London (Royal Academy of Arts)
1984

**Phoenix-Kansas City-The Hague
1998–1999**
M.K. Komanecky et al., *Copper as canvas:
Two centuries of masterpiece paintings on copper,
1575-1775*, Phoenix (Phoenix Art Museum),
Kansas City (The Nelson-Atkins Museum
of Art), The Hague (Mauritshuis) 1998–
1999

Van der Ploeg/Buvelot 2008
P. van der Ploeg & Q. Buvelot, *With heart and
soul: Frits Duparc as director of the Mauritshuis,
1991-2008*, The Hague-Zwolle 2008

Robinson 1987
W. Robinson, 'The Eavesdroppers and
Related Paintings by Nicolaes Maes', in
H. Bock, T.W. Gaehtgens (eds.), *Holländische
Genremalerei im 17. Jahrhundert: Symposium
Berlin 1984*, Berlin 1987, pp. 283–313

Robinson 1990
M.S. Robinson, *The Paintings of the Willem
van de Veldes*, 2 vols., Greenwich 1990

**Rotterdam-Frankfurt am Main
2004–2005**
J. Giltaij et al., *Senses and Sins: Dutch
painters of daily life in the seventeenth century*,
Rotterdam (Museum Boijmans Van
Beuningen), Frankfurt am Main
(Städelsches Kunstinstitut) 2004–2005

Russell 1975
M.A. Russell, *Jan van de Cappelle*, Leigh-
on-Sea 1975

Scholten 2003
F. Scholten, *Sumptuous memories: Studies
in seventeenth-century Dutch tomb sculpture*,
Zwolle 2003

Schumacher 2006
B. Schumacher, *Philips Wouwerman (1619-
1668): The horse painter of the golden age*, 2 vols.,
Doornspijk 2006

De Sitter 2010
S. de Sitter, 'Gedeeld belang: De betekenis
van professioneel advies en persoonlijke
betrokkenheid voor verzamelaars Eijk
and Rose-Marie de Mol van Otterloo en
adviseur Frits Duparc', in I. van Hamers-
veld & T. Gubbels (eds.), *Bondgenoten of
Tegenpolen? Samenwerking tussen kunstverzame-
laars en musea in Nederland*, Amsterdam-
The Hague 2010, pp. 67–81

Slive 1970–1974
S. Slive, *Frans Hals*, 3 vols., London 1970–
1974

Slive 2001
S. Slive, *Jacob van Ruisdael: A Complete Catalogue
of his Paintings, Drawings and Etchings*, New
Haven-London 2001

Smith 1829–1842
J. Smith, *A Catalogue Raisonné of the Works of
the Most Eminent Dutch, Flemish, and French
Painters*, 8 vols. and supplement, London
1829–1842

Stechow 1975
W. Stechow, *Salomon van Ruysdael*, Berlin
1975 (revised edition of 1938 publication)

Verhoef 2010
M. Verhoef, 'Van sneeuw naar verf',
Kunstschrift 53 (2010), no. 6, pp. 6–12

Vienna 2010
J. Kräftner (ed.), *Der Fürst als Sammler:*

Neuerwerbungen unter Hans-Adam II. von und zu Liechtenstein, Vienna (Liechtenstein Museum) 2010

Walsh 1971
J. Walsh, *Jan and Julius Porcellis: Dutch Marine Painters*, PhD thesis, Columbia 1971
Washington-Amsterdam 1996–1997
H. Perry Chapman, W.T. Kloek, A.K. Wheelock, *Jan Steen: Painter and Storyteller*, Washington (National Gallery of Art), Amsterdam (Rijksmuseum) 1996–1997
Washington-London-Amsterdam 2001–2002
A.K. Wheelock et al., *Aelbert Cuyp*, Washington (National Gallery of Art), London (National Gallery), Amsterdam (Rijksmuseum) 2001–2002
Washington-London-Haarlem 1989–1990
S. Slive et al., *Frans Hals*, Washington (National Gallery of Art), London (Royal Academy of Arts), Haarlem (Frans Hals Museum) 1989–1990
Washington-Milwaukee-Amsterdam 2008–2009
A. Wheelock et al., *Jan Lievens: A Dutch Master Rediscovered*, Washington (National Gallery of Art), Milwaukee (Milwaukee Art Museum), Amsterdam (Museum Het Rembrandthuis) 2008–2009

Index

Compilation and editorial responsibility
Quentin Buvelot, Mauritshuis

English translation
Beverley Jackson, Amsterdam

Design
DeLeeuwOntwerper(s), The Hague

Publishers/Printers
Waanders Publishers and Waanders
Printers, Zwolle

For more information about
the Mauritshuis and Waanders, see
www.mauritshuis.nl
www.waanders.nl

ISBN 978 90 400 7744 9 (hardcover)
NUR 640
A Dutch edition of this book is also
available.

Photo acknowledgments
The photographic material
was acquired from the owners.
Photograph of De Bray and Claesz:
Margareta Svensson, Amsterdam.
Photograph pp. 12–13:
Walter Silver, Salem, Mass.
Photograph shell p. 55:
Victor de Leeuw, The Hague

Front cover
Gerrit Dou, *A Resting Dog*, 1650.

Back cover
Rembrandt, *Portrait of Aeltje Uylenburgh*,
1632.

Nicolaes Berchem, Ambrosius Bosschaert the Elder, Isaack Koedijck, Adriaen Coorte, Jacob Backer, Willem Heda, Paulus Potter, Jan Baptist Weenix, Aelbert Cuyp, Jan van Goyen, Jan Davidsz de Heem, Jacob van Ruisdael, Balthasar van der Ast, Emanuel de Witte, Jan Steen, Jacob van Ruisdael, Simon de Vlieger, Jan van der Heyden, Frans van Mieris the Elder, Adam Pijnacker, Willem van Aelst, Philips Wouwerman, Gerard Houckgeest, Nicolaes Maes, Jan Porcellis, Jacob van Ruisdael, Willem van de Velde the Younger, Hendrick Avercamp, Jan van de Cappelle, Gerrit Dou, Rembrandt, Frans Hals, Karel du Jardin, Adriaen van Ostade, Salomon van Ruysdael, Jan Both, Jan Lievens, Rachel Ruysch, Willem van de Velde the Elder, Aert van der Neer, Esaias van de Velde, Salomon de Bray, Pieter Claesz, Gabriël Metsu, Nicolaes Berchem, Ambrosius Bosschaert the Elder, Isaack Koedijck, Adriaen Coorte, Jacob Backer, Willem Heda, Paulus Potter, Jan Baptist Weenix, Aelbert Cuyp, Jan van Goyen, Jan Davidsz de Heem, Jacob van Ruisdael, Balthasar van der Ast, Emanuel de Witte, Jan Steen, Jacob van Ruisdael, Simon de Vlieger, Jan van der Heyden, Frans van Mieris the Elder, Adam Pijnacker, Willem van Aelst, Philips Wouwerman, Gerard Houckgeest, Nicolaes Maes, Jan Porcellis, Jacob van Ruisdael, Willem van de Velde the Younger, Hendrick Avercamp, Jan van de Cappelle, Gerrit Dou, Rembrandt, Frans Hals, Karel du Jardin, Adriaen van Ostade, Salomon van Ruysdael, Jan Both, Jan Lievens, Rachel Ruysch, Willem van de Velde the Elder, Aert van der Neer, Esaias van de Velde, Salomon de Bray, Pieter Claesz, Gabriël Metsu, Nicolaes Berchem, Ambrosius Bosschaert the Elder, Isaack Koedijck, Adriaen Coorte, Jacob Backer, Willem Heda, Paulus Potter, Jan Baptist Weenix, Aelbert Cuyp, Jan van Goyen, Jan Davidsz de Heem, Jacob van Ruisdael, Balthasar van der Ast, Emanuel de Witte, Jan Steen, Jacob van Ruisdael, Simon de Vlieger, Jan van der Heyden, Frans van Mieris the Elder, Adam Pijnacker, Willem van Aelst, Philips Wouwerman, Gerard Houckgeest, Nicolaes Maes, Jan Porcellis, Jacob van Ruisdael, Willem van de Velde the Younger, Hendrick Avercamp, Jan van de Cappelle, Gerrit Dou, Rembrandt, Frans Hals, Karel du Jardin, Adriaen van Ostade, Salomon van Ruysdael, Jan Both, Jan Lievens, Rachel Ruysch, Willem van de Velde the Elder, Aert van der Neer, Jan Both, Esaias van de Velde, Salomon de Bray, Pieter Claesz, Gabriël Metsu, Nicolaes Berchem, Ambrosius Bosschaert the Elder, Isaack Koedijck, Adriaen Coorte, Jacob Backer, Willem Heda, Paulus Potter, Jan Baptist Weenix, Aelbert Cuyp, Jan van Goyen, Jan Davidsz de Heem, Jacob van Ruisdael, Balthasar van der Ast, Emanuel de Witte, Jan Steen, Jacob van Ruisdael, Simon de Vlieger, Jan van der Heyden, Frans van Mieris the Elder, Adam Pijnacker, Willem van Aelst, Philips Wouwerman, Gerard Houckgeest, Nicolaes Maes, Jan Porcellis, Jacob van Ruisdael, Willem van de Velde the Younger, Hendrick Avercamp, Jan van de Cappelle, Gerrit Dou, Rembrandt, Frans Hals, Karel du Jardin, Adriaen van Ostade, Salomon van Ruysdael, Jan Both, Jan Lievens, Rachel Ruysch, Willem van de Velde the Elder, Aert van der Neer, Esaias van de Velde, Salomon de Bray, Pieter Claesz, Gabriël Metsu, Nicolaes Berchem, Ambrosius Bosschaert de Oude, Isaack Koedijck, Adriaen Coorte, Jacob Backer, Willem Heda, Paulus Potter, Jan Baptist Weenix, Aelbert Cuyp, Jan van Goyen, Jan Davidsz de Heem, Jacob van Ruisdael, Balthasar van der Ast, Emanuel de Witte, Jan Steen, Jacob van Ruisdael, Simon de Vlieger, Jan van der Heyden, Frans van Mieris the Elder, Adam Pijnacker, Willem van Aelst, Philips Wouwerman, Gerard Houckgeest, Nicolaes Maes, Jan Porcellis, Jacob van Ruisdael, Willem van de Velde the Younger, Hendrick Avercamp, Jan van de Cappelle, Gerrit Dou, Rembrandt, Frans Hals, Karel du Jardin, Adriaen van Ostade, Salomon van Ruysdael, Jan Both, Jan Lievens, Rachel Ruysch, Willem van de Velde the Elder, Aert van der Neer, Esaias van de Velde, Salomon de Bray, Pieter Claesz, Gabriël Metsu, Nicolaes Berchem, Ambrosius Bosschaert the Elder, Isaack Koedijck, Adriaen Coorte, Jacob Backer, Willem Heda, Paulus Potter, Jan Baptist Weenix, Aelbert Cuyp, Jan van Goyen, Jan Davidsz de Heem, Jacob van Ruisdael, Balthasar van der Ast, Emanuel de Witte, Jan Steen, Jacob van Ruisdael, Simon de Vlieger, Jan van der Heyden, Frans van Mieris the Elder, Adam Pijnacker, Willem van Aelst, Philips Wouwerman, Gerard Houckgeest, Nicolaes Maes, Jan Porcellis, Jacob van Ruisdael, Willem van de Velde the Younger, Hendrick Avercamp, Jan van de Cappelle, Gerrit Dou, Rembrandt, Frans Hals, Karel du Jardin, Adriaen van Ostade, Salomon van Ruysdael, Jan Both, Jan Lievens, Rachel Ruysch, Willem van de Velde the Elder, Aert van der Neer, Esaias van de Velde, Salomon de Bray, Pieter Claesz, Gabriël Metsu, Nicolaes Berchem, Ambrosius Bosschaert the Elder, Isaack Koedijck, Adriaen Coorte, Jacob Backer, Willem Heda, Paulus Potter, Jan Baptist Weenix, Aelbert Cuyp, Jan van Goyen, Jan Davidsz de Heem, Jacob van Ruisdael, Balthasar van der Ast, Emanuel de Witte, Jan Steen, Jacob van Ruisdael, Simon de Vlieger, Jan van der Heyden, Frans van Mieris the Elder, Adam Pijnacker, Willem van Aelst, Philips Wouwerman, Gerard Houckgeest, Nicolaes Maes, Jan Porcellis, Jacob van Ruisdael, Willem van de Velde the Younger, Hendrick Avercamp, Jan van de Cappelle, Gerrit Dou, Rembrandt, Frans Hals, Karel du Jardin, Adriaen van Ostade, Salomon van Ruysdael, Jan Both, Jan Lievens, Rachel Ruysch, Willem van de Velde the Elder, Aert van der Neer, Esaias van de Velde, Salomon de Bray, Pieter Claesz, Gabriël Metsu, Nicolaes Berchem, Ambrosius Bosschaert the Elder, Isaack Koedijck, Adriaen Coorte, Jacob Backer, Willem Heda, Paulus Potter, Jan Baptist Weenix, Aelbert Cuyp, Jan van Goyen, Jan Davidsz de Heem, Jacob van Ruisdael, Balthasar van der Ast, Emanuel de Witte, Jan Steen, Jacob van Ruisdael, Simon de Vlieger, Jan van der Heyden, Frans van Mieris the Elder, Adam Pijnacker, Willem van Aelst, Philips Wouwerman, Gerard Houckgeest, Nicolaes Maes, Jan Porcellis, Jacob van Ruisdael, Willem van de Velde the Younger, Hendrick Avercamp, Jan van de Cappelle, Gerrit Dou, Rembrandt, Frans Hals, Karel du Jardin, Adriaen van Ostade, Salomon van Ruysdael, Jan Both, Jan Lievens, Rachel Ruysch, Willem van de Velde the Elder, Aert van der Neer, Esaias van de Velde, Salomon de Bray, Pieter Claesz, Gabriël Metsu, Nicolaes Berchem, Ambrosius Bosschaert the Elder, Isaack Koedijck, Adriaen Coorte, Jacob Backer, Willem Heda, Paulus Potter, Jan Baptist Weenix, Aelbert Cuyp, Jan van Goyen, Jan Davidsz de Heem, Jacob van Ruisdael, Balthasar van der Ast, Emanuel de Witte, Jan Steen, Jacob van Ruisdael, Simon de Vlieger, Jan van der Heyden, Frans van Mieris the Elder, Adam Pijnacker, Willem van Aelst, Philips Wouwerman, Gerard Houckgeest, Nicolaes Maes, Jan Porcellis, Jacob van Ruisdael, Willem van de Velde the Younger, Hendrick Avercamp, Jan van de Cappelle, Gerrit Dou, Rembrandt, Frans Hals, Karel du Jardin, Adriaen van Ostade, Salomon van Ruysdael, Jan Lievens, Rachel Ruysch, Willem van de Velde the Elder, Aert van der Neer, Esaias van de Velde, Salomon de Bray, Pieter Claesz, Gabriël Metsu, Nicolaes Berchem, Ambrosius Bosschaert the Elder, Isaack Koedijck, Adriaen Coorte, Jacob Backer, Willem Heda, Paulus Potter, Jan Baptist Weenix, Aelbert Cuyp, Jan van Goyen, Jan Davidsz de Heem, Jacob van Ruisdael, Balthasar van der Ast, Emanuel de Witte, Jan Steen, Jacob van Ruisdael, Simon de Vlieger, Jan van der Heyden, Frans van Mieris the Elder, Adam Pijnacker, Willem van Aelst, Philips Wouwerman, Gerard Houckgeest, Nicolaes Maes, Jan Porcellis, Jacob van Ruisdael, Willem van de Velde the Younger, Hendrick Avercamp, Jan van de Cappelle, Gerrit Dou, Rembrandt, Frans Hals, Karel du Jardin, Adriaen van Ostade, Salomon van Ruysdael, Jan Both, Jan Lievens, Rachel Ruysch, Willem van de Velde the Elder